THE WORKS OF SHAKESPEARE

EDITED FOR THE SYNDICS OF THE
CAMBRIDGE UNIVERSITY PRESS

BY

JOHN DOVER WILSON

KING HENRY V

KING HENRY V

CAMBRIDGE
AT THE UNIVERSITY PRESS
1968

PUBLISHED BY
THE SYNDICS OF THE CAMBRIDGE UNIVERSITY PRESS

Bentley House, 200 Euston Road, London, N.W. 1
American Branch: 32 East 57th Street, New York, N.Y. 10022

First edition 1947
Reprinted 1955
1964
First paperback edition 1968

Places where slight editorial changes or additions
introduce variants from the first edition are marked
by a date [1955] in square brackets.

First printed in Great Britain at the University Press, Cambridge
Reprinted in Great Britain by Hazell Watson & Viney Ltd,
Aylesbury, Bucks

CONTENTS

To

FIELD-MARSHAL THE VISCOUNT WAVELL
'Star of England' in her darkest night

INTRODUCTION

The First Folio gives us the only authoritative text for *Henry V*, and it is happily a good one, being printed as we shall see almost certainly from the author's manuscript; while a 'bad quarto', which is helpful now and then to an editor, has also come down to us[1]. In general, the play has received scant attention from scholars, and has not yet appeared in the invaluable American Variorum. I stand the more indebted, therefore, to Dr Duthie, who has prepared for me elaborate notes on the play, often approaching variorum fulness, together with a text based upon a fresh examination of the folio original. For what follows I must take full responsibility. But the fact that he had first traversed every step in the road greatly added to my speed and confidence; I have helped myself to his comments, as my Notes indicate; and I have adopted his text practically without change, the more readily that it is virtually a reprint in modern spelling of the folio text, punctuation and all, though with the addition of editorial stage-directions, mostly of my invention. Lastly, a comprehensive and masterly account of the historical events traversed in the play is now available in the three volumes of J. H. Wylie's monumental *Reign of Henry V*, 1914–29, the reading of which encourages us to believe that Shakespeare's account of the French campaign is substantially true to fact.

Henry V is a play which men of action have been wont silently to admire, and literary men, at any rate during the last hundred and thirty years, volubly to contemn. But even critics learn something from times like the present; or at least one humble member of the

[1] v. p. 111–13, below.

tribe imagines he has done so. Born in the penultimate decade of the nineteenth century, I grew up tutored by my betters to think of *Henry V* as a drum-and-trumpet show, thrown off by Shakespeare as a perfunctory concession to the popular taste of his age. But happening to witness a performance by Frank Benson and his company at Stratford in August or September 1914, I discovered for the first time what it was all about. The epic drama of Agincourt matched the temper of the moment, when Rupert Brooke was writing *The Soldier* and the Kaiser was said to be scoffing at our 'contemptible little army' which had just crossed the Channel, so exactly that it might have been written expressly for it. Details of the production have passed from my mind; but never can I forget the three hours' excitement which Shakespeare gave that audience. The truth is, he mirrors in his plays all sorts and conditions, not only of men and women, but also of national and social moods, so that any day one of them may suddenly become topical, even to the inflaming of political passions. Not many years since a performance of *Coriolanus* provoked a riot in Paris, which was followed by the dismissal of a cabinet minister. When, again, has *Troilus and Cressida* held English audiences spell-bound, except during the cynical years that divided the World War of 1914–18 from the World War of 1939–45?

But, indeed, the notion that there was anything perfunctory about *Henry V*, either for the dramatist or his original audience, will not easily survive consideration of the circumstances of its production. Sir Edmund Chambers sees it 'as the most complete expression of that heightened national self-consciousness, which is so characteristic a feature of the latter years of Elizabeth's chequered and anxious reign'; and finds it 'tempting to connect' its 'immediate inspiration...with the renewed stimulus given to the patriotic order of ideas by

the exploits of the Earl of Essex and his gallant company
during the filibustering expedition to Cadiz in 1596
and the less successful island voyage to the Azores in
1597[1]'. One can, I think, press the topicality even
closer home. In the eyes of ordinary Englishmen, of
whom politically speaking Shakespeare was one,
England at the beginning of 1599, when the play was
taking shape, must have appeared to 'stand upon the
top of happy hours'. The very real fears of a Spanish
invasion, which had hung over the country for fourteen
years and more, seemed suddenly lifted by the death of
Philip II in November 1598; and, as tangible proof,
it would appear, of this new-won security, there was
being fitted out at the same time the largest and most
elaborate military expedition launched from these
shores during Elizabeth's reign, with the object of
effecting the final conquest of Ireland[2]. At the head
of this force, which left England at the end of March
1599, was the young Earl; his appointment had been
hailed with satisfaction by the whole country; and he
made something like a royal procession through the
streets of London on the day of his departure, when
'the people pressed exceedingly to behold him for more
than four miles' space, crying out, "God save your
Lordship, God preserve your Honour"', some even
following him 'until the evening, only to behold him[3]'.

A reflection of these memorable events has been
commonly seen in the lines of the fifth Chorus which
compare Henry's triumphal entry into his capital after
Agincourt with the anticipated return of Essex himself.
Some years ago I drew attention also to a close resemblance between Fluellen and Sir Roger Williams, the
renowned Welsh soldier, with his professional pedantry,
his quaint and forcible turns of speech, his vanity and

---

[1] *Shakespeare: a Survey*, pp. 139–40.
[2] Cheyney, *History of England*, ii. 473–4.
[3] G. B. Harrison, *Elizabethan Journal*, iii. 13–14.

cool valour, who, as the familiar friend of Essex, would certainly have attended him to Ireland had he not died in 1595[1]. But it seems hitherto to have been hardly realized how intimately associated with the Irish expedition the play as a whole must have been, both in inception and composition. It was the crushing defeat of the English by Tyrone at Armagh in August 1598 which finally persuaded Elizabeth that unusual measures were needed if Ireland was not to be altogether lost to her crown; and by November, that is, just about the date when Shakespeare probably first took the play in hand, active preparations for a large-scale invasion were already on foot. Thus, while he was at work upon it during the winter of 1598–99, the whole country was agog with the pressing and mustering of troops; it was being finished about the time the expedition sailed; and was certainly produced not long after, seeing that the lines above mentioned, referring to the return of a conquering Essex, would be out of date by about the end of June, when doubts of the success of the campaign were being freely talked of in London[2], and it was an Essex in disgrace who returned on 28 September. In a word, *Henry V*, so apposite in theme and spirit, as I and many others discovered, to the dispatch of a great expeditionary force in 1914, was actually written for a similar occasion in 1599.

Yet it would have been written in any case about this time, and the occasion was for Shakespeare a stroke of luck. The two Parts of *Henry IV* had been drawing large audiences in 1597–8, and *Henry V* was not only their sequel, but a sequel promised in their Epilogue,

[1] 'Martin Marprelate and Shakespeare's Fluellen', *The Library*, 1912. For a possible historical original of Fluellen v. p. 118.

[2] *Chamberlain's Letters* (Camden Society), p. 51. If this dating be correct, the 'wooden O' must be the Curtain Theatre; cf. note 1 Prol. 13.

and no doubt eagerly looked for. A turn in national
affairs had unexpectedly placed at his disposal a miracu-
lously happy hour for a play upon which he had long
brooded, since he was already envisaging it in 1595
as the culmination of the historical series begun that
year with *Richard II*. And it crowned the series, not
merely because it filled the gap between *Henry IV* and
Henry VI, but also because its hero was Henry of
Monmouth, to Elizabethans the 'star of England' and
the most glorious of English kings. Mr Masefield tells
us that 'the play bears every mark of having been
hastily written[1]'. Yet other poets have gone wrong in
criticizing Shakespeare; and I dare to think that had
he at such a time set Arms and such a Man upon the
stage in any off-hand or hasty fashion, he would have
flouted a public not easily satisfied with second-rate
productions. More, he would have belied and falsified
the unmistakably genuine patriotism that burns in *King
John* and *Richard II*, to say nothing of the admiration
for Prince Hal which is evident in *Henry IV*[2]. Shakespeare was often careless; often obliged through pressure
of other work to offer his second best. But surely not
in *Henry V*. The national emergency, the height of his
great argument, the urge to equal if not surpass his
earlier successes in historical drama, the quickened
pulse of his own heart at the thought of England at
war; all these would stimulate him to put forth his
utmost strength.

But the spirit bloweth where it listeth, and resolution
is no guarantee of success in poetry or drama; too often
the reverse. Moreover, in chronicle-play the available
material may be an obstinately limiting factor. Dr
Duthie has suggested to me that, working forward from
Richard II, Shakespeare found when he reached

[1] *Shakespeare* (Home University Library), p. 120.
[2] Cf. ch. IV, *The Fortunes of Falstaff*.

Henry V that it was both inadequate in quantity and unsuitable in kind for drama, which demands plot, inner conflict, and development of character; none of them readily distilled from the facts of Henry V's reign. Thus, he concludes, Shakespeare was forced back upon the episodical treatment, accompanied by frequent description on the part of a presenter or chorus, which we find. I think there is a good deal in this, while it is relevant to observe that Shakespeare was less free than usual to manipulate or depart from his historical sources, seeing that, as his direct reference to readers of the story implies[1], the facts he dealt with were probably better known to his hearers than those of any other of his chronicle-plays. Certainly, he follows Holinshed here far more closely than elsewhere. Yet intractability in the medium has often provoked the highest flights of art; and though I do not rank *Henry V* as one of the highest flights of Shakespeare's genius, I am bold to claim that in the writing of it he 'turned his necessity to glorious gain'.

If the greatest story in English history, as he and his contemporaries thought it, was ill-suited for normal dramatic treatment, then a new form of drama must be invented. Theme and hero clearly called for epic; and the problem was how to use the theatre for this purpose. It was solved by setting a series of heroic episodes or tableaux upon the stage, interspersed indeed for comic relief with lighter scenes, which introduce bragging Frenchmen (at times extraordinarily like Mussolini), rascally camp-followers, or a couple of French ladies making pretty fritters of English, but never for long distracting the attention of the audience from the contemplation of one figure, that of the great King, which, exhibited in a variety of moods and situations, dominates the play as Æneas dominates the

[1] 5 Prol. 1–6.

Æneid. And the epical tone was emphasized by a Chorus, who speaks five prologues and an epilogue.

'In their sublimity and lyric fervour these monologues are unique', writes Dr Mackail; and he adds, 'we can hear in them, more certainly than elsewhere, more unquestionably than even in the *Sonnets*, the voice of Shakespeare speaking for himself, for his colleagues, and for his profession[1]'. I am inclined to believe, encouraged thereto by Mr George Skillan[2], that this voice was actually heard by the spectators of 1599; that, in other words, the part of Chorus, which with its 223 lines is next in importance to the part of Henry, and which David Garrick was to regard as not beneath his dignity[3], had been originally played by an actor called William Shakespeare. It is only a guess; but I find it helps me to understand Chorus and play alike, and think it may help others also. Certainly the diffident and apologetic tone, which the Chorus adopts throughout, and which sounds awkward, not to say ungracious, if interpreted, with most critics, as the impatience of an author girding against the resources of his theatre and the limitations of his actors, becomes at once natural and engaging when taken as a personal apology and plea by somebody who was author, player, and producer in one. And the lines of the Epilogue,

> Thus far, with rough and all-unable pen,
> Our bending author hath pursued the story,

gain much if we see in our mind's eye the modest playwright bowing to his audience as he speaks them. In any case, Shakespeare's references elsewhere to the art of the theatre almost always include the art of the dramatist, and the Epilogue proves that they should be

[1] *The Approach to Shakespeare*, 1930, pp. 56–7.
[2] v. his thoughtful and suggestive acting edition of the play (pub. Samuel French Ltd.).
[3] v. below, p. l.

taken as doing so in *Henry V* likewise. But, it may be
objected, why should the dramatist suddenly in 1599
begin apologizing for the incapacity of himself and his
theatre to cope with a historical theme and battle-
scenes[1], when such things had been one of their chief
stocks-in-trade for the past half-dozen years? Nor does
he make any bones later about confining the whole
Roman world or cramming the very casques of Antony,
Caesar and their legions within the 'wooden O' of
the Globe playhouse. The answer surely is that here
is no ordinary theme, but 'so great an object' that he
honestly doubts whether he can compass it, and doubts
the more that the nature of his material compels him
to launch forth upon an untried form of drama. The
diffidence of the Chorus is the expression of a genuine
attitude of mind. When the self-assured Milton sets out
upon his 'adventurous' flight, with intent 'to soar above
the Aonian mount', that is, to excel both Virgil and
Homer, he begins boldly 'Sing, Heavenly Muse!'
Shakespeare, with aims far less ambitious, can only
sigh, 'O, for a Muse of fire!' while he calls himself
a 'flat unraiséd spirit', a mere cipher in comparison
with the great 'accompt' he has to render. Yet one
can detect, I think, beneath the surface of sincere
humility an undertone of sly, almost Chaucerian
humour, together with not a little innocent guile
proper to the showman. We are here, says Master
Chorus in effect, to commemorate England's finest
hours, quite beyond the power of any dramatist, com-

---

[1] In this, as Aldis Wright observes, he was not entirely
without precedent, since the Chorus to *Captain Thomas
Stukely* (acted by Admiral's men, 1596) uses similar language of the battle of Alcazar:

> 'Your gentle favours must we needs entreat
> For rude presenting such a royal fight
> Which more imagination must supply
> Than all our utmost strength can reach unto.'

pany, or theatre to represent truly; but if you, as good patriots, will lend your aid, by allowing for our limitations and contributing the full force of your own powerful imaginations, the play cannot utterly fail, since as you 'sit and see' you will be all the while

Minding true things by what their mock'ries be.

Such an appeal, reiterated no less than twenty-five times[1], and comparable in the sphere of theatrical art to that of a priest leading his congregation in prayer or celebration, would be the more effective for its ingenuous modesty, confirmed, as I believe it was, by persuasive tones of eager entreaty from the playwright's own lips.

But his material set Shakespeare another problem, more serious still, a problem not of form but of spirit. What is the 'idea' of *Henry V*? Ever since 1817, when Hazlitt, in a fit of republican and anti-patriotic spleen, stigmatized Shakespeare's hero as a brute and a hypocrite, Henry has been a subject of debate among critics[2]. Let a modern representative of either side

[1] See an interesting letter by William Poel in *The Times Literary Supplement* of 15 Nov. 1928.

[2] The main English-speaking voices in this debate are: (i) *contra*, Hazlitt, *Characters*, 1817; Swinburne, *Study of Shakespeare*, 1880, pp. 112 ff.; Yeats, *Ideas of Good and Evil*, 1903, pp. 155 ff.; A. Bradley, *Oxford Lectures*, 1909, pp. 256 ff.; Masefield, *Shakespeare* (H.U.L.), 1911, pp. 121 ff.; Granville-Barker, *From 'Henry V' to 'Hamlet'*, 1925 (in *Aspects of Shakespeare*, pp. 57 ff.); M. van Doren, *Shakespeare*, 1939, pp. 170 ff.; J. Palmer, *Political Characters*, 1945, p. 180; (ii) *pro*, H. N. Hudson, *Shakespeare's Life*, etc., 1872, ii. pp. 122 ff.; Dowden, *Mind and Art*, 1875, (ed. 1909) pp. 210–21; Raleigh, *Shakespeare* ('English Men of Letters'), 1907, pp. 186 ff.; H. A. Evans, Introd. to *Henry V* (Arden ed. 1903), p. xl; John Bailey, *Shakespeare*, 1929, pp. 129 ff.; Charles Williams, *Henry V* (in *Shakespeare Criticism*, 1919–35, World's Classics, 1936, pp. 180 ff.).

speak for the rest. W. B. Yeats writes in a famous essay, inspired by Hazlitt but itself the inspiration of much later criticism, that

He has the gross vices, the coarse nerves, of one who is to rule among violent people....He is as remorseless and undistinguished as some natural force....Shakespeare has given him a resounding rhetoric that moves men, as a leading article does to-day. His purposes are so intelligible to everybody that everybody talks of him as if he succeeded. ...Shakespeare watched Henry V, not indeed as he watched the greater souls in the visionary procession, but cheerfully, as one watches some handsome spirited horse, and he spoke his tale, as he spoke all tales, with tragic irony [1].

In the view of the 'Arden' editor, on the other hand, he 'stands before us the embodiment of worldly success, and as such he is entitled to our unreserved admiration' [2]. This second statement would be almost unbelievable, were not its author clearly trying to outbid or to shout down a century of predecessors. Nearly all the critics, whether for or against Henry, are in fact agreed upon one point, that he typifies the successful Englishman, that the 'idea' of the play is, in a word, Success. Even Mr Granville-Barker sadly assents, and concludes therefrom that the writing of *Henry V* left Shakespeare disappointed with his hero and disillusioned with his art, since

he knew well enough that neither in the theatre nor in real life is it these 'embodiments of worldly success' that we carry closest in our hearts, or even care to spend an evening with....For behind the action, be the play farce or tragedy, there must be some spiritually significant idea, or it will hang lifeless. And this is what is lacking in *Henry V* [3].

Now had Shakespeare, embarking on a heroic play, enquired elsewhere than in his own breast for the

[1] *Op. cit.* pp. 163–4.   [2] *Op. cit.* p. xl.
[3] *Op. cit.* pp. 60–1.

meaning of heroic poetry, he might have found an answer in a little book called *An Apology for Poetry* by a favourite author of his, published in the year he produced his *Richard II*. To Sidney, as to every other Renaissance critic, the Heroical was the greatest of all the 'kinds' of poetry, and the heroical poet the loftiest of all poets,

who doth not only teach and move to a truth, but teacheth and moveth to the most high and excellent truth; who maketh magnanimity and justice shine throughout all misty fearfulness and foggy desires; who, if the saying of Plato and Tully be true that who could see Virtue would be wonderfully ravished with the love of her beauty—this man sets her out to make her more lovely in her holy-day apparel to the eye of any that will deign not to disdain until they understand.

Heroic poetry, it will be noted, is supreme for a *moral* reason, since it is above everything concerned with the greatest of men, whom it exhibits in action and in glory for our admiration and imitation. 'For', to quote Sidney once more,

as the image of each action stirreth and instructeth the mind, so the lofty image of such Worthies most inflameth the mind with desire to be worthy, and informs with counsel how to be worthy[1].

No Englishman in story or chronicle was more likely to inflame the minds of Englishmen of Sidney's and Shakespeare's day 'with desire to be worthy' than Henry of Monmouth. Turning regretfully from the theme of Agincourt, the poet Daniel, another of Shakespeare's favourite authors, exclaims

[1] *Apology for Poetry*, p. 179, vol. i, *Elizabethan Critical Essays*, ed. by Gregory Smith. I modernize the spelling and punctuation. The words of 4 Prol. 50 may be a conscious echo of Sidney's at p. 197; v. note below.

O, what eternal matter here is found!
Whence new immortal *Iliads* might proceed[1];

while even a short extract from Edward Hall's long
paean in his praise will make evident what Henry
stood for in the eyes of Tudor England:

This Henry was a king whose life was immaculate and
his living without spot. This king was a prince whom all
men loved and of none disdained. This prince was a captain
against whom fortune never frowned nor mischance once
spurned. This captain was a shepherd whom his flock
loved and lovingly obeyed. This shepherd was such a
justiciary that no offence was unpunished nor friendship
unrewarded. This justiciary was so feared, that all rebellion
was banished and sedition suppressed....He was merciful
to offenders, charitable to the needy, indifferent to all men,
faithful to his friends, and fierce to his enemies, toward
God most devout, toward the world moderate, and to his
realm a very father. What should I say? He was the blazing
comet and apparent lantern in his days; he was the mirror
of Christendom and the glory of his country; he was the
flower of kings past, and a glass to them that should succeed.
No Emperor in magnanimity ever him excelled[2].

Such was the idea of heroic poetry at that time, and
such was the traditional figure that confronted one
aspiring to write a heroic poem on Henry V. Neither
bears much relation to what we should to-day call the
'embodiment of worldly success'. Yet, as I shall now
try to show to 'any that will deign not to disdain until
they understand', they are to be found faithfully and
brilliantly imaged in the mirror that Shakespeare held
up in 1599.
    Let me begin by removing a fundamental and initial
misconception. 'Brute force, glossed over with a little
religious hypocrisy and archiepiscopal advice' is how

----

[1] *Civil Wars*, 1595, iv. 6. The words are placed in
Henry's own mouth.
[2] *Hall's Chronicle*, 1548, ed. 1809, pp. 112-13.

Hazlitt saw Henry's 'Virtue'; and the words take us
to the opening of the play and down to the roots of
the modern difficulties about it[1]. Practically every
critic since Hazlitt has assumed that the invasion of
France is an act of pure aggression, which is first suggested to Henry V by the Archbishop, who, in order
to avoid a wholesale expropriation of church lands,
cleverly directs his attention towards another victim.
Swinburne, for example, expands Hazlitt as follows:

The supple and shameless egotism of the churchmen on
whose political sophistries he relies for external support is
needed rather to varnish his project than to reassure his
conscience[2];

and Bradley, more temperate, though no less hostile,
writes:

When he adjures the Archbishop to satisfy him as to his
right to the French throne, he knows very well that the
Archbishop *wants* the war, because it will defer and perhaps
prevent what he considers the spoliation of the Church[3].

Now the actual invasion may have been quite un-
justifiable by modern Anglo-Saxon standards, and it is
possible to deduce the whole business of the Archbishop from Holinshed's version[4]; while it was pro-

---

[1] A large number of modern historians seem to assume
that hypocrisy was a conspicuous feature of the historical
Henry's character; a baseless charge as Wylie shows (ii. 245).

[2] *A Study of Shakespeare*, 1880, p. 112.

[3] *Oxford Lectures*, p. 257.

[4] Nineteenth-century historians generally emphasize the
'archiepiscopal advice', and though Wylie (*Henry V*, 1914,
vol. i, pp. 390–2) rejects the story altogether, he shows
that the Salic Law was debated, with all the subtilty of
scholastic argument, during negotiations between French
and English commissioners, in which Bishop Chichele took
part in 1413, and admits that Henry's claims were in fact
'monstrous' (*ibid*. i. pp. 153–5, 407).

bably Holinshed who led many of the critics astray. But history is one thing, drama another; and Holinshed's version is certainly not Shakespeare's. On the contrary, this is one of the few occasions on which Shakespeare departs from the chronicles, with the intention, I do not doubt, of guarding his hero from the very charges which modern writers have brought against him.

As Kingsford has shown, the story goes back to *Caxton's Chronicles*, 1480, which relates that the

bishops and men of the spiritualty doubted that he [Henry] would have had the temporalities out of their hands: wherefore they encouraged the King to challenge Normandy, and his right to France, to the end to set him awork there, so that he should not seek occasions to enter into such matters.

Hall, an ardent Protestant, always on the look out for evidence of chicanery in the unreformed Church, seized upon this hint, associated the business with a debate in the Parliament of Leicester, 1414, and invented appropriate speeches for the Archbishop, the Earl of Westmorland, and the Duke of Exeter[1]; Holinshed, as usual, borrowed from Hall, and thus the matter reached Shakespeare. He, however, though needing the speeches for reasons to be presently indicated, obliterated the anti-clerical implications of the incident, and entirely changed its relevance to Henry's claims on the French crown.

In the first place, it is clear from his text that before the Archbishop takes any hand in the affair at all, not only has the whole question of Henry's titles in France been broached, and, presumably in order to test the ground, a claim to 'certain dukedoms' already been lodged (the answer to which claim is brought by

[1] C. L. Kingsford, *English Historical Literature*, pp. 120–1; cf. Wylie, i. 390–2.

French ambassadors who arrive in the second scene), but the King's

> loyal subjects,
> Whose hearts have left their bodies here in England,
> And lie pavilioned in the fields of France,

have long since decided for an invasion. Next, so far from initiating anything, the Archbishop's speech on the Salic Law is delivered at the invitation of the King, who, though the general validity of the English claims has been recognized since the time of Edward III, when they were first put forward, is anxious to leave no corner of the legal position unexplored before taking the final step. It is not the Archbishop who sets the King awork, but the King the Archbishop; and we gather a general impression, which is everything in drama, of an imminent war, for which the country is all afire, only delayed by the uprightness of the young King, who wishes first to be absolutely certain of the justice of his cause. This is brought out in Henry's solemn 'conjuration' to the Archbishop to take heed how he 'incites' him to shed blood, a speech given him by Shakespeare to mark the gravity of the occasion and the scrupulosity of the King's conscience[1].

Lastly, the sole connection between the subject of the Archbishop's speech and the question of Church lands is that both are spoken of in the conversation of the two bishops which constitutes the opening scene. From this we glean the following information: that a bill for the wholesale expropriation of Church property is before Parliament; that the King, though, 'as a true lover of the holy Church', not in normal times likely to countenance such proceedings, might be tempted to

[1] Cf. *Henry V* ('Warwick Shakespeare'), p. 149, the best edition I know, whose editor, G. C. Moore Smith, alone seems to have understood what happens here.

use an opportunity of thus filling his coffers for the
French war; that the Archbishop, in the perfectly
legitimate desire of removing the temptation from his
path, waits upon him and offers, in the name of Convocation, a large subsidy towards the war; and that this
offer naturally leads to talk between them about the
diplomatic preliminaries, in the course of which Henry
learns for the first time of the Archbishop's knowledge
of French constitutional law, eagerly begs him to expound the matter, but is for the moment prevented
from hearing him by the arrival of the French ambassadors. Not a hint of a bribe on the Archbishop's part,
still less of his provoking the King to war in order to
protect Church property! Unhappy Shakespeare! He
little dreamed that learned doctors would read their
Holinshed or Holinshed's modern successors instead
of his play, and so draw precisely those cynical conclusions, the evidence for which he had been at pains
to erase from the record.

Yet he would not and could not dispense with the
Archbishop and his speech. For one thing, some discussion of the young King's conversion was needed at
the outset as a link with *Henry IV*, and who more apt
for this than a couple of clergymen? Secondly, he
wanted to preface his dramatic epic on an ideal King
by some disquisition on the character of good government, with allusions to parallels in music and the world
of nature; and for this a grave prelate would again be
the natural speaker. But the discourse on the Salic
Law is in a different category. Why did Shakespeare,
generally ready to sacrifice almost anything in his
sources likely to induce boredom in the audience,
transplant therefrom this tiresome genealogical lecture,
sixty-three lines long, and full of obscure names, some
of which he did not even trouble to transcribe correctly? Our producers, quite wisely, cut it drastically;
Shakespeare could no more do without something of
the kind than a modern historian can omit Magna

Carta from an account of the reign of John[1]. To the
Elizabethans France was a lost possession of the English
crown; lost during the disastrous Wars of the Roses,
which are the main theme of *Henry VI*, but never
prescriptively abandoned, even after the bitter humilia-
tion of the capture of Calais by the French in 1558.
Moreover, the English title seemed to Englishmen self-
evident. Edward III was the son of Isabella, daughter
of Philip IV, and thus after the death of her three
brothers, Louis X, Philip V, and Charles IV, he
became the rightful heir of his grandfather, whereas
it was Philip VI, a nephew of Philip IV, who had
actually ascended the French throne. As for the Salic
Law, supposedly derived from the old Frankish customs, which barred the rights of females to the suc-
cession, that was a fraudulent plea worked up by
French lawyers of the fourteenth century in order to
support the claims of Philip VI against those of Edward III. The Archbishop's demonstration, therefore,
that the said 'law' (i) has no relevance whatever to
'the realm of France', and, (ii) if it had, would bar the
rights of the entire French house, seeing that Hugh
Capet pretended to trace his descent from a daughter
of Charlemagne, was at once the legal vindication of
Henry's claims, an essential preliminary to any serious
treatment of the theme of the play, and a formal statement of the still valid rights of the English royal line.
Michael Drayton makes as much of Henry's claims in his
Battaile of Agincourt, 1627[2], and got Selden to append
a long 'illustration' on the question to the Seventeenth
Song of his *Polyolbion*[3]. Neither Elizabeth nor James

---

[1] The anonymous play, *Edward III* (1596), similarly
opens with a demonstration of Edward's rights to the French
throne (v. Tucker Brooke, *The Shakespeare Apocrypha*,
p. 69).

[2] This is, of course, the longer poem, not the well-known
ballad.

[3] v. *Poetical Works*, ed. R. Hooper, 1876, ii. pp. 246 ff.

was in a position to 'rouse him in his throne of France';
but the dynastic title was theirs to be jealously guarded
for assertion when a favourable moment came. Nor
was it merely the concern of the crown; it was no
doubt immensely popular. Few, if any, of the theatre
audience would know or care about the names in
question; but most would expect to hear the case
argued. And the Archbishop argues well. Being consti-
tutionally litigious, Elizabethans loved a good pleader,
while it flattered their national pride to hear it *proved*
that France belonged to them.

When the Henry of the play, therefore, affirms that
he puts forth his 'rightful hand in a well-hallowed
cause', he is speaking the simple truth. The war against
France is a righteous war; and seemed as much so to
Shakespeare's public as the war against the Nazis seems
to us. Once this is realized, a fog of suspicion and
detraction is lifted from the play; the mirror held up
in 1599 shines bright once more; and we are at liberty
to find a hero's face reflected within it. That face has
been hitherto dimmed by other misconceptions also;
but they are less serious than the one just considered,
and may be dealt with as the occasion arises.

There are, however, heroes and heroes. Assuming
that Shakespeare accepted the critical ideals of his age,
what sort of hero is he likely to have set before men's
eyes, so as to inflame their minds 'with desire to be
worthy' and inform them 'with counsel how to be
worthy'? One thing we can at any rate be certain of:
he would be content with nothing less than a human
being. The very nature of his genius, its instinctive
drive and bias, assures us of something very wrong in
a recent criticism of Henry's speeches as 'the golden
throatings of a hollow god[1]'. And it was of 'hollow
gods' that Johnson was thinking when he wrote:

---

[1] *Shakespeare*, by Mark van Doren, p. 179.

'Shakespeare has no heroes; his scenes are occupied only by men, who act and speak as the reader thinks that he would himself have spoken or acted on the same occasion[1].' Yet the criticism is just to this extent, that not until towards the end of act 3, as we read the play, does the humanity of the King begin to engage our hearts[2]. Is this because Shakespeare's creative imagination only at that point got to work upon his hero, that he took in fact some time to 'wind himself into his subject'? Or did he deliberately, and gradually, shift his focus as the action of the play developed? It is not easy to say. But a shift in the focus there certainly is, and it is one that might well have been adopted by a dramatist who set out to inflame an audience, prone to admire one kind of hero, with worship for another kind altogether.

To the ordinary Elizabethan, who did not read Sidney or even Hall, Henry V was first and foremost a great conqueror, a popular national hero who had been 'outstretched', as Hamlet might say, by two centuries of acclamation. In the opening words of the play Shakespeare gives this public what it wants, and in the most magnificent manner possible:

> O for a Muse of fire, that would ascend
> The brightest heaven of invention:
> A kingdom for a stage, princes to act,
> And monarchs to behold the swelling scene.
> Then should the warlike Harry, like himself,
> Assume the port of Mars, and at his heels,
> Leashed in like hounds, should Famine, Sword and Fire
> Crouch for employment.

The hero thus conjured up, in what Hazlitt, the admirer of Napoleon, calls 'perhaps one of the most

---

[1] *Preface to Shakespeare* (v. *Johnson on Shakespeare*, ed. W. Raleigh, 1908, p. 14).

[2] Burbage would, no doubt, have won them earlier.

striking images in all Shakespeare', springs from the
Marlovian sphere; he is a kind of English Tamburlaine.
We have the same Harry, once more outstretched
against the bright epical background, in the message
of Exeter, the English ambassador, which menaces the
French King with

> Bloody constraint: for if you hide the crown
> Even in your hearts, there will he rake for it.
> Therefore in fierce tempest is he coming,
> In thunder and in earthquake, like a Jove:
> That, if requiring fail, he will compel.

Nor is this vision of him in any way disturbed by his
words and actions before he leaves England, by his
dealings with the Archbishop and his Council, by his
sarcastic 'merry message' in answer to the Dauphin's
'tun of tennis-balls', or even by the long speech of
impassioned reproach to 'the man that was his bedfellow'. The last ends in a sob indeed, but we feel
that Friendship, not Harry, weeps. All this only teaches
us that the great King is as much above the stature of
ordinary men in statecraft as he is in conquest. Lastly,
in his summons to Harfleur to surrender, one of the
most dreadful speeches in Shakespeare, though based
upon the book of Deuteronomy and no doubt reflecting
contemporary Christian usage[1], we seem to hear the
voice of Tamburlaine himself.

Up to the taking of Harfleur, Henry is what John
Bailey calls 'the most royal, masterful, and victorious
of Shakespeare's kings'. And the impression has been
so firmly established that it remains with us for the rest
of the play. Yet Harfleur is a turning-point. For no
sooner does the governor yield than we become conscious that Henry's fierce intimidation is a mere device
to bring an end to the siege, on the part of a commander
anxious, because of sickness among his troops, to hurry

---

[1] v. note 3. 3. 1–43.

on to Calais; while in the brief order, 'Use mercy to them all[1]', given to Exeter whom he leaves in temporary command of the town, we have the first glimpse of a real man behind the traditional heroic mask. From this moment we are brought closer and closer to him, until we come, if not to know him well, at least to do him homage, even to think of him with affection; the homage and affection some of us pay to a Nelson or a Gordon. And that this change of focus was not just accidental, or occasioned by a character suddenly 'taking charge' of its creator, is suggested by the fact that it coincides with another change, equally interesting and structurally closely connected, a change of atmosphere.

The background of *Henry V* is war; and its atmosphere, as in most epics, is determined by the poet's attitude towards war. Now war may be conceived in two ways: as man's greatest vocation, the pursuit of Glory, at the risk of one's own life or those of others, and through the ruthless exercise of power; or as one of the greatest of human evils, with its miserable train of blood and anguish, horror and tears. The first, on the whole that of the traditional epic, is once again Marlowe's; the second, represented by Hardy's *Dynasts* and Tolstoi's *War and Peace*, is on the whole modern. Shakespeare gives both, one after the other. Yet there is no sudden transition, no violent contrast or crude incongruity: the change is so natural and inevitable that a spectator will not realize it is taking place; it corresponds with the development of the campaign, and reflects the mood of the nation and the army. The first two acts are concerned with the preparation for the descent upon France; and, once the legal and diplomatic preliminaries have been dealt with, the

[1] This, though historically correct (Wylie, ii. 58–9), finds no support in Holinshed. 'Harflue yeelded and sacked' is his marginal summary of the proceedings.

aspects of the war most emphasized are the light-
hearted enthusiasm of the nation, and ferocious descrip-
tions by its accredited representatives of what is coming
to the enemy. In other words, we see England going
to war after the fashion of all times and all countries:

> Now all the youth of England are on fire,
> And silken dalliance in the wardrobe lies,

says Shakespeare's Chorus;

> Now God be thanked Who has matched us with His hour,
> And caught our youth, and wakened us from sleeping,

echoes an English youth, Rupert Brooke, three hundred
and fifteen years later; while the preliminary phase of
bluster and threats, mirrored especially in 1. 2. 100–31,
274–98, has by now become so well known that in
'jingoism[1]' we have invented a special word for it.
There follows the sailing of the expeditionary force,
brilliantly presented in the third Prologue. And then,
suddenly, the audience is before Harfleur; and begins,
with the army, to face the realities of war for the first
time. For though Shakespeare quickens the pulse of
every patriot by Henry's charge to his troops, a speech
which opens,

> Once more unto the breach, dear friends, once more;
> Or close the wall up with our English dead,

shows that war is something more than 'a thing for an
editorial—a triumphal parade[2]'. And in the next scene

---

[1] Derived from a music-hall song of 1878 with the
refrain:

> 'We don't want to fight, yet by Jingo! if we do,
> We've got the ships, we've got the men, we've got
> the money too!'

Cf. 1. 2. 125: 'Your grace hath cause, and means, and
might.'

[2] Stephen Benét, *John Brown's Body*, Oxford, 1944,
p. 103.

but one Henry sets war before us in all its naked brutality, when he summons the town to surrender; while seeing that, as explained above, this speech has little relevance to character, I am persuaded that Shakespeare wrote it in order to bring home to his audience the meaning of war in terms of human agony.

Nor is this the only occasion on which he goes out of his way to do so. Honest Williams, concerned for the state of his soul before battle, gives us the following vivid glimpse of the stricken field:

But if the cause be not good, the king himself hath a heavy reckoning to make, when all those legs, and arms, and heads, chopped off in a battle, shall join together at the latter day, and cry all, 'We died at such a place'; some swearing, some crying for a surgeon; some upon their wives left poor behind them; some upon the debts they owe, some upon their children rawly left....I am afeard there are few die well, that die in a battle.

Montjoy gives us another glimpse after the fight is over[1]. And in the last scene of all Burgundy has a speech of forty lines describing the devastation which war has wrought upon the 'lovely visage' of fair France, lest the spectators should go away imagining that victory means nothing but fresh territory and the joyful homecoming of the conquerors. Of course, there is jesting also; but at what period have English soldiers not made fun of war?—behaviour which nations, to whom war is a vocation, find it hard to understand. It must be added that the English are also prone, too prone, to make fun of their enemies; and *Henry V* faithfully reflects this national characteristic as well. In short, as a recent writer has observed, while fighting is incidental to many other Shakespeare plays, 'In *Henry V* war is itself a theme—its glories, humours and passions; its dutiful courage and proud cruelty; its

[1] Cf. 4. 7. 74–80.

brilliant surface and the horrors that lie beneath it.'
Yet when the same writer goes on to characterize the
play as 'the glorification of a patriot king and an ex-
posure of the wicked futility of his enterprise', and
therefore a supreme instance of Shakespeare's 'ironic
detachment[1]', he misses the whole point. For, first,
the 'brilliant surface and the horrors' represent, not the
comment of some Epicurean divinity upon human
strife, but what war has ever seemed, first in prospect
and then in reality, and in particular what it looks like
to Henry and his army before and after they have
actual experience of it. And, second, the more they
experience it, the greater they become. In a word, the
'idea' of *Henry V* is not Success, but Heroism.

The turning-point, I have said, is Harfleur. Up to
then 'sits Expectation in the air'; after, the English
are dogged by sickness and despondency, utter weariness and sore peril, to say nothing of dilapidated boots,
tattered garments and the discomfort of 'rainy marching
in the painful field'; until, with their line of retreat
to Calais cut off and forced to give battle,

            The poor condemnéd English
Like sacrifices, by their watchful fires
Sit patiently, and inly ruminate
The morning's danger: and their gesture sad,
Investing lank-lean cheeks, and war-worn coats,
Presenteth them unto the gazing moon
So many horrid ghosts.

Agincourt was a great victory; great in its decisive
results, but greatest of all in its moral significance. For
it was the triumph of a much inferior army, diseased,
famished, weary, bedraggled, dispirited, over a mighty
French array, fresh, magnificently equipped, and entirely confident; a triumph which, under God, was

---

1 John Palmer, *Political Characters in Shakespeare*, 1945,
p. 228.

due to the heroic spirit of the great King. 'The most foolhardy and reckless adventure that ever an un-reasoning pietist·devised' is how a modern historian[1] describes the march from Harfleur. Yet the same writer calls it our English anabasis. And it is its heroic character which Shakespeare insists upon in scene after scene, speech after speech, and once even in a stage-direction, though the editors have obliterated it[2]. For the zenith of the play is not the victory—that is lightly passed over, and (in itself miraculous[3]) is ascribed to God alone—but the King's speeches before the battle is joined, the battle which all but the King think already lost. Every line of what Henry then says breathes the English temper, but one above all—

We few, we happy few, we band of brothers.

If History never repeats itself, the human spirit often does: Henry's words before Agincourt, and Churchill's after the Battle of Britain, come from the same national mint.

It is thus not to glory, or even to pride in 'the ex-pansion of England', that Shakespeare mainly ap-peals in *Henry V*, but to the admiration and homage which Englishmen and Scots, like the Greeks before them, instinctively pay to those who withstand an overwhelming force or power. Such battle, if fought to the death as at Thermopylae, or till victory as at Bannockburn, by a body of men united in affection and loyalty under an indomitable leader, has always appeared in their eyes the finest of war-plays. I use a word that often occurs in Anglo-Saxon poetry; for this sort of homage is as time-honoured as it is native. It goes back to the sea-rovers who colonized Iceland and these islands, and in whose heroic tales, as W. P. Ker

[1] Wylie, ii. 76.   [2] Cf. note 3. 6. 83 S.D.
[3] Cf. Wylie, ii. 190, n. 8.

has taught us, 'no kind of adventure is so common or better told in the earlier heroic manner than the defence of a narrow place against odds[1]'. It inspired what is perhaps the noblest fragment of Anglo-Saxon epic that has come down to us, *The Battle of Maldon,* which describes the glorious last stand of a small company of English, with their leader Byrhtnoth, against a superior force of Danes who landed on the shores of Essex in A.D. 991. And that English hearts in Shakespeare's day were as apt as those of their remote ancestors to thrill at such an appeal is shown by Raleigh's fervent account of *The Last Fight of the 'Revenge',* in which ship Sir Richard Grenville engaged a powerful Spanish fleet single-handed for fifteen hours in 1591[2]. Finally, to bring the record up to date, I quote a Swiss observer, who, giving his impressions of a visit to England last summer, exclaims:

How characteristic that of all the great events of the war it is not the victories of Alexander and Montgomery which have left the deepest impression upon the consciousness of the English people, but reverses which show English endurance put to the supreme test, the glorious reverses of Dunkirk and Arnhem![3]

Heroism is then the theme, and Henry the hero. In the humanizing of him that follows Harfleur Shakespeare breathes the spirit of Sidney's heroical 'worthy'. into the lay figure he found in Hall; and adds the vitalizing touch of his own divine genius. 'No emperor in magnanimity ever him excelled', says Hall. We have seen his quality of mercy shown towards the inhabitants of Harfleur. It is still further stressed in the words,

[1] *Epic and Romance,* 1897, p. 5.
[2] Some of these parallels are noted in *Shakespeare and his predecessors* (1896), by Dr F. S. Boas.
[3] v. an article by Martin Hürlimann in *Atlantis,* August, 1945, and *Time and Tide,* 8 Sept. 1945, p. 749, for a comment upon it.

based upon Holinshed[1], which he utters after the arrest
of Bardolph for plundering a church:

And we give express charge that in our marches through
the country there be nothing compelled from the villages;
nothing taken but paid for; none of the French upbraided
or abused in disdainful language; for when lenity and
cruelty play for a kingdom, the gentler gamester is the
soonest winner.

With such clemency his order for the slaying of the
prisoners at the height of the battle seems in strange
discord until it is realized that this episode, like the
speech of the Archbishop on the Salic Law, has been
altogether misapprehended by modern critics. Holinshed writes apologetically of the King's 'dolorous
decree', and explains that it is 'contrary to his accus-
tomed gentleness'; Shakespeare, who might have
omitted it[2], offers no apologies, but sets the decree in
a framework of circumstances which, when followed
on the stage, in scenes 4. 4 to 4. 7, which are in fact
one continuous battle-scene, makes it seem natural and
inevitable. Once again the critics have read the
chronicler instead of watching the dramatist at work;
and bemused themselves with attempts to unravel
Holinshed's tangled skein which Shakespeare had carefully straightened out.

  The whole situation is dominated by the fact that
the English are 'enrounded' by an army which out-
numbers them five to one[3]. Henry is indeed so short
of men that, as we are informed at the end of 4. 4,
he is obliged to leave his camp unguarded except by
boys, while even at the moment of their ignominious
flight one of the French nobles declares in 4. 5,

  [1] v. Wylie, ii. 90–1, for the historical evidence.
  [2] Cf. the omission of the 'sack' of Harfleur, referred
to above, p. xxvii.
  [3] Cf. notes 4 Prol. 36; 4. 3. 3, 4.

> We are enow yet living in the field
> To smother up the English in our throngs,
> If any order might be thought upon.

Encouraged by this recollection, and by the do-or-die determination of Bourbon, who recalls them to their duty, the French commanders, later in the same scene, return to the battle from which they had first fled, resolved to sell their lives dearly in some desperate counterstroke. It is a hazardous moment for the English, as spectators with any knowledge of warfare will be aware; since by a successful rally the French might not only offset their initial repulse, but, with the weight of numbers on their side, wrest the crown of victory from Henry's grasp. And Henry himself is well aware of this, as is shown us at the opening of 4. 6, when, congratulating his troops on what has so far been accomplished, he warns them at the same time

> But all's not done, yet keep the French the field.

Nor has he long to wait. The 'alarum' sounds, telling him of a rally, while we realize that some 'order' has been 'thought upon', and that Bourbon has managed to pull his men together for the counter-attack.

Henry's response is immediate and unhesitating. At the beginning of 4. 6 he had entered 'with prisoners', which on the stage should, I suggest, be represented as more numerous than the men who guard them[1]. In any case an encumbrance, since it is not possible for the same soldiers to guard and to fight, prisoners become a grave embarrassment under attack. Moreover, if rescued, they would add dangerously, if not fatally, to the enemy's already excessive numbers. Accordingly, the King issues the only command possible under the circumstances. 'But hark!' he cries,

[1] There is some contemporary evidence for this; v. Wylie, ii. 175.

> What new alarum is this same?
> The French have reinforced their scattered men:
> Then every soldier kill his prisoners,
> Give the word through—

and at once hurries forward to the quarter from which
the attack threatens. The order is one that, the security
of his whole force being at stake, any general then
would have given. Monstrelet, the contemporary Bur-
gundian chronicler, explains the situation clearly, and
never even suggests that the order requires justifica-
tion[1]. Further, there occurred during Shakespeare's
own lifetime an almost exact parallel in the massacre,
at Lord Grey's command in November, 1580, of five
or six hundred Spanish filibusters, captured at Smer-
wick in Ireland, prisoners who could not have been
conveyed through a hostile country by a force little
greater in number than themselves, without endangering
the whole position of the English rule in Ireland, and

---

[1] Cf. *Chroniques*, trans. T. Johnes, 1810, iv. pp. 180–2.
Wylie (ii. 175) sums it all up thus: 'In France even his
most furious critic [among contemporary writers]...vents
not a syllable of blame for this massacre on the battlefield.
For given the circumstances in those days the French would
have done the same themselves had they been in so perilous
a case. And so...[they] reserved their wrath for those
"wicked men" on their own side who would not recognise
that they were beaten by the rules of the game and whose
useless rally made this dreadful slaughter a necessity.'
A point on which Wylie throws no light is the tactical
problem. As an eminent living authority on the art of
war puts it to me, how could the troops have had time,
with an unforeseen counter-attack upon them, and without
machine-guns, to kill masses of prisoners who had been
only partially disarmed? But Shakespeare did not need to
worry about such questions, and in asking them we pass
from the sphere of drama into that of the historian, to
whom the problem must be left.

Spenser ardently defends the 'heroic spirit' of his chief for his conduct in this affair[1].

But Shakespeare had yet another point to make in favour of Henry's 'heroic spirit'. At the opening of 4. 7 he brings in Fluellen and Gower to tell us what the great counterstroke of the French had been. 'The cowardly rascals that ran from the battle' (i.e. Bourbon, the Constable, and the rest, whom we saw running in 4. 5) had 'reinforced their scattered men', and fallen—upon the undefended English camp, putting all the boys they found there to the sword! The attack is historical; and Fluellen's exclamation, "'Tis expressly against the law of arms, 'tis as arrant a piece of knavery, mark you now, as can be offert!' is in accordance with much contemporary comment on the battle, which shows that the treacherous assault left a deep stain upon the chivalry of France. Thus any lingering doubt about Henry's action is blotted from the minds of even the most squeamish in the audience, while his blazing anger and further threats at the sight of other bands of Frenchmen galloping about the field, on his return from avenging the boys, are fully justified[2]. In point of fact, it is only when the French herald appears and admits the victory to be an English one, that he

---

[1] Cf. Spenser, *View of the present state of Ireland*, ed. W. L. Renwick, pp. 139 ff., 244 ff. Prof. Renwick, who himself drew my attention to this parallel, comments on p. 245: 'Any court chosen from the most high-minded commanders of sixteenth-century Europe would certainly have declared unanimously that Grey's action was justified by the laws of war.' The truth is, commanders in the field often have dreadful decisions forced upon them, which civilians condemn because they shut their eyes to, or are ignorant of, the still more dreadful alternatives.

[2] Johnson, voicing the bewilderment of critics, exclaims: 'The King is in a very bloody disposition. He has already cut the throats of his prisoners, and threatens now to cut them again.'

can breathe freely at all. The slaughter of the prisoners might, I have said, have been omitted. Yet Shakespeare makes it central to his account of the battle. Indeed, it is almost the only aspect of it he sets upon the stage; for though the hubris of the French, which was the primary cause of their overthrow[1], is well brought out in scenes 3. 7 and 4. 2, strangely enough nothing whatever is said of the bowmen of England, who were the real victors. Clearly, Shakespeare's attention was concentrated upon Henry and he intended ours to be. Thus the general impression which the incident was designed to convey, and which I do not doubt was conveyed to the original audiences, is not one of brutality at all, but of a great commander's strength, decision, and presence of mind at the crisis of the battle. No wonder honest Gower cries, 'O, 'tis a gallant king!' and Fluellen goes on to speak of Alexander the Great.

The details of the story are to be found in Holinshed; but he has not linked them together. Shakespeare forges a link in the person of Bourbon[2]. He shows Bourbon reanimating the spirits of the runaway commanders in 4. 5; and he shows it was Bourbon who led the attack on the boys by the stage-direction for Henry's re-entry after the attack has been crushed, which stands thus in the Folio: 'Alarum. Enter King Harry and Burbon with priſoners. Flouriſh.' By dropping 'Burbon with priſoners' from the directions in his text Capell became largely responsible for the commentators' misunderstanding of what takes place, though it begins with Johnson, who still retained the direction in full.

I have run ahead. But the slaying of the prisoners is so famous and its misunderstanding is so generally entertained that it casts a baleful shadow over Henry's

[1] Wylie, ii. 199–204.
[2] That Bourbon actually distinguished himself there is contemporary evidence, v. Wylie, ii. 163.

earlier actions. It is therefore well to have it out of
the way before we consider him in those desperate
hours on the eve of the battle when he rises to the
supreme height of his heroic stature. As the ordeal
draws near Shakespeare reveals more and more of the
man to us, and his humanity is the argument at once
of his conversation with the soldiers and of the soliloquy that follows. Where else, too, in English poetry
is to be found our English notion of leadership better
expressed than in the fourth Chorus, which describes
him touring the camp throughout the night, and
cheering the 'ruined band' by his mere presence, words
of comfort being idle mockery in that awful predica-
ment? Above all, the grimmer things seem, the gayer
he becomes. Such gaiety is infectious; as recent experience has taught us, can even be caught by a whole
nation from the example of one man. For, as Henry
himself remarks,

'Tis good for men to love their present pains,
Upon example—so the spirit is eased:
And when the mind is quickened, out of doubt
The organs, though defunct and dead before,
Break up their drowsy grave, and newly move
With casted slough and fresh legerity.

Those who miss the gaiety of act 4 have missed one of
the finest effects of the play. It animates almost everything the King says or does before the battle. How
light-heartedly does he give good-morrow to his
brothers and old Erpingham! as if it had been a hunts-
man's horn in England that makes them 'early stirrers'.
Yet, as he tells the soldier Michael Williams not long
after, the whole army knows that they are 'even as
men wracked upon a sand, that look to be washed off
the next tide'. He is quite ready again to devise a jest
against the same soldier through the exchange of gloves
for a challenge, upon a morrow none of them may see.

And though he is grave in the discourses on Kingship, he is merry enough in that on Crispin Crispian over the stories the veterans will tell 'in their flowing cups' and the thought of 'gentlemen in England, now a-bed[1]'. Gaiety of this kind belongs to the genius of heroic leadership, a genius which, likely enough, the historical Henry himself possessed. Certainly Nelson did; and the lines in which Wordsworth describes the hero of Trafalgar might well have been written of the hero of Agincourt:

> But who, if he be called upon to face
> Some awful moment to which Heaven has joined
> Great issues, good or bad for human kind,
> Is happy as a lover; and attired
> With sudden brightness, like a man inspired[2].

No doubt the source of this inspiration differs with different leaders; but many great English soldiers have found it in their religion; and Shakespeare makes it clear that Henry does so likewise. In the first two and a half acts his references to God sound a little official. But the dangers of the campaign bring out the real man here as in other respects. After the crossing of the Somme the plight of the English host is made evident for the first time in an interview between Henry and Montjoy, who is sent to bid him face the facts and surrender. Henry admits the facts; but rejects the consequence. The interview over, Gloucester expresses the fears of all present in a fervently uttered 'I hope they will not come upon us now!' To which the King simply, almost casually, replies, 'We are in God's hand, brother, not in theirs', and turns directly to the duties of the day. The words sound a deeper,

---

[1] Cf. the suggestive essay on 'Henry V' by Charles Williams (v. *supra*, p. xv n.), and a fine treatment of the conversation with the soldiers by H. N. Hudson, *op. cit.*

[2] *Character of a Happy Warrior*, ll. 48–52.

humbler, more intimate note than we have heard
hitherto, and suggest a Henry who bows spirit as well
as knees, and finds in prayer a source of strength and
confidence. Nor is it the only hint of the kind. We may
infer that the implied counsel to his senior staff to
'dress' them 'fairly' for their 'end[1]', and the more
explicit counsel of the same sort to his soldiers later[2],
would not have been offered had he not already performed a like action himself, as his historical counterpart is known to have done[3].

But he has yet another prayer to utter, this time on
behalf of his army as king and leader; and that Shakespeare, as is fitting, allows us to overhear. It is one of
the most remarkable passages in the play, being as
central to the mighty wheel of the eight history plays
on the rise and fall of the house of Lancaster as are the
lines,

> So saying, her rash hand in evil hour
> Forth stretching to the Fruit, she pluck'd, she eat,

to *Paradise Lost*. On that topic, however, I have
already said something[4]. What I would stress here is
the spirit in which the prayer is uttered. No claims
of any kind are made; no reference to the justness of
the cause; not even a petition for victory. All Henry
asks is that courage be granted his soldiers to fight
against overwhelming odds, and that the crime of his
father, in compassing the throne by the deposition and
death of Richard, be not weighed in the balance against
them. And the attitude of the petitioner is evident
from the closing words, in which, after speaking of

---

[1] 4. 1. 10.   [2] 4. 1. 175 ff.
[3] Wylie, ii. 146.
[4] Cf. Introduction to *1 Henry IV*, pp. xxv–xxvi. It is
interesting to note that Drayton, probably copying Shakespeare, gives Henry a similar prayer in his *Battaile of
Agincourt.*

what he has tried to do by way of expiation, he continues:

> More will I do:
> Though all that I can do is nothing worth;
> Since that my penitence comes after all,
> Imploring pardon.

Is this bowed figure the 'warlike Harry' who 'assumes the port of Mars' and hurls himself upon France

> In thunder and in earthquake, like a Jove?

It is the same, seen no longer from without but from within; and all the more a hero, because now known as a man. Yet Shakespeare has a still finer moment for him, the last before battle, into which he sends his soldiers, no longer as at Harfleur with the war-cry 'God for England, Harry and Saint George!' but with a petition, 'How thou pleasest, God, dispose the day!' The words are not to be taken as implying despondency or resignation; on the contrary, as Charles Williams has observed, they are uttered gaily, like almost everything else the King says in the scene, and express the spiritual exaltation which inspires him, and through him the whole English army, at this crisis of their fate. One may paraphrase them roughly: 'Death or Victory, as God wills!—what matter which, since Honour comes either way, in heaven or on earth?[1]' It is a statement of the ultimate heroic faith, a faith which, like that of the martyrs, puts him who holds it beyond reach of mortal man.

After Agincourt anti-climax was hardly to be avoided, and most critics have complained of the emptiness of the fifth act. Yet, the fine description of Henry's home-

[1] For Henry's views of Honour in heaven, v. 4. 3. 98–103. Williams builds a rather fanciful structure, it seems to me, on this passage; but he is right to call attention to it, and to compare it with the lines about Fame in *Lycidas*.

coming, the eating of the leek by Pistol, and the wooing
of Katharine make a good mixture and the first two
ingredients have generally been approved. So I believe
the third would also have been, but for an unfortunate
misunderstanding about it, which is the last this Introduction must remove. It was Dr Johnson who here
first led the world astray; and his note, still being
quoted with approval by critics[1], runs as follows:

I know not why Shakespeare now gives the king nearly
such a character as he made him formerly ridicule in Percy.
This military grossness and unskilfulness in all the softer
arts, does not suit very well with the gaieties of his youth,
with the general knowledge ascribed to him at his accession,
or with the contemptuous message sent him by the Dauphin,
who represents him as fitter for the ball room than the field,
and tells him that he is not *to revel into duchies*, or win
provinces *with a nimble galliard*.

Johnson is usually so level-headed in judgment, and
so careful a reader of his text, that this criticism fills
one with astonishment. For Prince Hal ridicules no
such characteristics in Hotspur as he himself displays
as King Henry; nor does Hotspur's off-hand treatment
of his married Kate bear any real resemblance to
Henry's forthright conversation with his unmarried
one; while as for 'the gaieties of his youth', Johnson
has forgotten that their venue was the tavern and the
highway, not polite society, and that they brought him
into the company of topers and wenches, not of ladies
in ballrooms. The bishops, again, speak in I. I of his
proficiency in divinity, statecraft, and military affairs,
but say nothing at all of 'the softer arts'. Lastly, the
Dauphin's 'contemptuous message' was clearly worded
to show us that the French prince was totally ignorant
of the youthful habits he affected to despise in the
English one.

[1] Tillyard, *Shakespeare's History Plays*, p. 311; Van
Doren, *Shakespeare*, p. 175.

Yet Johnson's criticism serves to remind us of a fact that should never be forgotten, viz. that Henry is simply Hal grown up and grown wise[1], and that we have the story of his education in *Henry IV*. And is not the courtship of Katharine exactly the kind of wooing we might expect of the adult Hal, of a man who has had no experience or training in 'the softer arts', but despises what he knows of them, of a soldier genuinely in love, but to whom integrity of mind and plain dealing are the very pith of life? May we not even guess it to be the kind of wooing Shakespeare himself admired? Certainly, it is the way that men of the kind he admired, or was admiring up to the time he wrote *Henry V*, have with a maid. Imagine Benedick in love with a French Kate instead of a Beatrice of Messina; would he not go to work in just this fashion? Henry again seems like a more mature and self-confident Berowne, who has altogether forsworn the 'taffeta phrases, silken terms precise' which he always detested in his heart, and now woos 'in russet yeas and honest kersey noes'. Swinburne, in his second, shorter, and often better book on Shakespeare, truly remarks that in 'the noble and chivalrous Bastard' of *King John* we have 'a type which found its final and crowning expression in the person of King Henry V: the humorous-heroic[2]'. Agincourt shows us 'the humorous-heroic' man as leader; in the final scene we see 'the humorous-heroic' man in love, and making love as the Bastard might have made love to Blanche of Spain, had Shakespeare chosen to exhibit him so doing[3].

[1] Some critics deny that the boy Hal is father to the man Henry; e.g. Tillyard, *op. cit.* p. 306. A similar view in *The Essential Shakespeare*, p. 86, has since yielded to a further study of the plays in question. Cf. note 1. 2. 277-8.

[2] *Shakespeare*, 1909, p. 18.

[3] In *The Troublesome Reign* the Bastard is a suitor for the hand of Blanche; v. my *King John*, p. xxi.

Herford defines the 'norm of love' in Shakespeare as 'the healthy and natural self-fulfilment of man and woman, calling heart and wit and senses alike into vigorous play'. And such love, he remarks, 'not being itself ridiculous,' is only capable of comic treatment through 'the wit and humour of the lovers themselves' or because of 'some piquancy of situation[1]'. Shakespeare makes use of both humour and piquancy in the wooing of Katharine: the humour of the soldier-king and the piquancy of the language difficulty. And surely never was there a declaration which expressed the Shakespearian 'norm of love' more precisely and satisfactorily. 'Military grossness'? English lovers in the sixteenth century were wont to speak of the facts of life without mincing; and what may seem to modern ears the grossest portion of the dialogue is exchanged between the King and the Duke of Burgundy out of the ladies' earshot. Nor are we to be surprised if 'the mirror of Christendom' should in the age of Henry VIII, Elizabeth, and Henri Quatre allow himself such frankness. In any case, when Henry engages with his Katharine to 'compound a boy, half French half English, that shall go to Constantinople, and take the Turk by the beard', we could ill dispense with so 'signal a stroke of irony', which links *Henry V* with the sequel trilogy, dealing with the disastrous reign of the 'boy' in question.

The earliest critic to note the irony was the mid-nineteenth century American editor, H. N. Hudson, and I cannot do better than round off my attempted re-interpretation of a stupidly misapprehended scene by quoting some of the excellent things he has to say about it, which come like a fresh breeze into a stuffy chamber of criticism.

It is a real holiday of the spirits with him; his mouth overruns with play; he cracks jokes upon his own person

[1] *Shakespeare's Treatment of Love and Marriage*, pp. 21-2.

and his speaking of French; and sweetens his way to the lady's heart by genial frankness and simplicity of manner; wherein we relish nothing of the king indeed, but, which is better, much of the man. With the open and true-hearted pleasantry of a child, he laughs through his courtship; yet we feel all the while a deep undercurrent of seriousness beneath his laughter; and there is to our sense no lapse from dignity in his behaviour, because nothing is really so dignified as when a man forgets his dignity in the over-flowings of a right noble and generous heart. The King loves men who are better than their words; and it is his nature to be better than he speaks.

It is to be noted also that, notwithstanding the hero's sportive mood in the wooing, where he thinks the honour of his nation is involved, his mood is very different: then he purposely forgot the King in the man; now he resolutely forgets the man in the King; and will not budge a hair from the demands which he holds to be the right of his people. The dignity of his person he freely leaves to take care of itself; the dignity of his State is to him a sacred thing, and he will sooner die than compromise it a jot[1].

The courtship is written *con brio* because it was conceived *con amore*. For, so far from being disappointed in his hero, Shakespeare had, I believe, fallen pretty deeply in love with him before he had done. And having taught his audience too to hold him in their hearts, he will now show them that he is the 'King of good fellows', one whom they might 'even care to spend an evening with'. The 'port of Mars'? This hero, when he walks, treads on the ground.

Yet in the upshot neither he nor audience entirely escaped disappointment. He had promised them in the Epilogue to *Henry IV* that they should find Falstaff at Agincourt, and was then obliged, owing, I have suggested, to the desertion of Kempe from the company[2], to fob them off with Mistress Quickly's descrip-

[1] *Op. cit.* pp. 128–9.
[2] Cf. *The Fortunes of Falstaff*, pp. 124–5 and v. *infra*, pp. 113 ff.

tion of Sir John's death and the antics of Pistol, the former of his very best vintage in humorous tenderness, the latter amusing enough in their way, but of necessity light-weight in the scales with Falstaff. How the generality of spectators expressed their chagrin is not recorded, but legend has it that a 'judicious' lady at Whitehall gave utterance to hers in no uncertain fashion. The delicate flattery of the great speech on the Burden of Kingship sounded gratefully in her ears no doubt, while the similarity of Henry's sentiments with those she herself uttered to her last parliament[1] suggests that it had left its impress in her memory. But it could not be accepted as compensation, which she commanded peremptorily and without delay in the shape of another play exhibiting the fat man in love; a command Shakespeare complied with by producing *The Merry Wives of Windsor* at a fortnight's notice. Nevertheless, King Henry V is so much grander a figure than Prince Hal or his father, the war-scenes so infinitely more moving than anything of the kind in *Henry IV*, and the events of the hour, as explained at the beginning of this Introduction, so propitious for the original performances, that I cannot doubt of the play's success in the early summer of 1599.

Nor do I doubt that it would draw large audiences to-day, if interpreted by an intelligent producer and good actors who had not befuddled their brains with nineteenth-century criticism[2]. If they, or others, desirous of understanding Henry of Monmouth would con anything besides Shakespeare's play, let them study the character and exploits of the English heroes and explorers rather than our 'embodiments of worldly

---

[1] Cf. Introduction to *1 Henry IV*, p. xviii.

[2] Since writing this I have been able to see in London Mr Laurence Olivier's encouraging 'presentation' of *Henry V* on the films, a brief account of which will be found on p. lv.

success', or even turn to the records of those who aspire to climb, not the social escalator, but the great peaks of the globe. For myself, I have learnt more about Shakespeare's Henry from Wavell's *Life of Allenby* than from all the critics put together. I have learnt too, as Shakespeare himself may have done, from the character and career of a great sixteenth-century leader, in whose apparently forlorn cause most Englishmen took a deep interest, who was assassinated when the author of this play was in his twenty-first year, and with whom Henry of Monmouth has many points in common: I mean William the Silent[1].

[1947]   J. D. W.

P.S. [1955]. A more recent edition of the play by J. H. Walter was published in *The New Arden Shakespeare* (1954).

[1] Cf. an admirable biography by Miss C. V. Wedgwood, published in 1944.

THE STAGE HISTORY OF
HENRY V

Note. The stage-history of *Henry IV*, which failing
health prevented him from actually completing, though he
saw it in proof, was Harold Child's last contribution to
this edition. He had been my colleague since its inception
in June 1919, and constantly allowed me to consult him
on all sorts of points, apart from those connected with
the history of the stage; for he was as wise in Shakespeare
as he was generous in friendship. Thoughtful and kind
to the end, he sent me shortly before his death in November,
1945, a sheaf of notes for the stage-history of this and
future plays; and with their help Mr C. B. Young and
I must do what we can to uphold the high standard he
set. 'His life was gentle.'   J. D. W.

Apart from what we can infer about the original
performances in 1599, discussed on pp. ix–x above,
and referred to on the title-page of the Quarto of 1600,
which describes the play as 'sundry times playd by
the Right honourable the Lord Chamberlaine his
seruants[1]', no performance of *Henry V* is known during
Shakespeare's life except that of January 7, 1605, when,
according to the *Revels Accounts*, it was given at Court
by the King's Majesty's Players[2].

For the Restoration stage the record is equally scanty.
On July 6, 1668, Pepys was 'glad to see Betterton',
after his illness of 1667, act the King in Lincoln's Inn
Fields ('Duke's Old Theatre'). The rest is silence.
Truly, as Dr Johnson remarked a century later, 'the
Civil Wars...left in this nation scarcely any tradition
of more ancient history[3]'.

[1] This description is repeated on the title-pages of Q2
(1602) and Q3 (1619).

[2] v. Chambers, *William Shakespeare*, ii. 331.

[3] v. note on 4. 3. 57–9 below.

Not till a third of the eighteenth century was through
do notices begin to be frequent. Drury Lane, indeed,
put on a *Henry V* in 1723; but this was Aaron Hill's
play, which, while stealing lavishly from Shakespeare,
omitted all the comic scenes, and added a sub-plot
which turned the play into a sentimental drama of love
and intrigue. The first performance of Shakespeare's
Henry V, if Genest is right in thinking it not Hill's
once again, was at Goodman's Fields in November,
1735. Thereafter, the play was never long absent from
the London stage, Covent Garden and Drury Lane
monopolizing the honour of presenting it till the middle
of the nineteenth century, when Sadler's Wells first
comes into the picture. Covent Garden showed the
play ten times in 1738 and 1739, and again in 1740,
1744 and 1745. Drury Lane then took it up—in
December, 1747 (four times), and October, 1748; and
the *General Advertiser* announced it as promised here
for February, 1752. Meanwhile Covent Garden returned to it in 1750 (three times); and subsequently
every year but two from 1754 to 1770.

At the outset Delane played the King; and after being
succeeded in the part by Hale, he returned to it in
1750. At Drury Lane Barry displaced Delane in the
title rôle in 1747 (Delane acting the Archbishop of
Canterbury); and from November, 1750 to April,
1754, he took over the part in Covent Garden. In
1755, his mantle fell upon Smith, who, with one
resumption by Barry in 1758, continued to sustain the
rôle till 1769, though one year (1762) Hull took his
place on Easter Monday, which Smith, now an actor
of consequence, claimed as a holiday. In the early
years Hippisley made a hit as Fluellen; and the performance of March, 1739, was for his benefit. In 1747,
he was succeeded by Macklin, who in turn handed the
part on to Yates, Arthur, and Shuter successively. Two
other names stand out in the history of these revivals.

The younger Cibber acted Pistol at Covent Garden (first in 1740); while David Garrick recited the Prologues as Chorus in 1747 and 1748, and also in 1752, if a performance this year was carried out as advertised. To judge from the Acting Versions of Bell, Kemble and Oxberry, which omit them, the Prologues were commonly cut on the stage; but they must have been restored for most of the performances from 1747 to 1770, since Chorus constantly figures in Genest's notices of the casts, being usually assigned to Ryan. Even for later years Chorus not seldom appears in the lists of casts; the acting versions seem therefore to be a little misleading in this matter.

The 1761 series of performances added a new feature to the play in the shape of a Coronation scene[1], to celebrate the accession of George III, in which Mrs Bellamy, in her rôle as Katharine, 'walked in the procession from the Abbey as Queen'. The innovation proved popular; '*Henry V* with the Coronation', writes Genest, 'was acted 23 times successively, and 26 on the whole'. It was repeated in 1762, each year from 1766 to 1769, and again in 1778. The appetite for spectacle grew by what it fed on; for on September 22, 1769, the ancient 'Ceremony of the Champion' was added, and made realistic and impressive by mounting him on a real horse[2].

During the next seventy years, the play continued to be seen on the London stage, being shown at Covent Garden eight times between 1770 and 1782, Wroughton now appearing as the King; and during these years it was carried to the provinces also, and acted three times in Bath and Liverpool. In 1789 Drury Lane again took it up, and presented it more than a dozen times

[1] Cf. pp. xxxvi, xxxix, Stage History of *Henry IV*, for 'coronation scenes' in 2 *Henry IV*.

[2] Cf. Stage History of *Henry IV*, p. xxxix, for a use of this item with 2 *Henry IV* in 1821.

in this and the next two years; while in 1792 and 1793 the Company acted it at the Haymarket. For these revivals Drury Lane possessed an actor of genius in Kemble, who first played the King on October 1, 1789, to Baddeley's Fluellen; Mrs Booth was the Hostess, and Miss Collins Katharine. Kemble continued in the part till 1811 (Drury Lane, 1801; Covent Garden, 1811). But he subjected the play to a free handling, which, in the words of his biographer, Mr Herschel Baker, "cut the text to tatters". Meanwhile Elliston had presented the King three times, at Bath and at the Haymarket (1798–1803). Covent Garden also put on the play in 1803 for the benefit of the Patriotic Fund, but no cast is recorded. Macready succeeded Kemble in 1819, playing the title part twenty-eight times in all in five different years till 1839. These performances were mostly at Covent Garden; but once (1825) he acted it in one for his own benefit at Drury Lane. It was Drury Lane also that, on March 8, 1830, witnessed the miserable breakdown of Edmund Kean in his first and last presentation of the King, which proved the virtual end of his meteoric career. After 1839 there is a blank till Samuel Phelps's appearances in the part of the King at Sadler's Wells in 1852, and again in 1858–9. His 'scholarlike' rendering was praised by the *Morning Post* as 'among the best things which the modern European stage has produced'.

Macready's two productions at Covent Garden in 1837 are described as 'crude and incomplete'; 'the battle of Agincourt was fought in silken hose and velvet doublets, and not a single bowman was visible'. But this was exceptional; for from Macready onwards accurate realism in scenery and costume was increasingly aimed at, and scenic resources were more and more exploited. His own last production (Covent Garden, 1839) was grandly spectacular. A moving diorama ushered in the third act, depicting the voyage from

Southampton to Harfleur, the picture, as it were,
melting away into the actual siege, the acting of which
began before it had quite passed away. 'As scenic
spectacle', writes *The Times*, 'it merits unqualified
praise', though *John Bull* found it difficult to stomach
'the solemn strains of an organ', echoing across the
victorious battlefield, 'brought from England, we suppose for the purpose[1]'. Yet both Kean and Phelps
were to find this organ irresistible. On this occasion
Phelps played the Constable of France. Phelps's own
productions, while seeking scenic effect, aimed specially
at antiquarian fidelity. Both qualities mark even more
strongly Charles Kean's production in 1859, on the eve
of his retirement, at the Princess's Theatre, which
from 1850 to 1859 was 'the scene of the finest productions scenically of Shakespeare up to that date'. He
interpolated a pageant representing the triumphal entry
into London after Agincourt, reproducing in it with
meticulous care the details of an account in a chronicle
by an anonymous eye-witness[2]. (See Odell, *Shakespeare from Betterton to Irving*, vol. II, pp. 355–7.) But
the scholarly accuracy in dress, properties and scenes,
was counterbalanced by the usual free treatment of the
text. Largely following Kemble's Acting Version, he
cut out 1. 1, retained only the second of the two
scenes with the Hostess and Pistol, tagged on to the
end of it the Boy's speech ('As young as I am...')
from 3. 2. 28–53, and largely curtailed the longer
speeches throughout. Kean's production, in fact,
pointed forward to Irving and Tree in its subordina-
tion of dialogue and action to visual appeal. Charles
Calvert's series of Shakespearian revivals in Manchester

---

[1] Cited by A. C. Sprague, *Shakespeare and the Actors*,
p. 120.
[2] Evidently the *Gesta Henrici Quinti* (v. pp. 116 ff.) in
the trans. given by Nicholas, *Battle of Agincourt*, 1827.

from 1864 onwards displayed the same combination
of scenic splendour with historical accuracy. *Henry V*
was produced by him here in 1872, and three years
later carried to America.

Spectacle seems still in the ascendant in the two other
most notable London revivals of the century. At the
production in Queen's Theatre, Long Acre, with John
Coleman as King, in September, 1876, the playbill
requested 'indulgence for delays between Acts, as many
of the set scenes, especially the Interior of Westminster
Abbey, are of great magnitude'; while George Rignold's, at Drury Lane on November 1, 1879, reproduced the spectacular entry into London after Agincourt,
devised by Kean twenty years before. The Queen's
Theatre rendering, announced as an 'adaptation', em-
bellished the play with a poetic inaugural address by
Robert Buchanan, and a Prologue to the play proper,
consisting of the scenes between the King and Prince
Hal, and the Prince and the Chief Justice from
Henry IV, Part II. In this Prologue Phelps acted
King Henry IV for the last time to Coleman's Prince.
It is not altogether surprising to learn that this lavish
production was for Coleman the culminating financial
failure of a disastrous season. (See P. Hutchinson,
Masquerade, p. 170.)

The end of the century saw the advent at Stratford
of Benson as the King (1897), and for the next twenty
years and more he and Lewis Waller divided between
them the honours of the part. Between 1897 and 1931
the play was presented twenty separate times at Stratford, not counting the innovation of an 'all-women'
performance (Marie Slade as King) on the birthday
in 1921—'chiefly interesting as a curiosity[1]'. At the
Tercentenary in 1916 also it was the birthday play.

[1] A wholly feminine cast had previously acted the play
at Queen's Theatre in 1916, and the Stratford production
of 1921 was repeated at the Strand in the same year.

The first year of the new century witnessed a special matinée of the play by Ben Greet's Company under William Poel's direction with Elizabethan staging. The entire text was given without cuts, and with but one interval, on a bare stage hung with tapestries, a gallery running across the back. In the same year and in 1906 the play was one of a cycle of all the English Histories except Part I of *Henry IV*; and in 1905 of another cycle of Histories, beginning with Marlowe's *Edward II*. In 1914, the speeches made a special patriotic appeal[1]. From 1897 to 1916 Benson sustained the title part (though Waller took his place in 1908), with G. R. Weir as an admirable Fluellen for ten years; Mrs Benson playing Katharine, Oscar Asche Pistol, and H. O. Nicholson Nym and the French prisoner. With the same cast his Company made a hit with the play in 1900 at the Lyceum, and in 1914 they presented it at the Shaftesbury Theatre. After Benson had retired in 1919, Brydges-Adams produced the play in Stratford in 1920, and repeated it in a series of matinées at the Strand Theatre the same year. In 1927, after the fire at Stratford, the play was given on the birthday, with George Skillan as the King, in the temporary refuge of the old Picture House. The New Memorial Theatre has seen it three times, with John Wise (1934), McCallin (1937), and Baliol Holloway (1943) successively as the King. McCallin acted the part 'in rather too light a style', thinks Gordon Crosse[2]. He praises, however, Baliol Holloway's Pistol—'the best since Oscar Asche'—and Wolfit's speaking of the Prologues. In 1937, he notes, the play 'was mounted with colourful splendour'.

Lewis Waller's performances were mostly in London (Lyceum, December, 1900; Imperial, January, 1905;

---

[1] v. *supra*, p. viii.
[2] *Fifty Years of Shakespearean Playgoing*, pp. 104–5.

Lyric, November, 1908; His Majesty's, April, 1910).
His revivals stand out as among the most successful
in the scenic effects to which this play specially lends
itself; and both his and Benson's must rank high among
the renderings of the principal character. Among their
successors have been Martin Harvey (His Majesty's,
May, 1916); Baliol Holloway, Lewis Casson, Ralph
Richardson, and Laurence Olivier (all successively at
the Old Vic, 1926, 1928, 1931, and 1937). Other
twentieth-century revivals were the Elizabethan Society's by William Poel and Ben Greet in 1901
in the Lecture Theatre in Burlington Gardens
(reproduced, as already noted, at Stratford); Murray
Carrington's at the Strand Theatre (1930); the production at the Alhambra, with Godfrey Tearle as the
King, in January, 1934; by the Bankside Players at
the Ring, Blackfriars (producer, Robert Atkins) in
November, 1936; and by Lewis Casson at Drury Lane
with Ivor Novello as the King (September, 1938).
The latest and probably the most popular of all pre-
sentations is the film version by Laurence Olivier,
first seen in London on November 27, 1944, and
still (August, 1945) drawing large crowds. Prefaced
by a bird's-eye view of Shakespeare's London, the first
two acts take place in the Globe Theatre (A.D. 1600),
after which the spectators cross the Channel in the
fleet and watch the siege of Harfleur and the battle of
Agincourt in France (for which the Wicklow hills
provided the film background). The all-British cast
includes Laurence Olivier (Henry V), Robert Newton
(Pistol), Leslie Banks (Chorus), Esmund Knight
(Fluellen), Renée Asherson (Katharine), George Robey
(Falstaff, in a 'shot' of the death-bed, to explain 2. 1
and 2. 3 to those ignorant of *2 Henry IV*) and other
well-known actors and actresses. The excellence of the
production and its deserved popularity are encouraging
signs of the times.

In America, Macready played the King on his first visit, in December, 1826, in the Park Theatre, New York, where the play had previously been presented by Cooper in 1804, and by Wallack in 1819. But almost fifty years elapsed before it was staged again in New York, though it figured in Fanny Kemble's readings in 1849 and 1858, and in Tavernier's recitations in 1859. Then in 1875 Rignold scored a great success in the title rôle in 100 performances at Booth's Theatre, and the play became a feature of the theatres till 1878, Rignold returning to act in it each year. The 1875 production exactly reproduced that of Calvert in the Theatre Royal, Manchester (see above, p. lii), and Calvert, though too ill himself to act the King, supervised it. Rignold's greatest triumph in America was in 1876; but the furore he then created owed more, according to Odell, to 'his good looks' than to his acting; and the *New York Herald* commented on his faulty accent, his sing-song effects, and his unintelligibility. Yet his fame in the part surpassed all others, and from New York he carried his production triumphantly to London in 1879 (see above, p. liii) and afterwards to Australia.

J.D.W.

[1947]   C.B.Y.

TO THE READER

The following is a brief description of the punctuation and other typographical devices employed in the text, which have been more fully explained in the *Note on Punctuation* and the *Textual Introduction* to be found in *The Tempest* volume:

An obelisk (†) implies corruption or emendation, and suggests a reference to the Notes.

A single bracket at the beginning of a speech signifies an 'aside'.

Four dots represent a *full-stop* in the original, except when it occurs at the end of a speech, and they mark a long pause. Original *colons* or *semicolons*, which denote a somewhat shorter pause, are retained, or represented as three dots when they appear to possess special dramatic significance. Similarly, significant *commas* have been given as dashes.

Round brackets are taken from the original, and mark a significant change of voice; when the original brackets seem to imply little more than the drop in tone accompanying parenthesis, they are conveyed by commas or dashes.

Single inverted commas (' ') are editorial; double ones (" ") derive from the original, where they are used to draw attention to maxims, quotations, etc.

The reference number for the first line is given at the head of each page. Numerals in square brackets are placed at the beginning of the traditional acts and scenes.

THE LIFE OF HENRY V

The Scene: first England, then France

CHARACTERS IN THE PLAY

Chorus
KING HENRY *the Fifth*
HUMPHREY, DUKE OF GLOUCESTER
JOHN OF LANCASTER, DUKE OF BEDFORD ⎫ *brothers to*
THOMAS OF LANCASTER, DUKE OF ⎬ *the king*
   CLARENCE ⎭
DUKE OF EXETER, *uncle to the king*
DUKE OF YORK, *cousin to the king, formerly Aumerle*
EARLS OF SALISBURY, WESTMORELAND, *and* WARWICK
ARCHBISHOP OF CANTERBURY
BISHOP OF ELY
EARL OF CAMBRIDGE
LORD SCROOP
SIR THOMAS GREY
SIR THOMAS ERPINGHAM, GOWER, FLUELLEN, MAC-
   MORRIS, JAMY, *officers in King Henry's army*
BATES, COURT, WILLIAMS, *soldiers in the same*
PISTOL, NYM, BARDOLPH
BOY. A *Herald*
CHARLES *the Sixth, King of France*
LEWIS, *the Dauphin*
DUKES *of* BURGUNDY, ORLEANS, BRITAINE *and* BOURBON
The Constable of France
RAMBURES, *and* GRANDPRÉ, *French Lords*
Governor of Harfleur
MONTJOY, *a French herald*
Ambassadors to the King of England
ISABEL, *Queen of France*
KATHARINE, *daughter to Charles and Isabel*
ALICE, *a lady attending upon her*
Hostess, formerly MRS QUICKLY, *now Pistol's wife*
Lords, Ladies, Officers, French and English Soldiers,
   Messengers, and Attendants

THE LIFE OF HENRY V

[1. Prologue]

Enter CHORUS

Chorus. O for a Muse of fire, that would ascend
The brightest heaven of invention:
A kingdom for a stage, princes to act,
And monarchs to behold the swelling scene.
Then should the warlike Harry, like himself,
Assume the port of Mars, and at his heels,
Leashed in like hounds, should Famine, Sword, and Fire
Crouch for employment. But pardon, gentles all,
The flat unraiséd spirits that hath dared
On this unworthy scaffold to bring forth   10
So great an object. Can this cockpit hold
The vasty fields of France? or may we cram
Within this wooden O the very casques
That did affright the air at Agincourt?
O, pardon! since a crooked figure may
Attest in little place a million;
And let us, ciphers to this great accompt,
On your imaginary forces work....
Suppose within the girdle of these walls
Are now confined two mighty monarchies,   20
Whose high upre12réd and abutting fronts
The perilous narrow ocean parts asunder.
Piece out our imperfections with your thoughts:
Into a thousand parts divide one man,
And make imaginary puissance.
Think, when we talk of horses, that you see them

Printing their proud hoofs i'th'receiving earth:
For 'tis your thoughts that now must deck our kings,
Carry them here and there: jumping o'er times;
30 Turning th'accomplishment of many years
Into an hour-glass: for the which supply,
Admit me Chorus to this history;
Who prologue-like your humble patience pray,
Gently to hear, kindly to judge, our play.   ['*exit*.']

[I. I.]   *London. An antechamber in the King's palace*

Enter the ARCHBISHOP *of* CANTERBURY *and
the* BISHOP *of* ELY

Canterbury. My lord, I'll tell you—that self bill
      is urged,
Which in th' eleventh year of the last king's reign
Was like, and had indeed against us passed,
But that the scambling and unquiet time
Did push it out of farther question.
    Ely. But how, my lord, shall we resist it now?
    Canterbury. It must be thought on...If it pass
      against us,
We lose the better half of our possession:
For all the temporal lands which men devout
10 By testament have given to the Church
Would they strip from us; being valued thus—
As much as would maintain, to the king's honour,
Full fifteen earls, and fifteen hundred knights,
Six thousand and two hundred good esquires:
And, to relief of lazars and weak age,
Of indigent faint souls past corporal toil,
A hundred almshouses right well supplied:

And to the coffers of the king beside,
A thousand pounds by th'year: thus runs the bill.
  Ely. This would drink deep.
  Canterbury.   'Twould drink the cup and all.   20
  Ely. But what prevention?
  Canterbury. The king is full of grace and fair regard,
    and a true lover of the holy Church.
  Ely. The courses of his youth promised it not.
  Canterbury. The breath no sooner left his father's body,
But that his wildness, mortified in him,
Seemed to die too: yea, at that very moment,
Consideration like an angel came,
And whipped th' offending Adam out of him;
Leaving his body as a Paradise,   30
T'envelop and contain celestial spirits....
Never was such a sudden scholar made:
Never came reformation in a flood,
With such a heady currance, scouring faults:
Nor never Hydra-headed wilfulness
So soon did lose his seat—and all at once—
As in this king.
  Ely.   We are blessèd in the change.
  Canterbury. Hear him but reason in divinity;
And, all-admiring, with an inward wish
You would desire the king were made a prelate: 40
Hear him debate of commonwealth affairs;
You would say it hath been all in all his study:
List his discourse of war; and you shall hear
A fearful battle rendered you in music.
Turn him to any cause of policy,
The Gordian knot of it he will unloose,
Familiar as his garter: that, when he speaks,
The air, a chartered libertine, is still,
And the mute wonder lurketh in men's ears,

50 To steal his sweet and honeyed sentences:
   So that the art and practic part of life
   Must be the mistress to this theoric;
   Which is a wonder, how his grace should glean it,
   Since his addiction was to courses vain,
   His companies unlettered, rude, and shallow,
   His hours filled up with riots, banquets, sports;
   And never noted in him any study,
   Any retirement, any sequestration,
   From open haunts and popularity.

60   *Ely*. The strawberry grows underneath the nettle,
   And wholesome berries thrive and ripen best
   Neighboured by fruit of baser quality:
   And so the prince obscured his contemplation
   Under the veil of wildness, which, no doubt,
   Grew like the summer grass, fastest by night,
   Unseen, yet crescive in his faculty.

   Canterbury. It must be so; for miracles are ceased:
   And therefore we must needs admit the means
   How things are perfected.

   Ely.   But, my good lord,
70 How now for mitigation of this bill
   Urged by the commons? Doth his majesty
   Incline to it, or no?

   Canterbury.   He seems indifferent—
   Or rather swaying more upon our part
   Than cherishing th' exhibiters against us:
   For I have made an offer to his majesty,
   Upon our spiritual convocation,
   And in regard of causes now in hand,
   Which I have opened to his grace at large,
   As touching France, to give a greater sum
80 Than ever at one time the clergy yet
   Did to his predecessors part withal.

Ely. How did this offer seem received, my lord?
Canterbury. With good acceptance of his majesty:
Save that there was not time enough to hear,
As I perceived his grace would fain have done,
The severals and unhidden passages
Of his true titles to some certain dukedoms,
And generally to the crown and seat of France
Derived from Edward, his great-grandfather.
  Ely. What was th' impediment that broke this off?   90
  Canterbury. The French ambassador upon that instant
Craved audience; and the hour, I think, is come
To give him hearing: is it four o'clock?
  Ely. It is.
  Canterbury. Then go we in, to know his embassy:
Which I could with a ready guess declare,
Before the Frenchman speak a word of it.
  Ely. I'll wait upon you, and I long to hear it.
                                              [*they go*

[1. 2.]   *The Presence-chamber in the palace*

KING HENRY *in his chair of state;* GLOUCESTER,
BEDFORD, EXETER, WARWICK, WESTMORELAND *at a
table below; attendants*

  King Henry. Where is my gracious Lord
      of Canterbury?
  Exeter. Not here in presence.
  King Henry.   Send for him, good uncle.
  Westmoreland. Shall we call in th'ambassador,
      my liege?
  King Henry. Not yet, my cousin: we would
      be resolved,
Before we hear him, of some things of weight
That task our thoughts, concerning us and France.

*The Archbishop of CANTERBURY and the Bishop of ELY
enter and make obeisance*

    Canterbury. God and his angels guard your
      sacred throne,
And make you long become it!
    King Henry.   Sure, we thank you....
My learnéd lord, we pray you to proceed,
10 And justly and religiously unfold
Why the law Salic that they have in France
Or should or should not bar us in our claim:
And God forbid, my dear and faithful lord,
That you should fashion, wrest, or bow your reading,
Or nicely charge your understanding soul
With opening titles miscreate, whose right
Suits not in native colours with the truth:
For God doth know how many now in health
Shall drop their blood in approbation
20 Of what your reverence shall incite us to.
Therefore take heed how you impawn our person,
How you awake our sleeping sword of war;
We charge you in the name of God, take heed:
For never two such kingdoms did contend
Without much fall of blood, whose guiltless drops
Are every one a woe, a sore complaint
'Gainst him whose wrongs gives edge unto the swords
That makes such waste in brief mortality....
Under this conjuration, speak, my lord:
30 For we will hear, note, and believe in heart,
That what you speak is in your conscience washed
As pure as sin with baptism.
    Canterbury. Then hear me, gracious sovereign, and
      you peers,
That owe yourselves, your lives, and services

To this imperial throne....There is no bar
To make against your highness' claim to France,
But this which they produce from Pharamond:
"In terram Salicam mulieres ne succedant"—
"No woman shall succeed in Salic land":
Which Salic land the French unjustly gloze   40
To be the realm of France, and Pharamond
The founder of this law and female bar.
Yet their own authors faithfully affirm
That the land Salic is in Germany,
Between the floods of Sala and of Elbe:
Where Charles the Great, having subdued the Saxons,
There left behind and settled certain French:
Who holding in disdain the German women
For some dishonest manners of their life,
Established then this law—to wit, no female   50
Should be inheritrix in Salic land:
Which Salic, as I said, 'twixt Elbe and Sala,
Is at this day in Germany called Meisen.
Then doth it well appear the Salic law
Was not devised for the realm of France:
Nor did the French possess the Salic land
Until four hundred one and twenty years
After defunction of King Pharamond,
Idly supposed the founder of this law,
Who died within the year of our redemption   60
Four hundred twenty-six: and Charles the Great
Subdued the Saxons, and did seat the French
Beyond the river Sala, in the year
Eight hundred five....Besides, their writers say,
King Pepin, which deposéd Childeric,
Did, as heir general, being descended
Of Blithild, which was daughter to King Clothair,
Make claim and title to the crown of France.

Hugh Capet also, who usurped the crown
70 Of Charles the duke of Lorraine, sole heir male
Of the true line and stock of Charles the Great,
To find his title with some shows of truth,
Though in pure truth it was corrupt and naught,
Conveyed himself as th'heir to th'Lady Lingare,
Daughter to Charlemain, who was the son
To Lewis the emperor, and Lewis the son
Of Charles the Great: also King Lewis the tenth,
Who was sole heir to the usurper Capet,
Could not keep quiet in his conscience,
80 Wearing the crown of France, till satisfied
That fair Queen Isabel, his grandmother,
Was lineal of the Lady Ermengare,
Daughter to Charles the foresaid duke of Lorraine:
By the which marriage the line of Charles the Great
Was re-united to the crown of France.
So that, as clear as is the summer's sun,
King Pepin's title and Hugh Capet's claim,
King Lewis his satisfaction, all appear
To hold in right and title of the female:
90 So do the kings of France unto this day.
Howbeit they would hold up this Salic law
To bar your highness claiming from the female,
And rather choose to hide them in a net
†Than amply to imbare their crooked titles,
Usurped from you and your progenitors.
   King Henry. May I with right and conscience make
     this claim?
   Canterbury. The sin upon my head, dread sovereign!
For in the book of Numbers is it writ,
When the man dies, let the inheritance
100 Descend unto the daughter....Gracious lord.
Stand for your own, unwind your bloody flag,

Look back into your mighty ancestors:
Go, my dread lord, to your great-grandsire's tomb,
From whom you claim; invoke his warlike spirit,
And your great-uncle's, Edward the Black Prince,
Who on the French ground played a tragedy,
Making defeat on the full power of France,
Whiles his most mighty father on a hill
Stood smiling to behold his lion's whelp
Forage in blood of French nobility....   110
O noble English, that could entertain
With half their forces the full pride of France,
And let another half stand laughing by,
All out of work and cold for action!

  Ely. Awake remembrance of these valiant dead,
And with your puissant arm renew their feats;
You are their heir, you sit upon their throne:
The blood and courage that renownéd them
Runs in your veins: and my thrice-puissant liege
Is in the very May-morn of his youth,   120
Ripe for exploits and mighty enterprises.

  Exeter. Your brother kings and monarchs of the earth
Do all expect that you should rouse yourself,
As did the former lions of your blood.

  Westmoreland. They know your grace hath cause, and
      means, and might;
So hath your highness: never king of England
Had nobles richer, and more loyal subjects,
Whose hearts have left their bodies here in England,
And lie pavilioned in the fields of France.

  Canterbury. O let their bodies follow, my dear liege, 130
With blood and sword and fire, to win your right:
In aid whereof, we of the spiritualty
Will raise your highness such a mighty sum
As never did the clergy at one time

Bring in to any of your ancestors.

  King Henry. We must not only arm t'invade
    the French,
But lay down our proportions to defend
Against the Scot, who will make road upon us
With all advantages.

140 *Canterbury.* They of those marches, gracious sovereign,
Shall be a wall sufficient to defend
Our inland from the pilfering borderers.

  King Henry. We do not mean the coursing
    snatchers only,
But fear the main intendment of the Scot,
Who hath been still a giddy neighbour to us:
For you shall read that my great-grandfather
Never went with his forces into France,
But that the Scot on his unfurnished kingdom
Came pouring like the tide into a breach,

150 With ample and brim fulness of his force,
Galling the gleanéd land with hot assays,
Girding with grievous siege castles and towns:
That England, being empty of defence,
Hath shook and trembled at th'ill neighbourhood.

  Canterbury. She hath been then more feared than
    harmed, my liege:
For hear her but exampled by herself—
When all her chivalry hath been in France,
And she a mourning widow of her nobles,
She hath herself not only well defended,

160 But taken and impounded as a stray
The King of Scots: whom she did send to France,
To fill King Edward's fame with prisoner kings,
And make her chronicle as rich with praise
As is the ooze and bottom of the sea
With sunken wrack and sumless treasuries.

Ely. But there's a saying very old and true—
  "If that you will France win,
   Then with Scotland first begin:"
For once the eagle England being in prey,
To her unguarded nest the weasel Scot   170
Comes sneaking, and so sucks her princely eggs,
Playing the mouse in absence of the cat,
To 'tame and havoc more than she can eat.
 Exeter. It follows then the cat must stay at home.
Yet that is but a crushed necessity,
Since we have locks to safeguard necessaries,
And pretty traps to catch the petty thieves.
While that the arméd hand doth fight abroad
Th'adviséd head defends itself at home:
For government, though high, and low, and lower, 180
Put into parts, doth keep in one consent,
Congreeing in a full and natural close,
Like music.
 Canterbury.   Therefore doth heaven divide
The state of man in divers functions,
Setting endeavour in continual motion:
To which is fixéd, as an aim or butt,
Obedience: for so work the honey-bees,
Creatures that by a rule in nature teach
The act of order to a peopled kingdom.
They have a king and officers of sorts: 190
Where some, like magistrates, correct at home,
Others, like merchants, venture trade abroad:
Others, like soldiers, arméd in their stings
Make boot upon the summer's velvet buds:
Which pillage they with merry march bring home
To the tent-royal of their emperor:
Who, busied in his majesty, surveys
The singing masons building roofs of gold,

The civil citizens kneading up the honey;
200 The poor mechanic porters crowding in
Their heavy burdens at his narrow gate:
The sad-eyed justice, with his surly hum,
Delivering o'er to executors pale
The lazy yawning drone...I this infer,
That many things, having full reference
To one consent, may work contrariously—
As many arrows looséd several ways
Come to one mark:
†As many several ways meet in one town:
210 As many fresh streams meet in one salt sea:
As many lines close in the dial's centre:
So may a thousand actions, once afoot,
End in one purpose, and be all well borne
Without defeat....Therefore to France, my liege—
Divide your happy England into four,
Whereof take you one quarter into France,
And you withal shall make all Gallia shake.
If we, with thrice such powers left at home,
Cannot defend our own doors from the dog,
220 Let us be worried, and our nation lose
The name of hardiness and policy.
    King Henry. Call in the messengers sent from
        the Dauphin.   [*attendants go forth*
Now are we well resolved, and by God's help
And yours, the noble sinews of our power,
France being ours, we'll bend it to our awe,
Or break it all to pieces. Or there we'll sit,
Ruling in large and ample empery
O'er France and all her almost kingly dukedoms,
Or lay these bones in an unworthy urn,
230 Tombless, with no remembrance over them:
Either our history shall with full mouth

Speak freely of our acts, or else our grave,
Like Turkish mute, shall have a tongueless mouth,
Not worshipped with a waxen epitaph....

'Enter Ambassadors of France,' followed by
a servitor, trundling a gilded barrel

Now are we well prepared to know the pleasure
Of our fair cousin Dauphin: for we hear
Your greeting is from him, not from the king.
　Ambassador. May't please your majesty to give
　　us leave
Freely to render what we have in charge:
Or shall we sparingly show you far off　　　　　　　240
The Dauphin's meaning and our embassy?
　King Henry. We are no tyrant, but a Christian king,
Unto whose grace our passion is as subject
As is our wretches fettered in our prisons;
Therefore with frank and with uncurbéd plainness
Tell us the Dauphin's mind.
　Ambassador.　　　　　　Thus then, in few:
Your highness, lately sending into France,
Did claim some certain dukedoms, in the right
Of your great predecessor, King Edward the third.
In answer of which claim, the prince our master　　250
Says that you savour too much of your youth,
And bids you be advised there's nought in France
That can be with a nimble galliard won:
You cannot revél into dukedoms there....
He therefore sends you, meeter for your spirit,
This tun of treasure; and, in lieu of this,
Desires you let the dukedoms that you claim
Hear no more of you....This the Dauphin speaks.
　King Henry. What treasure, uncle?
　Exeter. [*opening the barrel*] Tennis-balls, my liege.

260   *King Henry.* We are glad the Dauphin is so pleasant
        with us—
     His present and your pains we thank you for:
     When we have matched our rackets to these balls,
     We will in France, by God's grace, play a set
     Shall strike his father's crown into the hazard.
     Tell him he hath made a match with such a wrangler
     That all the courts of France will be disturbed
     With chases....And we understand him well,
     How he comes o'er us with our wilder days,
     Not measuring what use we made of them.
270 We never valued this poor seat of England,
     And therefore, living hence, did give ourself
     To barbarous licence: as 'tis ever common
     That men are merriest when they are from home....
     But tell the Dauphin I will keep my state,
     Be like a king, and show my sail of greatness,
     When I do rouse me in my throne of France.
     For that I have laid by my majesty,
     And plodded like a man for working-days:
     But I will rise there with so full a glory
280 That I will dazzle all the eyes of France,
     Yea, strike the Dauphin blind to look on us.
     And tell the pleasant prince this mock of his
     Hath turned his balls to gun-stones, and his soul
     Shall stand sore chargéd for the wasteful vengeance
     That shall fly with them: for many a thousand widows
     Shall this his mock mock out of their dear husbands;
     Mock mothers from their sons, mock castles down:
     And some are yet ungotten and unborn
     That shall have cause to curse the Dauphin's scorn.
290 But this lies all within the will of God,
     To whom I do appeal, and in whose name,
     Tell you the Dauphin, I am coming on,

To venge me as I may, and to put forth
My rightful hand in a well-hallowed cause.
So get you hence in peace...And tell the Dauphin
His jest will savour but of shallow wit,
When thousands weep more than did laugh at it....
Convey them with safe conduct. Fare you well.

       ['*Exeunt Ambassadors*'
Exeter. This was a merry message.
King Henry. We hope to make the sender blush at it: 300
Therefore, my lords, omit no happy hour
That may give furth'rance to our expedition:
For we have now no thought in us but France,
Save those to God, that run before our business.
Therefore let our proportions for these wars
Be soon collected, and all things thought upon
That may with reasonable swiftness add
More feathers to our wings: for, God before,
We'll chide this Dauphin at his father's door.
Therefore let every man now task his thought, 310
That this fair action may on foot be brought.

    [*he rises and departs, the rest following*

[2. *Prologue*]

'*Flourish. Enter* CHORUS'

Chorus. Now all the youth of England are on fire,
And silken dalliance in the wardrobe lies:
Now thrive the armourers, and honour's thought
Reigns solely in the breast of every man.
They sell the pasture now, to buy the horse;
Following the mirror of all Christian kings,
With wingéd heels, as English Mercuries.
For now sits Expectation in the air,

And hides a sword, from hilts unto the point,
10 With crowns imperial, crowns and coronets,
Promised to Harry and his followers.
The French, advised by good intelligence
Of this most dreadful preparation,
Shake in their fear, and with pale policy
Seek to divert the English purposes.
O England! model to thy inward greatness,
Like little body with a mighty heart:
What might'st thou do, that honour would thee do,
Were all thy children kind and natural!
20 But see, thy fault France hath in thee found out,
A nest of hollow bosoms, which he fills
With treacherous crowns: and three corrupted men,
One, Richard Earl of Cambridge, and the second,
Henry Lord Scroop of Masham, and the third,
Sir Thomas Grey, knight of Northumberland,
Have for the gilt of France (O guilt indeed!)
Confirmed conspiracy with fearful France,
And by their hands this grace of kings must die,
If hell and treason hold their promises,
30 Ere he take ship for France, and in Southampton....
Linger your patience on, and we'll digest
Th'abuse of distance; force a play:
The sum is paid, the traitors are agreed,
The king is set from London, and the scene
Is now transported, gentles, to Southampton,
There is the playhouse now, there must you sit,
And thence to France shall we convey you safe,
And bring you back: charming the narrow seas
To give you gentle pass: for if we may,
40 We'll not offend one stomach with our play....
But till the king come forth, and not till then,
Unto Southampton do we shift our scene.   ['*exit*'

[2. 1.]   *London. A street*

NYM and BARDOLPH meeting

Bardolph. Well met, Corporal Nym.

Nym. Good morrow, Lieutenant Bardolph.

Bardolph. What, are Ancient Pistol and you friends yet?

Nym. For my part, I care not: I say little: but when time shall serve, there shall be smiles—but that shall be as it may. I dare not fight, but I will wink and hold out mine iron: it is a simple one, but what though? It will toast cheese, and it will endure cold, as another man's sword will: and there's an end.   10

Bardolph. I will bestow a breakfast to make you friends, and we'll be all three sworn brothers to France: let't be so, good Corporal Nym.

Nym. Faith, I will live so long as I may, that's the certain of it: and when I cannot live any longer, I will do as I may: that is my rest, that is the rendezvous of it.

Bardolph. It is certain, corporal, that he is married to Nell Quickly, and certainly she did you wrong, for you were troth-plight to her.

Nym. I cannot tell—things must be as they may: men 20 may sleep, and they may have their throats about them at that time, and some say knives have edges...It must be as it may—though patience be a tired mare, yet she will plod—there must be conclusions—well, I cannot tell.

Ancient PISTOL and the Hostess approach

Bardolph. Here comes Ancient Pistol and his wife: good corporal, be patient here.

†*Nym.* How now, mine host Pistol!

Pistol. Base tike, call'st thou me host?

30 Now by this hand I swear I scorn the term:
Nor shall my Nell keep lodgers.

Hostess. No, by my troth, not long: for we cannot
lodge and board a dozen or fourteen gentlewomen that
live honestly by the prick of their needles, but it will be
thought we keep a bawdy-house straight. [*Nym draws
his sword*] O well-a-day, Lady, if he be not hewn now,
we shall see wilful adultery and murder committed.

Bardolph. Good lieutenant, good corporal, offer
nothing here.

40 *Nym.* Pish!

Pistol. Pish for thee, Iceland dog! thou prick-eared
cur of Iceland!

Hostess. Good Corporal Nym, show thy valour, and
put up your sword.

Nym. Will you shog off? I would have you solus.

                        . [*he sheathes his sword*

Pistol. 'Solus', egregious dog? O viper vile!
The 'solus' in thy most marvellous face,
The 'solus' in thy teeth, and in thy throat,
And in thy hateful lungs, yea in thy maw, perdy—
50 And, which is worse, within thy nasty mouth!
I do retort the 'solus' in thy bowels,
For I can take, and Pistol's cock is up,
And flashing fire will follow.

Nym. I am not Barbason, you cannot conjure me:
I have an humour to knock you indifferently well...If
you grow foul with me, Pistol, I will scour you with my
rapier, as I may, in fair terms. If you would walk off,
I would prick your guts a little in good terms, as I may,
and that's the humour of it.

60 *Pistol.* O braggart vile, and damnéd furious wight,
The grave doth gape, and doting death is near,
Therefore exhale!   [*they both draw*

Bardolph. [*also drawing*] Hear me, hear me what I
say: he that strikes the first stroke, I'll run him up to the
hilts, as I am a soldier.

Pistol. An oath of mickle might, and fury shall abate....
　　　　　　　　　　　　　　　　　　　　　　[*they sheathe*
Give me thy fist, thy fore-foot to me give:
Thy spirits are most tall.

Nym. I will cut thy throat one time or other in fair
terms, that is the humour of it.　　　　　　　　　　　　70

Pistol. 'Couple a gorge',
That is the word. I thee defy again.
O hound of Crete, think'st thou my spouse to get?
No, to the spital go,
And from the powdering-tub of infamy
Fetch forth the lazar kit of Cressid's kind,
Doll Tearsheet she by name, and her espouse.
I have, and I will hold, the quondam Quickly
For the only she: and—pauca, there's enough.
Go to.　　　　　　　　　　　　　　　　　　　　80
　　　　　　　　　　　'*Enter the Bor*'

Boy. Mine host Pistol, you must come to my master,
and you, hostess: he is very sick, and would to bed.
Good Bardolph, put thy face between his sheets, and do
the office of a warming-pan: faith, he's very ill.

Bardolph. Away, you rogue.　　　　　　[*the Boy runs off*
Hostess. By my troth, he'll yield the crow a pudding
one of these days...The king has killed his heart. Good
husband, come home presently.
　　　　　　　　　　　　　　　[*Hostess follows the Boy*
Bardolph. Come, shall I make you two friends? We
must to France together: why the devil should we keep 90
knives to cut one another's throats?

Pistol. Let floods o'erswell, and fiends for food howl on!

Nym. You'll pay me the eight shillings I won of you at betting?

Pistol. Base is the slave that pays.

Nym. That now I will have: that's the humour of it.

Pistol. As manhood shall compound: push home.

[*they 'draw'*

Bardolph. By this sword, he that makes the first thrust, I'll kill him: by this sword, I will.

100 *Pistol*. Sword is an oath, and oaths must have their course.

Bardolph. Corporal Nym, an thou wilt be friends, be friends, an thou wilt not, why then be enemies with me too: prithee put up.

†*Nym*. I shall have my eight shillings I won of you at betting?

Pistol. A noble shalt thou have, and present pay, And liquor likewise will I give to thee, And friendship shall combine, and brotherhood.

110 I'll live by Nym, and Nym shall live by me— Is not this just? for I shall sutler be Unto the camp, and profits will accrue. Give me thy hand.   [*they sheathe again*

Nym. I shall have my noble?

Pistol. In cash, most justly paid.

Nym. Well, then that's the humour of 't.

[*they strike hands*
Hostess returns

Hostess. As ever you come of women, come in quickly to Sir John. Ah, poor heart! he is so shaked of a burning quotidian tertian, that it is most lamentable to behold. 120 Sweet men, come to him.

Nym. The king hath run bad humours on the knight, that's the even of it.

Pistol. Nym, thou hast spoke the right,
His heart is fracted and corroborate.

Nym. The king is a good king, but it must be as it may:
he passes some humours and careers.

Pistol. Let us condole the knight, for, lambkins, we
will live.   [*they go*

[2. 2.]   *Southampton. A council-chamber*

'*Enter* EXETER, BEDFORD, *and* WESTMORELAND'

Bedford. 'Fore God, his grace is bold to trust
          these traitors.

Exeter. They shall be apprehended by and by.

Westmoreland. How smooth and even they do
          bear themselves,
As if allegiance in their bosoms sat
Crownéd with faith, and constant loyalty.

Bedford. The king hath note of all that they intend,
By interception which they dream not of.

Exeter. Nay, but the man that was his bedfellow,
Whom he hath dulled and cloyed with gracious favours—
That he should for a foreign purse so sell   10
His sovereign's life to death and treachery.

Trumpets sound. '*Enter the King,* SCROOP,
     CAMBRIDGE, *and* GREY', *with attendants*

King Henry. Now sits the wind fair, and we
          will aboard....
My Lord of Cambridge, and my kind Lord of Masham,
And you, my gentle knight, give me your thoughts:
Think you not that the powers we bear with us
Will cut their passage through the force of France,

K.H.V.—5

Doing the execution, and the act
For which we have in head assembled them?
Scroop. No doubt, my liege, if each man do his best.
20 *King Henry.* I doubt not that, since we are
    well persuaded
We carry not a heart with us from hence,
That grows not in a fair consent with ours:
Nor leave not one behind, that doth not wish
Success and conquest to attend on us.
   Cambridge. Never was monarch better feared
    and loved
Than is your majesty; there's not, I think, a subject
That sits in heart-grief and uneasiness
Under the sweet shade of your government.
   Grey. True: those that were your father's enemies
30 Have steeped their galls in honey, and do serve you
With hearts create of duty and of zeal.
   King Henry. We therefore have great cause
    of thankfulness,
And shall forget the office of our hand
Sooner than quittance of desert and merit,
According to the weight and worthiness.
   Scroop. So service shall with steeléd sinews toil,
And labour shall refresh itself with hope
To do your grace incessant services.
   King Henry. We judge no less....Uncle of Exeter,
40 Enlarge the man committed yesterday,
That railed against our person: we consider
It was excess of wine that set him on,
And on his more advice we pardon him.
   Scroop. That's mercy, but too much security:
Let him be punished, sovereign, lest example
Breed, by his sufferance, more of such a kind.
   King Henry. O let us yet be merciful.

Cambridge. So may your highness, and yet punish too.

Grey. Sir,

You show great mercy if you give him life,   50

After the taste of much correction.

King Henry. Alas, your too much love and care of me

Are heavy orisons 'gainst this poor wretch…

If little faults, proceeding on distemper,

Shall not be winked at, how shall we stretch our eye

When capital crimes, chewed, swallowed, and digested,

Appear before us? We'll yet enlarge that man,

Though Cambridge, Scroop, and Grey, in their

     dear care

And tender preservation of our person

Would have him punished….And now to our   60

     French causes,   [*he takes up papers*

Who are the late commissioners?

Cambridge. I one, my lord,

Your highness bade me ask for it to-day.

Scroop. So did you me, my liege.

Grey. And I, my royal sovereign.

King Henry. [*delivering the papers*] Then, Richard,

     Earl of Cambridge, there is yours:

There yours, Lord Scroop of Masham: and, sir knight,

Grey of Northumberland, this same is yours:

Read them, and know I know your worthiness….

My Lord of Westmoreland, and uncle Exeter,   70

We will aboard to night….Why, how now, gentlemen?

What see you in those papers, that you lose

So much complexion? Look ye how they change:

Their cheeks are paper. Why, what read you there,

That have so cowarded and chased your blood

Out of appearance?   [*they fall upon their knee*

Cambridge.   I do confess my fault,

And do submit me to your highness' mercy.

Grey.
Scroop. } To which we all appeal.

King Henry. The mercy that was quick in us but late,
80 By your own counsel is suppressed and killed:
You must not dare, for shame, to talk of mercy,
For your own reasons turn into your bosoms,
As dogs upon their masters, worrying you...
See you, my princes, and my noble peers,
These English monsters: my Lord of Cambridge here,
You know how apt our love was to accord
To furnish him with all appertinents
Belonging to his honour; and this man
Hath for a few light crowns lightly conspired
90 And sworn unto the practices of France
To kill us here in Hampton. To the which
This knight, no less for bounty bound to us
Than Cambridge is, hath likewise sworn....But O,
What shall I say to thee, Lord Scroop, thou cruel,
Ingrateful, savage, and inhuman creature?
Thou that didst bear the key of all my counsels,
That knew'st the very bottom of my soul,
That (almost) mightst have coined me into gold,
Wouldst thou have practised on me, for thy use?
100 May it be possible, that foreign hire
Could out of thee extract one spark of evil
That might annoy my finger? 'Tis so strange,
That though the truth of it stands off as gross
†As black on white, my eye will scarcely see it.
Treason and murder ever kept together,
As two yoke-devils sworn to either's purpose,
Working so grossly in a natural cause,
That admiration did not hoop at them.
But thou, 'gainst all proportion, didst bring in
110 Wonder to wait on treason and on murder:

And whatsoever cunning fiend it was
That wrought upon thee so preposterously,
Hath got the voice in hell for excellence:
All other devils that suggest by treasons
Do botch and bungle up damnation,
With patches, colours, and with forms being fetched
From glist'ring semblances of piety:
But he that tempered thee, bade thee stand up,
Gave thee no instance why thou shouldst do treason,
Unless to dub thee with the name of traitor.　　　120
If that same demon that hath gulled thee thus
Should with his lion gait walk the whole world,
He might return to vasty Tartar back,
And tell the legions, "I can never win
A soul so easy as that Englishman's."
O, how hast thou with jealousy infected
The sweetness of affiance? Show men dutiful?
Why, so didst thou: seem they grave and learnéd?
Why, so didst thou: come they of noble family?
Why, so didst thou: seem they religious?　　　130
Why, so didst thou. Or are they spare in diet,
Free from gross passion, or of mirth, or anger,
Constant in spirit, not swerving with the blood,
Garnished and decked in modest complement,
Not working with the eye without the ear,
And but in purgéd judgement trusting neither?
Such and so finely bolted didst thou seem:
And thus thy fall hath left a kind of blot,
To mark the full-fraught man and best indued
With some suspicion. I will weep for thee.　　　140
For this revolt of thine, methinks, is like
Another fall of man....Their faults are open,
Arrest them to the answer of the law,
And God acquit them of their practices.

Exeter. I arrest thee of high treason, by the name of
Richard Earl of Cambridge.
I arrest thee of high treason, by the name of Henry
Lord Scroop of Masham.
I arrest thee of high treason, by the name of Thomas
150 Grey, knight of Northumberland.

Scroop. Our purposes God justly hath discovered,
And I repent my fault more than my death,
Which I beseech your highness to forgive,
Although my body pay the price of it.

Cambridge. For me, the gold of France did not seduce,
Although I did admit it as a motive,
The sooner to effect what I intended:
But God be thankéd for prevention,
Which I in sufferance heartily will rejoice,
160 Beseeching God, and you, to pardon me.

Grey. Never did faithful subject more rejoice
At the discovery of most dangerous treason,
Than I do at this hour joy o'er myself,
Prevented from a damnéd enterprise;
My fault, but not my body, pardon, sovereign.

King Henry. God quit you in his mercy! Hear
　　　your sentence.
You have conspired against our royal person,
Joined with an enemy proclaimed, and from his coffers
Received the golden earnest of our death:
170 Wherein you would have sold your king to slaughter,
His princes and his peers to servitude,
His subjects to oppression and contempt,
And his whole kingdom into desolation...
Touching our person, seek we no revenge,
But we our kingdom's safety must so tender,
Whose ruin you have sought, that to her laws
We do deliver you. Get you therefore hence,

Poor miserable wretches, to your death:
The taste whereof God of his mercy give
You patience to endure, and true repentance   180
Of all your dear offences....Bear them hence....
        [*Exeunt Cambridge, Scroop, and Grey, guarded*
Now, lords, for France: the enterprise whereof
Shall be to you as us, like glorious.
We doubt not of a fair and lucky war,
Since God so graciously hath brought to light
This dangerous treason lurking in our way
To hinder our beginnings. We doubt not now
But every rub is smoothéd on our way....
Then forth, dear countrymen: let us deliver
Our puissance into the hand of God,   190
Putting it traight in expedition....
Cheerly to sea, the signs of war advance,
No king of England, if not king of France.
                        ['*Flourish*'; *they go*

[2. 3.]   *London. Before a tavern*

    Enter PISTOL, HOSTESS, NYM, BARDOLPH, *and Boy*

  Hostess. Prithee, honey-sweet husband, let me bring
thee to Staines.
  Pistol. No: for my manly heart doth earn.
Bardolph, be blithe: Nym, rouse thy vaunting veins:
Boy, bristle thy courage up: for Falstaff he is dead,
And we must earn therefore.
  Bardolph. Would I were with him, wheresome'er he
is, either in heaven or in hell!
  Hostess. Nay sure, he's not in hell: he's in Arthur's
bosom, if ever man went to Arthur's bosom: a' made 10
a finer end, and went away an it had been any christom

child: a' parted e'en just between twelve and one, e'en
at the turning o'th'tide: for after I saw him fumble with
the sheets, and play with flowers, and smile upon his
finger's end, I knew there was but one way: for his nose
was as sharp as a pen, and a' babbled of green fields.
'How now, Sir John?' quoth I. 'What, man! be o'
good cheer': so a' cried out, 'God, God, God!' three
or four times: now I, to comfort him, bid him a' should
20 not think of God; I hoped there was no need to trouble
himself with any such thoughts yet: so a' bade me lay
more clothes on his feet: I put my hand into the bed,
and felt them, and they were as cold as any stone: then
I felt to his knees, and so up'ard and up'ard, and all was
as cold as any stone.

Nym. They say he cried out of sack.

Hostess. Ay, that a' did.

Bardolph. And of women.

Hostess. Nay, that a' did not.

30 *Boy.* Yes, that a' did, and said they were devils incarnate.

Hostess. A' could never abide carnation—'twas a colour
he never liked.

Boy. A' said once, the devil would have him about
women.

Hostess. A' did in some sort, indeed, handle women:
but then he was rheumatic, and talked of the whore of
Babylon.

Boy. Do you not remember a' saw a flea stick upon
Bardolph's nose, and a' said it was a black soul burning
40 in hell?

Bardolph. Well, the fuel is gone that maintained that
fire: that's all the riches I got in his service.

Nym. Shall we shog? the king will be gone from
Southampton.

Pistol. Come, let's away....My love, give me thy lips...

Look to my chattels and my movables:
Let senses rule: the word is 'Pitch and pay':
Trust none:
For oaths are straws, men's faiths are wafer-cakes,
And Hold-fast is the only dog, my duck: 50
Therefore, Caveto be thy counsellor....
Go, clear thy crystals....Yoke-fellows in arms,
Let us to France, like horse-leeches, my boys,
To suck, to suck, the very blood to suck!
   Boy. And that's but unwholesome food, they say.
   Pistol. Touch her soft mouth, and march.
   Bardolph. Farewell, hostess.   *[kissing her*
   Nym. I cannot kiss, that is the humour of it: but adieu.
   Pistol. Let housewifery appear: keep close, I thee
command.   60
   Hostess. Farewell: adieu.   *[they march off*

[2. 4.]   *The French King's Palace*

'*Flourish. Enter the French* KING, *the* DAUPHIN, *the
Dukes of* BERRI *and* BRITAINE,' *the* CONSTABLE, *and
others*

   French King. Thus comes the English with full power
      upon us,
And more than carefully it us concerns
To answer royally in our defences.
Therefore the Dukes of Berri and of Britaine,
Of Brabant and of Orleans, shall make forth,
And you, Prince Dauphin, with all swift dispatch
To line and new repair our towns of war
With men of courage and with means defendant:
For England his approaches makes as fierce
As waters to the sucking of a gulf.   10

It fits us then to be as provident
As fear may teach us, out of late examples
Left by the fatal and neglected English
Upon our fields.
   Dauphin.   My most redoubted father,
It is most meet we arm us 'gainst the foe:
For peace itself should not so dull a kingdom,
(Though war nor no known quarrel were in question)
But that defences, musters, preparations,
Should be maintained, assembled, and collected,
20 As were a war in expectation.
   Therefore I say 'tis meet we all go forth
To view the sick and feeble parts of France:
And let us do it with no show of fear,
No, with no more than if we heard that England
Were busied with a Whitsun morris-dance:
For, my good liege, she is so idly kinged,
Her sceptre so fantastically borne
By a vain, giddy, shallow, humorous youth,
That fear attends her not.
   Constable.   O peace, Prince Dauphin!
30 You are too much mistaken in this king:
Question your grace the late ambassadors,
With what great state he heard their embassy,
How well supplied with noble counsellors,
How modest in exception; and, withal,
How terrible in constant resolution:
And you shall find his vanities forespent
Were but the outside of the Roman Brutus,
Covering discretion with a coat of folly;
As gardeners do with ordure hide those roots
40 That shall first spring, and be most delicate.
   Dauphin. Well, 'tis not so, my lord high constable.
But though we think it so, it is no matter:

In cases of defence, 'tis best to weigh
The enemy more mighty than he seems,
So the proportions of defence are filled:
Which, of a weak and niggardly projection,
Doth like a miser spoil his coat with scanting
A little cloth.

   French King. Think we King Harry strong:
And, princes, look you strongly arm to meet him.
The kindred of him hath been fleshed upon us:　　　50
And he is bred out of that bloody strain,
That haunted us in our familiar paths:
Witness our too much memorable shame,
When Cressy battle fatally was struck,
And all our princes captived, by the hand
Of that black name, Edward, Black Prince of Wales:
Whiles that his mountain sire, on mountain standing
Up in the air, crowned with the golden sun,
Saw his heroical seed, and smiled to see him
Mangle the work of nature, and deface　　　60
The patterns that by God and by French fathers
Had twenty years been made....This is a stem
Of that victorious stock: and let us fear
The native mightiness and fate of him.

             '*Enter a* MESSENGER'

   Messenger. Ambassadors from Harry King of England
Do crave admittance to your majesty.
   French King. We'll give them present audience. Go,
     and bring them.
        [*the Messenger departs, with certain lords*
You see this chase is hotly followed, friends.
   Dauphin. Turn head, and stop pursuit: for
     coward dogs

70 Most spend their mouths, when what they seem
    to threaten
Runs far before them. Good my sovereign,
Take up the English short, and let them know
Of what a monarchy you are the head:
Self-love, my liege, is not so vile a sin
As self-neglecting.

Re-enter LORDS, *with* EXETER *and his train*

French King.   From our brother of England?
  Exeter. From him, and thus he greets your majesty:
He wills you, in the name of God Almighty,
That you divest yourself, and lay apart
The borrowed glories that by gift of heaven,
80 By law of nature, and of nations, 'longs
To him and to his heirs, namely, the crown,
And all wide-stretchéd honours, that pertain
By custom, and the ordinance of times,
Unto the crown of France: that you may know
'Tis no sinister, nor no awkward claim,
Picked from the worm-holes of long-vanished days,
Nor from the dust of old oblivion raked,
He sends you this most memorable line, [*gives a paper*
In every branch truly demonstrative;
90 Willing you overlook this pedigree:
And when you find him evenly derived
From his most famed of famous ancestors,
Edward the third, he bids you then resign
Your crown and kingdom, indirectly held
From him the native and true challenger.
  French King. Or else what follows?
  Exeter. Bloody constraint: for if you hide the crown
Even in your hearts, there will he rake for it.
Therefore in fierce tempest is he coming,

In thunder and in earthquake, like a Jove: 100
That, if requiring fail, he will compel.
And bids you, in the bowels of the Lord,
Deliver up the crown, and to take mercy
On the poor souls, for whom this hungry war
Opens his vasty jaws: and on your head
Turning the widows' tears, the orphans' cries,
The dead men's blood, the pining maidens' groans,
For husbands, fathers, and betrothéd lovers,
That shall be swallowed in this controversy.
This is his claim, his threatening, and my message: 110
Unless the Dauphin be in presence here;
To whom expressly I bring greeting too.
   French King. For us, we will consider of this further:
To-morrow shall you bear our full intent
Back to our brother of England.
   Dauphin.   For the Dauphin,
I stand here for him: what to him from England?
   Exeter. Scorn and defiance, slight regard, contempt,
And any thing that may not misbecome
The mighty sender, doth he prize you at.
Thus says my king: an if your father's highness   120
Do not, in grant of all demands at large,
Sweeten the bitter mock you sent his majesty,
He'll call you to so hot an answer of it,
That caves and womby vaultages of France
Shall chide your trespass, and return your mock
In second accent of his ordinance.
   Dauphin. Say: if my father render fair return,
It is against my will; for I desire
Nothing but odds with England. To that end,
As matching to his youth and vanity,   130
I did present him with the Paris-balls.
   Exeter. He'll make your Paris Louvre shake for it,

Were it the mistress-court of mighty Europe:
And, be assured, you'll find a difference,
As we his subjects have in wonder found,
Between the promise of his greener days,
And these he masters now: now he weighs time
Even to the utmost grain: that you shall read
In your own losses, if he stay in France.

140 *French King* [*rises*] To-morrow shall you know our
          mind at full.   ['*Flourish*'
  Exeter. Dispatch us with all speed, lest that our king
Come here himself to question our delay;
For he is footed in this land already.
  French King. You shall be soon dispatched, with
      fair conditions.
A night is but small breath, and little pause,
To answer matters of this consequence.
              [*the King and his Courtiers leave,*
                Exeter with his train following

[3. Prologue]

'*Flourish. Enter* CHORUS'

  Chorus. Thus with imagined wing our swift scene flies,
In motion of no less celerity
Than that of thought....Suppose that you have seen
The well-appointed king at Hampton pier
Embark his royalty: and his brave fleet
With silken streamers the young Phœbus fanning;
Play with your fancies: and in them behold,
Upon the hempen tackle, ship-boys climbing;
Hear the shrill whistle, which doth order give
10 To sounds confused: behold the threaden sails,
Borne with th'invisible and creeping wind,

Draw the huge bottoms through the furrowed sea,
Breasting the lofty surge....O, do but think
You stand upon the rivage, and behold
A city on th'inconstant billows dancing:
For so appears this fleet majestical,
Holding due course to Harfleur....Follow, follow!
Grapple your minds to sternage of this navy,
And leave your England as dead midnight, still,
Guarded with grandsires, babies, and old women,   20
Either past or not arrived to pith and puissance...
For who is he, whose chin is but enriched
With one appearing hair, that will not follow
These culled and choice-drawn cavaliers to France?
Work, work your thoughts, and therein see a siege:
Behold the ordinance on their carriages,
With fatal mouths gaping on girded Harfleur....
Suppose th'ambassador from the French comes back:
Tells Harry that the king doth offer him
Katharine his daughter, and with her, to dowry,   30
Some petty and unprofitable dukedoms.
The offer likes not: and the nimble gunner
With linstock now the devilish cannon touches,

                    ['*Alarum, and chambers go off*'

And down goes all before them....Still be kind,
And eke out our performance with your mind.

                                        ['*exit*'

[3. 1.] *France. Before the gates* '*at Harfleur*'

'*Alarum.*' '*Enter the King,* EXETER, BEDFORD, *and*
GLOUCESTER,' *followed by soldiers with* '*scaling ladders*'

   King Henry. Once more unto the breach, dear friends,
      onee more;
Or close the wall up with our English dead...

In peace, there's nothing so becomes a man,
As modest stillness, and humility:
But when the blast of war blows in our ears,
Then imitate the action of the tiger:
†Stiffen the sinews, conjure up the blood,
Disguise fair nature with hard-favoured rage:
Then lend the eye a terrible aspect:
10 Let it pry through the portage of the head,
Like the brass cannon: let the brow o'erwhelm it
As fearfully as doth a galléd rock
O'erhang and jutty his confounded base,
Swilled with the wild and wasteful ocean.
Now set the teeth, and stretch the nostril wide,
Hold hard the breath, and bend up every spirit
To his full height! On, on, you noblest English,
Whose blood is fet from fathers of war-proof:
Fathers, that like so many Alexanders,
20 Have in these parts from morn till even fought,
And sheathed their swords for lack of argument.
Dishonour not your mothers: now attest
That those whom you called fathers did beget you!
Be copy now to men of grosser blood,
And teach them how to war! And you, good yeomen,
Whose limbs were made in England; show us here
The mettle of your pasture: let us swear,
That you are worth your breeding—which I doubt not:
For there is none of you so mean and base,
30 That hath not noble lustre in your eyes.
I see you stand like greyhounds in the slips,
Straining upon the start. The game's afoot:
Follow your spirit; and upon this charge,
Cry, 'God for Harry, England, and Saint George!'
                    [*They pass forward to the breach.*
                      '*Alarum, and chambers go off*'

[3. 2.] '*NYM, BARDOLPH, PISTOL,*' *and the*
         '*Boy' come up*

Bardolph. On, on, on, on, on! to the breach, to the
breach!

Nym. Pray thee, corporal, stay, the knocks are too hot:
and for mine own part, I have not a case of lives: the
humour of it is too hot, that is the very plain-song of it.

Pistol. The plain-song is most just: for humours
    do abound:
Knocks go and come: God's vassals drop and die:
       And sword and shield,
       In bloody field,
       Doth win immortal fame.   10

Boy. Would I were in an alehouse in London! I would
give all my fame for a pot of ale, and safety.

Pistol. And I:
       If wishes would prevail with me,
       My purpose should not fail with me;
       But thither would I hie.

Boy. As duly,
       But not as truly,
       As bird doth sing on bough.

*FLUELLEN marches up with supply troops for the breach;
he belabours Bardolph, Nym and Pistol with the flat of
his sword; the Boy hides behind a bush*

Fluellen. Up to the breach, you dogs; avaunt, you 20
cullions!

Pistol. Be merciful, great duke, to men of mould:
Abate thy rate, abate thy manly rage;
Abate thy rage, great duke!
Good bawcock, bate thy rage: use lenity, sweet chuck!

Nym. These be good humours…Your honour wins bad
humours.   [*Fluellen drives them forward with his men*

Boy. [*stealing forth*] As young as I am, I have observed
these three swashers: I am boy to them all three, but all
30 they three, though they would serve me, could not be
man to me; for indeed three such antics do not amount
to a man...For Bardolph, he is white-livered and red-
faced; by the means whereof a' faces it out, but fights
not: for Pistol, he hath a killing tongue, and a quiet
sword; by the means whereof a' breaks words, and keeps
whole weapons: for Nym, he hath heard that men of
few words are the best men, and therefore he scorns to
say his prayers, lest a' should be thought a coward: but
his few bad words are matched with as few good deeds;
40 for a' never broke any man's head but his own, and that
was against a post, when he was drunk. They will steal
any thing, and call it purchase. Bardolph stole a lute-
case, bore it twelve leagues, and sold it for three half-
pence. Nym and Bardolph are sworn brothers in
filching: and in Calais they stole a fire-shovel. I knew
by that piece of service, the men would carry coals. They
would have me as familiar with men's pockets as their
gloves or their handkerchers: which makes much against
my manhood, if I should take from another's pocket, to
50 put into mine; for it is plain pocketing up of wrongs....
I must leave them, and seek some better service: their
villany goes against my weak stomach, and therefore I
must cast it up.   [*he goes back towards the camp*

FLUELLEN returns with GOWER

Gower. Captain Fluellen, you must come presently to
the mines; the Duke of Gloucester would speak with you.
Fluellen. To the mines? Tell you the duke, it is not
so good to come to the mines: for look you, the mines
is not according to the disciplines of the war; the con-
cavities of it is not sufficient: for look you, th'athversary—

you may discuss unto the duke—look you, is digt himself 60
four yard under the counter-mines: by Cheshu, I think
a' will plow up all, if there is not better directions.

Gower. The Duke of Gloucester, to whom the order
of the siege is given, is altogether directed by an Irish-
man, a very valiant gentleman, i'faith.

Fluellen. It is Captain Macmorris, is it not?

Gower. I think it be.

Fluellen. By Cheshu, he is an ass, as in the world,
I will verify as much in his beard: he has no more
directions in the true disciplines of the wars, look you, 70
of the Roman disciplines, than is a puppy-dog.

'*Enter MACMORRIS and Captain JAMY*'

Gower. Here a' comes, and the Scots captain, Captain
Jamy, with him.

Fluellen. Captain Jamy is a marvellous falorous gentleman, that is certain, and of great expedition and
knowledge in th'ancient wars, upon my particular
knowledge of his directions: by Cheshu, he will maintain his argument as well as any military man in the
world, in the disciplines of the pristine wars of the
Romans.   80

Jamy. I say gud-day, Captain Fluellen.

Fluellen. God-den to your worship, good Captain
James.

Gower. How now, Captain Macmorris, have you quit
the mines? have the pioners given o'er?

Macmorris. By Chrish, la! tish ill done: the work ish
give over, the trompet sound the retreat. By my hand
I swear, and my father's soul, the work ish ill done:
it ish give over: I would have blowed up the town, so
Chrish save me, la, in an hour. O tish ill done, tish ill 90
done: by my hand, tish ill done!

Fluellen. Captain Macmorris, I beseech you now, will you voutsafe me, look you, a few disputations with you, as partly touching or concerning the disciplines of the war, the Roman wars, in the way of argument, look you, and friendly communication: partly to satisfy my opinion, and partly for the satisfaction, look you, of my mind: as touching the direction of the military discipline, that is the point.

100 *Jamy.* It sall be vary gud, gud feith, gud captains bath, and I sall quit you with gud leve, as I may pick occasion: that sall I, marry.

Macmorris. It is no time to discourse, so Chrish save me: the day is hot, and the weather, and the wars, and the king, and the dukes: it is no time to discourse, the town is beseeched: an the trumpet call us to the breach, and we talk, and, be Chrish, do nothing, 'tis shame for us all: so God sa' me, 'tis shame to stand still, it is shame, by my hand: an there is throats to be cut, and works to 110 be done, and there ish nothing done, so Chrish sa' me, la!

Jamy. By the mess, ere these eyes of mine take themselves to slomber, ay'll de gude service, or ay'll lig i'th'grund for it; ay, or go to death: and ay'll pay't as valorously as I may, that sal I suerly do, that is the breff and the long...Mary, I wad full fain hear some question 'tween you tway.

Fluellen. Captain Macmorris, I think, look you, under your correction, there is not many of your nation—

Macmorris. Of my nation! What ish my nation? Ish 120 a villain, and a bastard, and a knave, and a rascal— What ish my nation? Who talks of my nation?

Fluellen. Look you, if you take the matter otherwise than is meant, Captain Macmorris, peradventure I shall think you do not use me with that affability as in discretion you ought to use me, look you, being as good

a man as yourself, both in the disciplines of war, and in
the derivation of my birth, and in other particularities.

Macmorris. I do not know you so good a man as
myself: so Chrish save me, I will cut off your head.

Gower. Gentlemen both, you will mistake each other. 130

Jamy. Ah! that's a foul fault.

'A parley' sounded from the walls

Gower. The town sounds a parley.

Fluellen. Captain Macmorris, when there is more
better opportunity to be required, look you, I will be
so bold as to tell you I know the disciplines of war: and
there is an end.   [*they stand aside*

[3. 3.] *The* GOVERNOR *and some* CITIZENS *appear upon
the walls. 'Enter the King and all his train before
the gates'*

King. How yet resolves the governor of the town?
This is the latest parle we will admit:
Therefore to our best mercy give yourselves,
Or, like to men proud of destruction,
Defy us to our worst: for, as I am a soldier,
A name that in my thoughts becomes me best,
If I begin the battery once again,
I will not leave the half-achieved Harfleur
Till in her ashes she lie buriéd.
The gates of mercy shall be all shut up,   10
And the fleshed soldier, rough and hard of heart,
In liberty of bloody hand, shall range
With conscience wide as hell, mowing like grass
Your fresh fair virgins, and your flowering infants.
What is it then to me, if impious war,
Arrayed in flames like to the prince of fiends,
Do with his smirched complexion all fell feats

K.H.V.—6

Enlinked to waste and desolation?
What is't to me, when you yourselves are cause,
20 If your pure maidens fall into the hand
Of hot and forcing violation?
What rein can hold licentious wickedness,
When down the hill he holds his fierce career?
We may as bootless spend our vain command
Upon th'enragéd soldiers in their spoil,
As send precépts to the leviathan
To come ashore. Therefore, you men of Harfleur,
Take pity of your town and of your people,
Whiles yet my soldiers are in my command,
30 Whiles yet the cool and temperate wind of grace
O'erblows the filthy and contagious clouds
Of heady murder, spoil, and villany.
If not—why, in a moment look to see
The blind and bloody soldier with foul hand
Defile the locks of your shrill-shrieking daughters:
Your fathers taken by the silver beards,
And their most reverend heads dashed to the walls:
Your naked infants spitted upon pikes,
Whiles the mad mothers with their howls confused
40 Do break the clouds; as did the wives of Jewry,
At Herod's bloody-hunting slaughtermen.
What say you? Will you yield, and this avoid?
Or, guilty in defence, be thus destroyed?
   Governor. Our expectation hath this day an end:
The Dauphin, whom of succours we entreated,
Returns us that his powers are yet not ready
To raise so great a siege...Therefore, great king,
We yield our town and lives to thy soft mercy:
Enter our gates, dispose of us and ours,
50 For we no longer are defensible.
   King. Open your gates...Come, uncle Exeter,

Go you and enter Harfleur; there remain,
And fortify it strongly 'gainst the French:
Use mercy to them all. For us, dear uncle,
The winter coming on, and sickness growing
Upon our soldiers, we will retire to Calais.
To-night in Harfleur will we be your guest,
To-morrow for the march are we addrest.

['*Flourish.*' *The King and his forces* '*enter the town*'

[3. 4.]   *Rouen. The French King's palace*

The Princess KATHARINE *and* ALICE, '*an old
Gentlewoman*', *and other ladies-in-waiting*

Katharine. Alice, tu as été en Angleterre, et tu bien
parles le langage.

Alice. Un peu, madame.

Katharine. Je te prie, m'enseignez—il faut que j'ap-
prenne à parler...Comment appelez-vous la main en
Anglais?

Alice. La main? elle est appelée de hand.

Katharine. De hand. Et les doigts?

Alice. Les doigts? ma foi, j'oublie les doigts; mais je
me souviendrai. Les doigts? je pense qu'ils sont appelés 10
de fingres: oui, de fingres.

Katharine. La main, de hand: les doigts, de fingres.
Je pense que je suis le bon écolier. J'ai gagné deux mots
d'Anglais vitement. Comment appelez-vous les ongles?

Alice. Les ongles? nous les appelons de nailès.

Katharine. De nailès. Ecoutez: dites moi si je parle
bien: de hand, de fingres, et de nailès.

Alice. C'est bien dit, madame; il est fort bon Anglais.

Katharine. Dites moi l'Anglais pour le bras.

Alice. De arm, madame.   20

Katharine. Et le coude.

Alice. D' elbow.

Katharine. D' elbow. Je m'en fais la répétition de tous les mots que vous m'avez appris dès à présent.

Alice. Il est trop difficile, madame, comme je pense.

Katharine. Excusez-moi, Alice; écoutez: d' hand, de fingre, de nailès, d' arma, de bilbow.

Alice. D' elbow, madame.

Katharine. O Seigneur Dieu, je m'en oublie! d'
30 elbow. Comment appelez-vous le col?

Alice. De nick, madame.

Katharine. De nick. Et le menton?

Alice. De chin.

Katharine. De sin. Le col, de nick: le menton, de sin.

Alice. Oui. Sauf votre honneur, en vérité, vous pro-noncez les mots aussi droit que les natifs d'Angleterre.

Katharine. Je ne doute point d'apprendre, par la grace de Dieu, et en peu de temps.

Alice. N'avez vous pas déjà oublié ce que je vous ai
40 enseigné?

Katharine. Non, je réciterai à vous promptement: d' hand, de fingre, de mailès,—

Alice. De nailès, madame.

Katharine. De nailès, de arm, de ilbow.

Alice. Sauf votre honneur, d' elbow.

Katharine. Ainsi dis-je: d' elbow, de nick, et de sin. Comment appelez-vous le pied et la robe?

Alice. Le foot, madame, et le count.

Katharine. Le foot, et le count? O Seignieur Dieu!
50 ils sont mots de son mauvais, corruptible, gros, et im-pudique, et non pour les dames d'honneur d'user: je ne voudrais prononcer ces mots devant les seigneurs de France pour tout le monde. Foh! le foot et le count. Néanmoins, je réciterai une autre fois ma leçon ensemble:

d' hand, de fingre, de nailès, d' arm, d' elbow, de nick,
de sin, de foot, le count.

   Alice. Excellent, madame!

   Katharine. C'est assez pour une fois: allons-nous à
dîner.   *[they go*

[3. 5.] '*Enter the* KING *of France, the* DAUPHIN,' *the
Duke of* BRITAINE, '*the* CONSTABLE *of France, and
others*'

   French King. 'Tis certain he hath passed the
     river Somme.

   Constable. And if he be not fought withal, my lord,
Let us not live in France: let us quit all,
And give our vineyards to a barbarous people.

   Dauphin. O Dieu vivant! shall a few sprays of us,
The emptying of our fathers' luxury,
Our scions, put in wild and savage stock,
Spirt up so suddenly into the clouds,
And overlook their grafters?

   Britaine. Normans, but bastard Normans,
     Norman bastards!   10
Mort Dieu! ma vie! if they march along
Unfought withal, but I will sell my dukedom,
To buy a slobbery and a dirty farm
In that nook-shotten isle of Albion.

   Constable. Dieu de batailles! where have they
     this mettle?
Is not their climate foggy, raw, and dull?
On whom, as in despite, the sun looks pale,
Killing their fruit with frowns. Can sodden water,
A drench for sur-reined jades, their barley broth,
Decoct their cold blood to such valiant heat?   20
And shall our quick blood, spirited with wine,
Seem frosty? O, for honour of our land,

Let us not hang like roping icicles
Upon our houses' thatch, whiles a more frosty people
Sweat drops of gallant youth in our rich fields...
Poor we may call them in their native lords.
  Dauphin. By faith and honour,
Our madams mock at us, and plainly say
Our mettle is bred out, and they will give
30 Their bodies to the lust of English youth,
To new-store France with bastard warriors.
  Britaine. They bid us to the English dancing-
    schools,
And teach lavoltas high, and swift corantos,
Saying our grace is only in our heels,
And that we are most lofty runaways.
  French King. Where is Montjoy the herald? speed
    him hence,
Let him greet England with our sharp defiance....
Up, princes, and, with spirit of honour edged
More sharper than your swords, hie to the field:
40 Charles Delabreth, high constable of France,
You Dukes of Orleans, Bourbon, and of Berri,
Alençon, Brabant, Bar, and Burgundy,
Jacques Chatillon, Rambures, Vaudemont,
Beaumont, Grandpré, Roussi, and Faulconbridge,
Foix, Lestrake, Bouciqualt, and Charolois,
High dukes, great princes, barons, lords, and knights;
For your great seats now quit you of great shames...
Bar Harry England, that sweeps through our land
With pennons painted in the blood of Harfleur:
50 Rush on his host, as doth the melted snow
Upon the valleys, whose low vassal seat
The Alps doth spit and void his rheum upon....
Go down upon him—you have power enough—
†And in a chariot, captive into Rouen

Bring him our prisoner.

Constable.　　　　　　This becomes the great.
Sorry am I his numbers are so few,
His soldiers sick and famished in their march:
For I am sure, when he shall see our army,
He'll drop his heart into the sink of fear,
And for achievement offer us his ransom.　　　　　60

　French King. Therefore, lord constable, haste
　　on Montjoy,
And let him say to England, that we send
To know what willing ransom he will give....
Prince Dauphin, you shall stay with us in Rouen.

　Dauphin. Not so, I do beseech your majesty.

　French King. Be patient, for you shall remain
　　with us....
Now forth, lord constable and princes all,
And quickly bring us word of England's fall. [*they go*

[3. 6.]　　　　*Near a river in Picardy*

The English and Welsh captains, GOWER *and*
FLUELLEN, *meeting*

　Gower. How now, Captain Fluellen! come you from
the bridge?

　Fluellen. I assure you, there is very excellent services
committed at the bridge.

　Gower. Is the Duke of Exeter safe?

　Fluellen. The Duke of Exeter is as magnanimous as
Agamemnon, and a man that I love and honour with
my soul, and my heart, and my duty, and my live, and
my living, and my uttermost power. He is not—God be
praised and blessed!—any hurt in the world, but keeps 10
the bridge most valiantly, with excellent discipline.

There is an ancient lieutenant there at the pridge,
I think in my very conscience he is as valiant a man as
Mark Antony, and he is a man of no estimation in the
world, but I did see him do as gallant service.

Gower. What do you call him?

Fluellen. He is called Ancient Pistol.

Gower. I know him not.

PISTOL *is seen approaching*

Fluellen. Here is the man.

20   *Pistol.* Captain, I thee beseech to do me favours:
The Duke of Exeter doth love thee well.

Fluellen. Ay, I praise God, and I have merited some
love at his hands.

Pistol. Bardolph, a soldier firm and sound of heart,
And of buxom valour, hath, by cruel fate,
And giddy Fortune's furious fickle wheel,
That goddess blind,
That stands upon the rolling restless stone—

Fluellen. By your patience, Ancient Pistol...Fortune
30 is painted blind, with a muffler afore his eyes, to
signify to you that Fortune is blind; and she is painted
also with a wheel, to signify to you, which is the moral
of it, that she is turning and inconstant, and mutability,
and variation: and her foot, look you, is fixed upon a
spherical stone, which rolls, and rolls, and rolls: in good
truth, the poet makes a most excellent description of it:
Fortune is an excellent moral.

Pistol. Fortune is Bardolph's foe, and frowns on him:
For he hath stolen a pax, and hangéd must a' be
40 A damnéd death!
Let gallows gape for dog, let man go free,
And let not hemp his wind-pipe suffocate:
But Exeter hath given the doom of death,

For pax of little price.
Therefore go speak, the duke will hear thy voice;
And let not Bardolph's vital thread be cut
With edge of penny cord, and vile reproach.
Speak, captain, for his life, and I will thee requite.

   Fluellen. Ancient Pistol, I do partly understand
     your meaning.

   Pistol. Why then rejoice therefore.　　　　　　　50

   Fluellen. Certainly, ancient, it is not a thing to
rejoice at: for if, look you, he were my brother, I would
desire the duke to use his good pleasure, and put him
to execution; for discipline ought to be used.

   Pistol. Die and be damned! and figo for thy friendship!
                                [*he turns away*

   Fluellen. It is well.

   Pistol. [*he bites his thumb*] The fig of Spain!

   Fluellen. Very good.

   Gower. Why, this is an arrant counterfeit rascal, I
remember him now: a bawd, a cutpurse.　　　　　60

   Fluellen. I'll assure you, a' uttered as prave words at
the pridge as you shall see in a summer's day: but it is
very well: what he has spoke to me, that is well, I warrant
you, when time is serve.

   Gower. Why, 'tis a gull, a fool, a rogue, that now and
then goes to the wars, to grace himself at his return into
London, under the form of a soldier...And such fellows
are perfect in the great commanders' names, and they
will learn you by rote where services were done; at such
and such a sconce, at such a breach, at such a convoy: 70
who came off bravely, who was shot, who disgraced,
what terms the enemy stood on; and this they con
perfectly in the phrase of war, which they trick up with
new-tuned oaths: and what a beard of the general's cut,
and a horrid suit of the camp, will do among foaming

bottles, and ale-washed wits, is wonderful to be thought on. But you must learn to know such slanders of the age, or else you may be marvellously mistook.

Fluellen. I tell you what, Captain Gower: I do per-
80 ceive he is not the man that he would gladly make show to the world he is: if I find a hole in his coat, I will tell him my mind...[*Drum heard*] Hark you, the king is coming, and I must speak with him from the pridge.

'*Drum and colours. Enter King*' HENRY, GLOUCESTER,
'*and his poor soldiers*'

Fluellen. God pless your majesty!

King Henry. How now, Fluellen, cam'st thou from the bridge?

Fluellen. Ay, so please your majesty...The Duke of Exeter has very gallantly maintained the pridge; the French is gone off, look you, and there is gallant and
90 most prave passages: marry, th'athversary was have possession of the pridge, but he is enforced to retire, and the Duke of Exeter is master of the pridge...I can tell your majesty, the duke is a prave man.

King Henry. What men have you lost, Fluellen?

Fluellen. The perdition of th'athversary hath been very great, reasonable great: marry, for my part, I think the duke hath lost never a man, but one that is like to be executed for robbing a church, one Bardolph, if your majesty know the man: his face is all bubukles and
100 whelks, and knobs, and flames afire, and his lips blows at his nose, and it is like a coal of fire, sometimes plue, and sometimes red, but his nose is executed, and his fire's out.

King Henry. We would have all such offenders so cut off: and we give express charge that in our marches through the country there be nothing compelled from

the villages; nothing taken but paid for; none of the
French upbraided or abused in disdainful language;
for when lenity and cruelty play for a kingdom, the
gentler gamester is the soonest winner.　　　　　110

A 'tucket' sounds. Montjoy *approaches*

Montjoy. You know me by my habit.

King Henry. Well then, I know thee: what shall I
know of thee?

Montjoy. My master's mind.

King Henry. Unfold it.

Montjoy. Thus says my king: Say thou to Harry of
England, Though we seemed dead, we did but sleep:
advantage is a better soldier than rashness....Tell him,
we could have rebuked him at Harfleur, but that we
thought not good to bruise an injury till it were full 120
ripe. Now we speak upon our cue, and our voice is
imperial: England shall repent his folly, see his weak-
ness, and admire our sufferance. Bid him therefore
consider of his ransom, which must proportion the losses
we have borne, the subjects we have lost, the disgrace
we have digested; which in weight to re-answer, his
pettiness would bow under. For our losses, his exchequer
is too poor; for th'effusion of our blood, the muster of
his kingdom too faint a number; and for our disgrace,
his own person kneeling at our feet, but a weak and 130
worthless satisfaction....To this add defiance: and tell
him, for conclusion, he hath betrayed his followers,
whose condemnation is pronounced...So far my king
and master; so much my office.

King Henry. What is thy name? I know thy quality.

Montjoy. Montjoy.

King Henry. Thou dost thy office fairly. Turn
　　thee back,

And tell thy king I do not seek him now,
But could be willing to march on to Calais
140 Without impeachment: for, to say the sooth,
Though 'tis no wisdom to confess so much
Unto an enemy of craft and vantage,
My people are with sickness much enfeebled,
My numbers lessened: and those few I have,
Almost no better than so many French;
Who when they were in health, I tell thee, herald,
I thought upon one pair of English legs
Did march three Frenchmen....Yet forgive me, God,
That I do brag thus! This your air of France
150 Hath blown that vice in me. I must repent...
Go therefore, tell thy master here I am;
My ransom is this frail and worthless trunk;
My army, but a weak and sickly guard:
Yet, God before, tell him we will come on,
Though France himself, and such another neighbour,
Stand in our way....There's for thy labour, Montjoy.
                              [*he gives a purse of gold*
Go bid thy master well advise himself.
If we may pass, we will: if we be hindered,
We shall your tawny ground with your red blood
160 Discolour...And so, Montjoy, fare you well.
The sum of all our answer is but this:
We would not seek a battle as we are,
Nor, as we are, we say we will not shun it:
So tell your master.
     Montjoy. I shall deliver so...Thanks to your highness.
                              [*he bows low and departs*
     Gloucester. I hope they will not come upon us now.
     King Henry. We are in God's hand, brother, not
          in theirs...
March to the bridge—it now draws toward night—

Beyond the river we'll encamp ourselves,
And on to-morrow bid them march away.   [*they go* 170

[3. 7.]   *A tent in the French camp, near Agincourt*

'*Enter the* CONSTABLE *of* FRANCE, *the Lord* RAM-
BURES, ORLEANS, DAUPHIN, *with others*'

Constable. Tut! I have the best armour of the world:
would it were day!

Orleans. You have an excellent armour: but let my
horse have his due.

Constable. It is the best horse of Europe.

Orleans. Will it never be morning?

Dauphin. My Lord of Orleans, and my lord high
constable, you talk of horse and armour?

Orleans. You are as well provided of both as any
prince in the world.   10

Dauphin. What a long night is this! I will not change
my horse with any that treads but on four pasterns.
Ça, ha! he bounds from the earth, as if his entrails were
hairs: le cheval volant, the Pegasus, chez les narines de
feu! When I bestride him, I soar, I am a hawk: he trots
the air: the earth sings when he touches it: the basest
horn of his hoof is more musical than the pipe of Hermes.

Orleans. He's of the colour of the nutmeg.

Dauphin. And of the heat of the ginger. It is a beast
for Perseus: he is pure air and fire; and the dull elements 20
of earth and water never appear in him, but only in
patient stillness while his rider mounts him: he is indeed
a horse, and all other jades you may call beasts.

Constable. Indeed, my lord, it is a most absolute and
excellent horse.

Dauphin. It is the prince of palfreys—his neigh is like

the bidding of a monarch, and his countenance enforces homage.

Orleans. No more, cousin.

30 *Dauphin.* Nay, the man hath no wit that cannot, from the rising of the lark to the lodging of the lamb, vary deserved praise on my palfrey: it is a theme as fluent as the sea: turn the sands into eloquent tongues, and my horse is argument for them all: 'tis a subject for a sovereign to reason on, and for a sovereign's sovereign to ride on: and for the world, familiar to us and unknown, to lay apart their particular functions and wonder at him—I once writ a sonnet in his praise, and began thus, "Wonder of nature"—

40 *Orleans.* I have heard a sonnet begin so to one's mistress.

Dauphin. Then did they imitate that which I composed to my courser, for my horse is my mistress.

Orleans. Your mistress bears well.

Dauphin. Me well, which is the prescript praise and perfection of a good and particular mistress.

Constable. Nay, for methought yesterday your mistress shrewdly shook your back.

Dauphin. So perhaps did yours.

50 *Constable.* Mine was not bridled.

Dauphin. O then belike she was old and gentle, and you rode like a kern of Ireland, your French hose off, and in your strait strossers.

Constable. You have good judgement in horsemanship.

Dauphin. Be warned by me then: they that ride so, and ride not warily, fall into foul bogs: I had rather have my horse to my mistress.

Constable. I had as lief have my mistress a jade.

Dauphin. I tell thee, constable, my mistress wears his
60 own hair.

Constable. I could make as true a boast as that, if I had a sow to my mistress.

Dauphin. "Le chien est retourné à son propre vomissement, et la truie lavée au bourbier": thou mak'st use of any thing.

Constable. Yet do I not use my horse for my mistress, or any such proverb so little kin to the purpose.

Rambures. My lord constable, the armour that I saw in your tent to-night, are those stars or suns upon it?

Constable. Stars, my lord. 70

Dauphin. Some of them will fall to-morrow, I hope.

Constable. And yet my sky shall not want.

Dauphin. That may be, for you bear a many superfluously, and 'twere more honour some were away.

Constable. Ev'n as your horse bears your praises, who would trot as well, were some of your brags dismounted.

Dauphin. Would I were able to load him with his desert! Will it never be day? I will trot to-morrow a mile, and my way shall be paved with English faces. 80

Constable. I will not say so, for fear I should be faced out of my way: but I would it were morning, for I would fain be about the ears of the English.

Rambures. Who will go to hazard with me for twenty prisoners?

Constable. You must first go yourself to hazard, ere you have them.

Dauphin. 'Tis midnight, I'll go arm myself.

　　　　　　　　　　　　　　[he leaves the tent

Orleans. The Dauphin longs for morning.

Rambures. He longs to eat the English. 90

Constable. I think he will eat all he kills.

Orleans. By the white hand of my lady, he's a gallant prince.

Constable. Swear by her foot, that she may tread out the oath.

Orleans. He is simply the most active gentleman of France.

Constable. Doing is activity, and he will still be doing.

Orleans. He never did harm, that I heard of.

100 *Constable.* Nor will do none to-morrow: he will keep that good name still.

Orleans. I know him to be valiant.

Constable. I was told that, by one that knows him better than you.

Orleans. What's he?

Constable. Marry, he told me so himself, and he said he cared not who knew it.

Orleans. He needs not, it is no hidden virtue in him.

Constable. By my faith, sir, but it is: never any body

110 saw it, but his lackey: 'tis a hooded valour, and when it appears, it will bate.

Orleans. Ill will never said well.

Constable. I will cap that proverb with "There is flattery in friendship."

Orleans. And I will take up that with "Give the devil his due."

Constable. Well placed: there stands your friend for the devil: have at the very eye of that proverb with "A pox of the devil."

120 *Orleans.* You are the better at proverbs, by how much "A fool's bolt is soon shot."

Constable. You have shot over.

Orleans. 'Tis not the first time you were overshot.

'*Enter a* MESSENGER'

Messenger. My lord high constable, the English lie within fifteen hundred paces of your tents.

Constable. Who hath measured the ground?

Messenger. The lord Grandpré.

Constable. A valiant and most expert gentleman.... Would it were day! Alas, poor Harry of England! he longs not for the dawning, as we do.   130

Orleans. What a wretched and peevish fellow is this King of England, to mope with his fat-brained followers so far out of his knowledge!

Constable. If the English had any apprehension, they would run away.

Orleans. That they lack: for if their heads had any intellectual armour, they could never wear such heavy head-pieces.

Rambures. That island of England breeds very valiant creatures; their mastiffs are of unmatchable courage.   140

Orleans. Foolish curs, that run winking into the mouth of a Russian bear, and have their heads crushed like rotten apples! You may as well say, that's a valiant flea that dare eat his breakfast on the lip of a lion.

Constable. Just, just: and the men do sympathize with the mastiffs in robustious and rough coming on, leaving their wits with their wives: and then give them great meals of beef, and iron and steel; they will eat like wolves, and fight like devils.

Orleans. Ay, but these English are shrewdly out of   150 beef.

Constable. Then shall we find to-morrow they have only stomachs to eat, and none to fight....Now is it time to arm: come, shall we about it?

Orleans. It is now two o'clock: but, let me see, by ten We shall have each a hundred Englishmen.

                                             [*they go out*

[4. Prologue]

Enter 'CHORUS'

Chorus. Now entertain conjecture of a time
When creeping murmur and the poring dark
Fills the wide vessel of the universe.
From camp to camp, through the foul womb of night
The hum of either army stilly sounds;
That the fixed sentinels almost receive
The secret whispers of each other's watch.
Fire answers fire, and through their paly flames
Each battle sees the other's umbered face.
10 Steed threatens steed, in high and boastful neighs
Piercing the night's dull ear: and from the tents
The armourers, accomplishing the knights,
With busy hammers closing rivets up,
Give dreadful note of preparation.
The country cocks do crow, the clocks do toll,
And the third hour of drowsy morning name.
Proud of their numbers, and secure in soul,
The confident and over-lusty French
Do the low-rated English play at dice;
20 And chide the cripple tardy-gaited night,
Who like a foul and ugly witch doth limp
So tediously away. The poor condemnéd English,
Like sacrifices, by their watchful fires
Sit patiently, and inly ruminate
The morning's danger: and their gesture sad,
Investing lank-lean cheeks, and war-worn coats,
Presenteth them unto the gazing moon
So many horrid ghosts. O now, who will behold
The royal captain of this ruined band
30 Walking from watch to watch, from tent to tent,

Let him cry, "Praise and glory on his head!"
For forth he goes, and visits all his host,
Bids them good morrow with a modest smile,
And calls them brothers, friends, and countrymen.
Upon his royal face there is no note,
How dread an army hath enrounded him;
Nor doth he dedicate one jot of colour
Unto the weary and all-watchéd night:
But freshly looks, and over-bears attaint
With cheerful semblance, and sweet majesty: 40
That every wretch, pining and pale before,
Beholding him, plucks comfort from his looks.
A largess universal, like the sun,
His liberal eye doth give to every one,
Thawing cold fear, that mean and gentle all
Behold, as may unworthiness define,
A little touch of Harry in the night.
And so our scene must to the battle fly:
Where—O for pity!—we shall much disgrace,
With four or five most vile and ragged foils,   50
Right ill-disposed, in brawl ridiculous,
The name of Agincourt: yet sit and see,
Minding true things by what their mock'ries be.

                                                  ['*Exit*'

[4. 1.] *A passage between the tents of the English camp
                  at Agincourt. Before dawn*

          King HENRY, BEDFORD, *and* GLOUCESTER

King Henry. Gloucester, 'tis true that we are in
     great danger,
The greater therefore should our courage be....
Good morrow, brother Bedford...God Almighty!

There is some soul of goodness in things evil,
Would men observingly distil it out.
For our bad neighbour makes us early stirrers,
Which is both healthful, and good husbandry.
Besides, they are our outward consciences·
And preachers to us all, admonishing
10 That we should dress us fairly for our end.
Thus may we gather honey from the weed,
And make a moral of the devil himself.

ERPINGHAM comes up

Good morrow, old Sir Thomas Erpingham:
A good soft pillow for that good white head
Were better than a churlish turf of France.
　Erpingham. Not so, my liege—this lodging likes
　　me better,
Since I may say 'Now lie I like a king.'
　King Henry. 'Tis good for men to love their
　　present pains,
Upon example—so the spirit is eased:
20 And when the mind is quickened, out of doubt
The organs, though defunct and dead before,
Break up their drowsy grave, and newly move
With casted slough and fresh legerity....
Lend me thy cloak, Sir Thomas...Brothers both,
Commend me to the princes in our camp;
Do my good morrow to them, and anon
Desire them all to my pavilion.
　Gloucester. We shall, my liege.
　Erpingham. Shall I attend your grace?
　King Henry.　　　　　　　No, my good knight:
30 Go with my brothers to my lords of England:
I and my bosom must debate awhile,
And then I would no other company.

Erpingham. The Lord in heaven bless thee,
  noble Harry!
King Henry. God-a-mercy, old heart! thou
  speak'st cheerfully. [*they take leave of the King*

PISTOL *steals into view, is about to pilfer from a tent,*
  but starts as he perceives someone in the dark

Pistol. Qui va là?
King Henry. A friend.
Pistol. Discuss unto me, art thou officer,
Or art thou base, common, and popular?
King Henry. I am a gentleman of a company.
Pistol. Trail'st thou the puissant pike?   40
King Henry. Even so: what are you?
Pistol. As good a gentleman as the emperor.
King Henry. Then you are a better than the king.
Pistol. The king's a bawcock, and a heart of gold,
A lad of life, an imp of Fame,
Of parents good, of fist most valiant:
I kiss his dirty shoe, and from heart-string
I love the lovely bully....What is thy name?
King Henry. Harry le Roy.
Pistol. Le Roy? a Cornish name: art thou of 50
  Cornish crew?
King Henry. No, I am a Welshman.
Pistol. Know'st thou Fluellen?
King Henry. Yes.
Pistol. Tell him I'll knock his leek about his pate
Upon Saint Davy's day.
King Henry. Do not you wear your dagger in your
cap that day, lest he knock that about yours.
Pistol. Art thou his friend?
King Henry. And his kinsman too.
Pistol. The figo for thee then!   60

King Henry. I thank you: God be with you!
Pistol. My name is Pistol called. [*he goes*
King Henry. It sorts well with your fierceness.

The King withdraws a little; FLUELLEN and GOWER encounter, coming different ways.

Gower. Captain Fluellen!
Fluellen. So! in the name of Jesu Christ, speak fewer... It is the greatest admiration in the universal world, when the true and ancient prerogatifes and laws of the wars is not kept: if you would take the pains but to examine the wars of Pompey the Great, you shall find, I warrant
70 you, that there is no tiddle taddle nor pibble pabble in Pompey's camp: I warrant you, you shall find the ceremonies of the wars, and the cares of it, and the forms of it, and the sobriety of it, and the modesty of it, to be otherwise.
Gower. Why, the enemy is loud, you hear him all night.
Fluellen. If the enemy is an ass and a fool, and a prating coxcomb, is it meet, think you, that we should also, look you, be an ass and a fool, and a prating coxcomb? in
80 your own conscience now?
Gower. I will speak lower.
Fluellen. I pray you, and beseech you, that you will.
[*they depart severally*
King Henry. Though it appear a little out of fashion, There is much care and valour in this Welshman.

'*Three soldiers, JOHN BATES, ALEXANDER COURT, and MICHAEL WILLIAMS,*' *come up*

Court. Brother John Bates, is not that the morning which breaks yonder?

Bates. I think it be: but we have no great cause to desire the approach of day.

Williams. We see yonder the beginning of the day, but I think we shall never see the end of it....Who goes 90 there?

King Henry. A friend.

Williams. Under what captain serve you?

King Henry. Under Sir Thomas Erpingham.

Williams. A good old commander, and a most kind gentleman: I pray you, what thinks he of our estate?

King Henry. Even as men wracked upon a sand, that look to be washed off the next tide.

Bates. He hath not told his thought to the king?

King Henry. No: nor it is not meet he should: for, 100 though I speak it to you, I think the king is but a man, as I am: the violet smells to him as it doth to me; the element shows to him as it doth to me; all his senses have but human conditions: his ceremonies laid by, in his nakedness he appears but a man; and though his affections are higher mounted than ours, yet, when they stoop, they stoop with the like wing: therefore, when he sees reason of fears, as we do, his fears, out of doubt, be of the same relish as ours are: yet, in reason, no man should possess him with any appearance of fear, lest he, 110 by showing it, should dishearten his army.

Bates. He may show what outward courage he will: but I believe, as cold a night as 'tis, he could wish himself in Thames up to the neck; and so I would he were, and I by him, at all adventures, so we were quit here.

King Henry. By my troth, I will speak my conscience of the king: I think he would not wish himself any where but where he is.

Bates. Then I would he were here alone; so should 120

he be sure to be ransomed, and a many poor men's lives saved.

King Henry. I dare say you love him not so ill, to wish him here alone: howsoever you speak this to feel other men's minds. Methinks I could not die any where so contented as in the king's company; his cause being just, and his quarrel honourable.

Williams. That's more than we know.

Bates. Ay, or more than we should seek after; for we
130 know enough, if we know we are the king's subjects: if his cause be wrong, our obedience to the king wipes the crime of it out of us.

Williams. But if the cause be not good, the king himself hath a heavy reckoning to make, when all those legs, and arms, and heads, chopped off in a battle, shall join together at the latter day, and cry all "We died at such a place"; some swearing, some crying for a surgeon; some upon their wives, left poor behind them; some upon the debts they owe; some upon their children rawly
140 left...I am afeard there are few die well, that die in a battle: for how can they charitably dispose of any thing, when blood is their argument? Now, if these men do not die well, it will be a black matter for the king, that led them to it; who to disobey were against all proportion of subjection.

King Henry. So, if a son that is by his father sent about merchandise do sinfully miscarry upon the sea, the imputation of his wickedness, by your rule, should be imposed upon his father that sent him: or if a servant,
150 under his master's command, transporting a sum of money, be assailed by robbers, and die in many irreconciled iniquities, you may call the business of the master the author of the servant's damnation...But this is not so: the king is not bound to answer the particular endings

of his soldiers, the father of his son, nor the master of his servant; for they purpose not their death, when they purpose their services. Besides, there is no king, be his cause never so spotless, if it come to the arbitrement of swords, can try it out with all unspotted soldiers: some, peradventure, have on them the guilt of premeditated 160 and contrived murder; some, of beguiling virgins with the broken seals of perjury; some, making the wars their bulwark, that have before gored the gentle bosom of peace with pillage and robbery. Now, if these men have defeated the law, and outrun native punishment, though they can outstrip men, they have no wings to fly from God. War is His beadle, war is His vengeance: so that here men are punished, for before breach of the king's laws, in now the king's quarrel: where they feared the death, they have borne life away; and where they would 170 be safe, they perish. Then if they die unprovided, no more is the king guilty of their damnation than he was before guilty of those impieties for the which they are now visited. Every subject's duty is the king's, but every subject's soul is his own. Therefore should every soldier in the wars do as every sick man in his bed, wash every mote out of his conscience: and dying so, death is to him advantage; or not dying, the time was blessedly lost, wherein such preparation was gained: and in him that escapes, it were not sin to think that, making God so free 180 an offer, He let him outlive that day, to see His greatness, and to teach others how they should prepare.

Williams. 'Tis certain, every man that dies ill, the ill upon his own head, the king is not to answer it.

Bates. I do not desire he should answer for me, and yet I determine to fight lustily for him.

King Henry. I myself heard the king say he would not be ransomed.

Williams. Ay, he said so, to make us fight cheerfully:
190 but when our throats are cut, he may be ransomed, and
we ne'er the wiser.

King Henry. If I live to see it, I will never trust his
word after.

Williams. You pay him then! That's a perilous shot
out of an elder-gun, that a poor and a private displeasure
can do against a monarch! you may as well go about to
turn the sun to ice, with fanning in his face with a
peacock's feather...You'll never trust his word after!
come, 'tis a foolish saying.

200 *King Henry.* Your reproof is something too round—
I should be angry with you, if the time were convenient.

Williams. Let it be a quarrel between us, if you live.

King Henry. I embrace it.

Williams. How shall I know thee again?

King Henry. Give me any gage of thine, and I will
wear it in my bonnet: then, if ever thou dar'st acknow-
ledge it, I will make it my quarrel.

Williams. Here's my glove: give me another of thine.

King Henry. There.

210 *Williams.* This will I also wear in my cap: if ever
thou come to me and say, after to-morrow, "This is my
glove", by this hand I will take thee a box on the ear.

King Henry. If ever I live to see it, I will challenge it.

Williams. Thou dar'st as well be hanged.

King Henry. Well, I will do it, though I take thee in
the king's company.

Williams. Keep thy word: fare thee well.

Bates. Be friends, you English fools, be friends; we
have French quarrels enow, if you could tell how to
220 reckon.

King Henry. Indeed, the French may lay twenty
French crowns to one, they will beat us, for they bear

them on their shoulders: but it is no English treason to
cut French crowns, and to-morrow the king himself will
be a clipper.   [*the soldiers go their way*
Upon the king! let us our lives, our souls,
Our debts, our careful wives,
Our children, and our sins, lay on the king!
We must bear all. O hard condition,
Twin-born with greatness, subject to the breath   230
Of every fool, whose sense no more can feel
But his own wringing! What infinite heart's ease
Must kings neglect that private men enjoy!
And what have kings, that privates have not too,
Save Ceremony, save general Ceremony?
And what art thou, thou idol Ceremony?
What kind of god art thou, that suffer'st more
Of mortal griefs than do thy worshippers?
What are thy rents? what are thy comings in?
O Ceremony, show me but thy worth!   240
What! Is thy soul of adoration?
Art thou aught else but place, degree, and form,
Creating awe and fear in other men?
Wherein thou art less happy, being feared,
Than they in fearing.
What drink'st thou oft, instead of homage sweet,
But poisoned flattery? O, be sick, great greatness,
And bid thy ceremony give thee cure!
Thinkst thou the fiery fever will go out
With titles blown from adulation?   250
Will it give place to flexure and low bending?
Canst thou, when thou command'st the beggar's knee,
Command the health of it? No, thou proud dream,
That play'st so subtly with a king's repose.
I am a king that find thee: and I know,
'Tis not the balm, the sceptre, and the ball,

The sword, the mace, the crown imperial,
The intertissued robe of gold and pearl,
The farcéd title running 'fore the king,
260 The throne he sits on: nor the tide of pomp
That beats upon the high shore of this world:
No, not all these, thrice-gorgeous ceremony,
Not all these, laid in bed majestical,
Can sleep so soundly as the wretched slave:
Who, with a body filled, and vacant mind,
Gets him to rest, crammed with distressful bread,
Never sees horrid night, the child of hell:
But, like a lackey, from the rise to set,
Sweats in the eye of Phœbus; and all night
270 Sleeps in Elysium: next day, after dawn,
Doth rise, and help Hyperion to his horse,
And follows so the ever-running year
With profitable labour to his grave:
And, but for ceremony, such a wretch,
Winding up days with toil, and nights with sleep,
Had the fore-hand and vantage of a king.
The slave, a member of the country's peace,
Enjoys it; but in gross brain little wots
What watch the king keeps to maintain the peace,
280 Whose hours the peasant best advantages.

ERPINGHAM returns

Erpingham. My lord, your nobles, jealous of
        your absence,
Seek through your camp to find you.
    King Henry.   Good old knight,
Collect them all together at my tent:
I'll be before thee.
    Erpingham.   I shall do't, my lord.   [*he goes*
    King Henry. [*kneels apart*] O God of battles, steel my
        soldiers' hearts,

Possess them not with fear: take from them now
†The sense of reck'ning, or th'opposéd numbers
Pluck their hearts from them. Not to-day, O Lord,
O not to-day, think not upon the fault
My father made in compassing the crown!   290
I Richard's body have interréd new,
And on it have bestowed more contrite tears,
Than from it issued forcéd drops of blood.
Five hundred poor I have in yearly pay,
Who twice a day their withered hands hold up
Toward heaven, to pardon blood: and I have built
Two chantries, where the sad and solemn priests
Sing still for Richard's soul. More will I do:
Though all that I can do is nothing worth;
Since that my penitence comes after all,   300
Imploring pardon.   [*he continues in prayer*

GLOUCESTER *returns calling*

Gloucester. My liege!
King Henry. [*rises*] My brother Gloucester's voice?
Ay:
I know thy errand, I will go with thee:
The day, my friends, and all things stay for me.
               [*they go together*

[4. 2.]   *A tent in the French camp (as before); daybreak*

The DAUPHIN, ORLEANS, RAMBURES, *and others,*
awaking

Orleans. The sun doth gild our armour. Up, my lords!
Dauphin. Montez à cheval! My horse! varlet!
laquais! ha!
Orleans. O brave spirit!
Dauphin. Via! les eaux et la terre!

Orleans. Rien puis? l'air et le feu?

Dauphin. Ciel! cousin Orleans.

CONSTABLE *enters*

Now, my lord Constable?

Constable. Hark how our steeds for present
service neigh.

Dauphin. Mount them, and make incision in
their hides,

10 That their hot blood may spin in English eyes,
·And dout them with superfluous courage, ha!

Rambures. What, will you have them weep our
horses' blood?

How shall we then behold their natural tears?

'*Enter* MESSENGER'

Messenger. The English are embattled, you
French peers.

Constable. To horse, you gallant princes, straight
to horse!

Do but behold yon poor and starvéd band,
And your fair show shall suck away their souls,
Leaving them but the shales and husks of men.
There is not work enough for all our hands,
20 Scarce blood enough in all their sickly veins,
To give each naked curtle-axe a stain,
That our French gallants shall to-day draw out,
And sheathe for lack of sport. Let us but blow on them,
The vapour of our valour will o'erturn them.
'Tis positive 'gainst all exceptions, lords,
That our superfluous lackeys, and our peasants,
Who in unnecessary action swarm
About our squares of battle, were enow
To purge this field of such a hilding foe;

Though we upon this mountain's basis by   30
Took stand for idle speculation:
But that our honours must not. What's to say?
A very little little let us do,
And all is done...Then let the trumpets sound
The tucket sonance, and the note to mount:
For our approach shall so much dare the field,
That England shall couch down in fear, and yield.

'*Enter* GRANDPRÉ'

Grandpré. Why do you stay so long, my lords
    of France?
Yon island carrions, desperate of their bones,
Ill-favouredly become the morning field: 40
Their ragged curtains poorly are let loose,
And our air shakes them passing scornfully.
Big Mars seems bankrout in their beggared host,
And faintly through a rusty beaver peeps.
The horsemen sit like fixéd candlesticks,
With torch-staves in their hand: and their poor jades
Lob down their heads, dropping the hides and hips,
The gum down-roping from their pale-dead eyes,
And in their pale dull mouths the gimmaled bit
Lies foul with chawed-grass, still and motionless.   50
And their executors, the knavish crows,
Fly o'er them all, impatient for their hour.
Description cannot suit itself in words,
To demonstrate the life of such a battle,
In life so lifeless as it shows itself.
  Constable. They have said their prayers, and they stay
    for death.
  Dauphin. Shall we go send them dinners, and
    fresh suits,
And give their fasting horses provender,

And after fight with them?

60 *Constable.* I stay but for my guidon: to the field!
I will the banner from a trumpet take,
And use it for my haste....Come, come away!
The sun is high, and we outwear the day.

[they hurry forth

[4. 3.]　*The English camp; before the King's pavilion*

'*Enter* GLOUCESTER, BEDFORD, EXETER, ERPINGHAM
with all his host: SALISBURY *and* WESTMORELAND,'
with others

Gloucester. Where is the king?
Bedford. The king himself is rode to view their battle.
Westmoreland. Of fighting men they have full three-
score thousand.
Exeter. There's five to one, besides they all are fresh.
Salisbury. God's arm strike with us! 'tis a
fearful odds....
God bye you, princes all; I'll to my charge:
If we no more meet till we meet in heaven,
Then joyfully, my noble Lord of Bedford,
My dear Lord Gloucester, and my good Lord Exeter,
10 And my kind kinsman, warriors all, adieu!
Bedford. Farewell, good Salisbury, and good luck go
with thee!
Exeter. Farewell, kind lord: fight valiantly to-day:
And yet I do thee wrong, to mind thee of it,
For thou art framed of the firm truth of valour.

[Salisbury goes

Bedford. He is as full of valour as of kindness,
Princely in both.

The King approaches

Westmoreland.   O that we now had here
But one ten thousand of those men in England,
That do no work to-day!

King Henry.   What's he that wishes so?
My cousin Westmoreland? No, my fair cousin:
If we are marked to die, we are enow   20
To do our country loss: and if to live,
The fewer men, the greater share of honour.
God's will, I pray thee wish not one man more.
By Jove, I am not covetous for gold,
Nor care I who doth feed upon my cost:
It earns me not if men my garments wear;
Such outward things dwell not in my desires.
But if it be a sin to covet honour,
I am the most offending soul alive.
No, faith, my coz, wish not a man from England: 30
God's peace, I would not lose so great an honour,
As one man more, methinks, would share from me,
For the best hope I have. O, do not wish one more:
Rather proclaim it, Westmoreland, through my host,
That he which hath no stomach to this fight,
Let him depart, his passport shall be made,
And crowns for convoy put into his purse:
We would not die in that man's company
That fears his fellowship, to die with us.
This day is called the feast of Crispian: 40
He that outlives this day, and comes safe home,
Will stand a tip-toe when this day is named,
And rouse him at the name of Crispian.
He that shall see this day, and live old age,
Will yearly on the vigil feast his neighbours,
And say, "To-morrow is Saint Crispian."

Then will he strip his sleeve, and show his scars,
And say, "These wounds I had on Crispin's day."
Old men forget; yet all shall be forgot,
50 But he'll remember, with advantages,
What feats he did that day. Then shall our names,
Familiar in his mouth as household words,
Harry the king, Bedford and Exeter,
Warwick and Talbot, Salisbury and Gloucester,
Be in their flowing cups freshly remembered.
This story shall the good man teach his son:
And Crispin Crispian shall ne'er go by,
From this day to the ending of the world,
But we in it shall be rememberéd;
60 We few, we happy few, we band of brothers:
For he to-day that sheds his blood with me
Shall be my brother: be he ne'er so vile,
This day shall gentle his condition.
And gentlemen in England, now a-bed,
Shall think themselves accursed they were not here;
And hold their manhoods cheap, whiles any speaks
That fought with us upon Saint Crispin's day.

SALISBURY returns

Salisbury. My sovereign lord, bestow yourself
with speed:
The French are bravely in their battles set,
70 And will with all expedience charge on us.
    King Henry. All things are ready, if our minds be so.
    Westmoreland. Perish the man whose mind is
    backward now!
    King Henry. Thou dost not wish more help from
    England, coz?
    Westmoreland. God's will, my liege, would you and
    I alone,

Without more help, could fight this royal battle!
  King Henry. Why, now thou hast unwished five
    thousand men:
Which likes me better than to wish us one....
You know your places: God be with you all!

A 'tucket' sounds and MONTJOY *approaches*

  Montjoy. Once more I come to know of thee,
    King Harry,
If for thy ransom thou wilt now compound,   80
Before thy most assuréd overthrow:
For certainly thou art so near the gulf,
Thou needs must be englutted. Besides, in mercy,
The Constable desires thee thou wilt mind
Thy followers of repentance; that their souls
May make a peaceful and a sweet retire
From off these fields: where, wretches, their poor bodies
Must lie and fester.
  King Henry.   Who hath sent thee now?
  Montjoy. The Constable of France.
  King Henry. I pray thee bear my former answer back: 90
Bid them achieve me, and then sell my bones.
Good God! why should they mock poor fellows thus?
The man that once did sell the lion's skin
While the beast lived, was killed with hunting him.
A many of our bodies shall no doubt
Find native graves: upon the which, I trust,
Shall witness live in brass of this day's work.
And those that leave their valiant bones in France,
Dying like men, though buried in your dunghills,
They shall be famed: for there the sun shall greet them, 100
And draw their honours reeking up to heaven,
Leaving their earthly parts to choke your clime,
The smell whereof shall breed a plague in France.

Mark then abounding valour in our English:
That being dead, like to the bullet's crasing,
Break out into a second course of mischief,
Killing in relapse of mortality....
Let me speak proudly: tell the Constable
We are but warriors for the working-day:
110 Our gayness and our gilt are all besmirched
With rainy marching in the painful field.
There's not a piece of feather in our host—
Good argument, I hope, we will not fly—
And time hath worn us into slovenry.
But, by the mass, our hearts are in the trim:
And my poor soldiers tell me, yet ere night
They'll be in fresher robes, or they will pluck
The gay new coats o'er the French soldiers' heads,
And turn them out of service. If they do this—
120 As, if God please, they shall—my ransom then
Will soon be levied. Herald, save thou thy labour:
Come thou no more for ransom, gentle herald,
They shall have none, I swear, but these my joints:
Which if they have, as I will leave 'em them,
Shall yield them little, tell the Constable.
  Montjoy. I shall, King Harry. And so fare thee well:
Thou never shalt hear herald any more.   [*he goes*
  King Henry. I fear thou wilt once more come again
for a ransom.

The Duke of YORK *comes up*

130 *York.* My lord, most humbly on my knee I beg
The leading of the vaward.
  King Henry. Take it, brave York....Now soldiers,
      march away,
And how thou pleasest, God, dispose the day!
                              [*the host marches forward*

[4. 4.]   *Near the field of battle*

'Alarum. Excursions. Enter PISTOL,
FRENCH SOLDIER,*' and '*BOY*'*

Pistol. Yield, cur!

French Soldier. Je pense que vous êtes le gentilhomme
de bonne qualité.

Pistol. Qualtitie! Calen o custure me! Art thou a
gentleman? what is thy name? discuss.

French Soldier. O Seigneur Dieu!

Pistol. O, Signieur Dew should be a gentleman:
Perpend my words, O Signieur Dew, and mark:
O Signieur Dew, thou diest on point of fox,
Except, O signieur, thou do give to me   10
Egregious ransom.

French Soldier. O, prenez miséricorde! ayez pitié de
moi!

Pistol. Moy shall not serve, I will have forty moys:
Or I will fetch thy rim out at thy throat,
In drops of crimson blood.

French Soldier. Est-il impossible d'échapper la force
de ton bras?

Pistol. Brass, cur?
Thou damnéd and luxurious mountain goat,   20
Offer'st me brass?

French Soldier. O pardonnez moi!

Pistol. Say'st thou me so? is that a ton of moys?
Come hither, boy, ask me this slave in French
What is his name.

Boy. Écoutez: comment êtes-vous appelé?

French Soldier. Monsieur le Fer.

Boy. He says his name is Master Fer.

Pistol. Master Fer! I'll fer him, and firk him, and
ferret him: discuss the same in French unto him.   30

Boy. I do not know the French for fer, and ferret, and firk.

Pistol. Bid him prepare, for I will cut his throat.

French Soldier. Que dit-il, monsieur?

Boy. Il me commande à vous dire que vous faites vous prêt, car ce soldat ici est disposé tout à cette heure de couper votre gorge.

Pistol. Owy, cuppele gorge, permafoy,
Peasant, unless thou give me crowns, brave crowns;
40 Or mangled shalt thou be by this my sword.

French Soldier. O, je vous supplie, pour l'amour de Dieu, me pardonner! Je suis le gentilhomme de bonne maison, gardez ma vie, et je vous donnerai deux cents écus.

Pistol. What are his words?

Boy. He prays you to save his life, he is a gentleman of a good house, and for his ransom he will give you two hundred crowns.

Pistol. Tell him my fury shall abate, and I
50 The crowns will take.

French Soldier. Petit monsieur, que dit-il?

Boy. Encore qu'il est contre son jurement de pardonner aucun prisonnier: néanmoins, pour les écus que vous l'avez promis, il est content à vous donner la liberté, le franchisement.

French Soldier. Sur mes genoux je vous donne mille remercîments, et je m'estime heureux que je suis tombé entre les mains d'un chevalier, je pense, le plus brave, vaillant, et très distingué seigneur d'Angleterre.

60　*Pistol.* Expound unto me, boy.

Boy. He gives you upon his knees a thousand thanks, and he esteems himself happy that he hath fallen into the hands of one, as he thinks, the most brave, valorous, and thrice-worthy signieur of England.

Pistol. As I suck blood, I will some mercy show.
Follow me!   [*Pistol passes in*
  Boy. Suivez-vous le grand capitaine!
                              [*the French soldier follows*
I did never know so full a voice issue from so empty
a heart: but the saying is true, "The empty vessel makes
the greatest sound." Bardolph and Nym had ten times 70
more valour than this roaring devil i'th'old play, that
every one may pare his nails with a wooden dagger, and
they are both hanged, and so would this be, if he durst
steal any thing adventurously....I must stay with the
lackeys with the luggage of our camp; the French might
have a good prey of us, if he knew of it, for there is none
to guard it but boys.   [*he goes*

[4. 5.]   '*Enter* CONSTABLE, ORLEANS, BOURBON,
                DAUPHIN, *and* RAMBURES' *in flight*

Constable. O diable!
  Orleans. O Seigneur! le jour est perdu, tout est perdu!
  Dauphin. Mort Dieu! ma vie! all is confounded, all!
Reproach and everlasting shame
Sits mocking in our plumes.   ['*a short alarum*'
O méchante fortune! Do not run away.
  Constable. Why, all our ranks are broke.
  Dauphin. O perdurable shame! let's stab ourselves:
Be these the wretches that we played at dice for?
  Orleans. Is this the king we sent to for his ransom? 10
  Bourbon. Shame, and eternal shame, nothing but
        shame!
†Let us die in harness: once more back again,
And he that will not follow Bourbon now,
Let him go hence, and with his cap in hand
Like a base pandar hold the chamber-door,
Whilst by a slave, no gentler than my dog,

His fairest daughter is contaminated.

    Constable. Disorder, that hath spoiled us, friend
      us now!

Let us on heaps go offer up our lives.

20 *Orleans.* We are enow yet living in the field

To smother up the English in our throngs,

If any order might be thought upon.

    Bourbon. The devil take order now! I'll to the throng;

Let life be short, else shame will be too long.

                        [they return to the field

    [4. 6.]   '*Alarum. Enter the King and his train,*
           with prisoners,' EXETER *and others*

    King Henry. Well have we done, thrice-
      valiant countrymen,

But all's not done—yet keep the French the field.

    Exeter. The Duke of York commends him to
      your majesty.

    King Henry. Lives he, good uncle? thrice within
      this hour

I saw him down; thrice up again, and fighting,

From helmet to the spur all blood he was.

    Exeter. In which array, brave soldier, doth he lie,

Larding the plain: and by his bloody side,

Yoke-fellow to his honour-owing wounds,

10 The noble Earl of Suffolk also lies.

Suffolk first died, and York, all haggled over,

Comes to him, where in gore he lay insteeped,

And takes him by the beard, kisses the gashes

That bloodily did yawn upon his face,

And cries aloud, 'Tarry, my cousin Suffolk!

My soul shall thine keep company to heaven:

Tarry, sweet soul, for mine, then fly abreast:

As in this glorious and well-foughten field

We kept together in our chivalry.'
Upon these words I came, and cheered him up,   20
He smiled me in the face, raught me his hand,
And, with a feeble gripe, says, 'Dear my lord,
Commend my service to my sovereign.'
So did he turn, and over Suffolk's neck
He threw his wounded arm, and kissed his lips,
And so espoused to death, with blood he sealed
A testament of noble-ending love:
The pretty and sweet manner of it forced
Those waters from me which I would have stopped,
But I had not so much of man in me,   30
And all my mother came into mine eyes,
And gave me up to tears.
 King Henry.   I blame you not,
For, hearing this, I must perforce compound
With mistful eyes, or they will issue too.... ['*alarum*'
But hark! what new alarum is this same?
The French have reinforced their scattered men:
Then every soldier kill his prisoners,
Give the word through.   [*they hasten forward*

[4. 7.] '*Enter* FLUELLEN *and* GOWER'

 Fluellen. Kill the poys and the luggage! 'tis expressly
against the law of arms, 'tis as arrant a piece of knavery,
mark you now, as can be offert. In your conscience
now, is it not?
 Gower. 'Tis certain there's not a boy left alive, and
the cowardly rascals that ran from the battle ha' done
this slaughter: besides, they have burned and carried
away all that was in the king's tent, wherefore the king
most worthily hath caused every soldier to cut his
prisoner's throat. O, 'tis a gallant king!   10
 Fluellen. Ay, he was porn at Monmouth, Captain

Gower: what call you the town's name where Alexander the pig was born?

Gower. Alexander the Great.

Fluellen. Why, I pray you, is not pig great? The pig, or the great, or the mighty, or the huge, or the magnanimous, are all one reckonings, save the phrase is a little variations.

Gower. I think Alexander the Great was born in
20 Macedon, his father was called Philip of Macedon, as I take it.

Fluellen. I think it is in Macedon where Alexander is porn: I tell you, captain, if you look in the maps of the 'orld, I warrant you sall find, in the comparisons between Macedon and Monmouth, that the situations, look you, is both alike. There is a river in Macedon, and there is also moreover a river at Monmouth, it is called Wye at Monmouth: but it is out of my prains what is the name of the other river: but 'tis all one, 'tis
30 alike as my fingers is to my fingers, and there is salmons in both. If you mark Alexander's life well, Harry of Monmouth's life is come after it indifferent well, for there is figures in all things. Alexander, God knows, and you know, in his rages, and his furies, and his wraths, and his cholers, and his moods, and his displeasures, and his indignations, and also being a little intoxicates in his prains, did in his ales and his angers, look you, kill his best friend Cleitus.

Gower. Our king is not like him in that, he never killed
40 any of his friends.

Fluellen. It is not well done, mark you now, to take the tales out of my mouth, ere it is made and finished. I speak but in the figures and comparisons of it: as Alexander killed his friend Cleitus, being in his ales and his cups; so also Harry Monmouth, being in his right

wits and his good judgements, turned away the fat
knight with the great-belly doublet: he was full of jests,
and gipes, and knaveries, and mocks, I have forgot his
name.

Gower. Sir John Falstaff.　　　　　　　　　　　　50

Fluellen. That is he: I'll tell you, there is good men
porn at Monmouth.

Gower. Here comes his majesty.

'*Alarum. Enter King* HARRY *and* BOURBON *with
prisoners,*' *meeting* WARWICK, GLOUCESTER, EXETER,
heralds and soldiers, WILLIAMS *among them.* '*Flourish.*'

King Henry. I was not angry since I came to France
Until this instant....Take a trumpet, herald,
Ride thou unto the horsemen on yon hill:
If they will fight with us, bid them come down,
Or void the field: they do offend our sight.
If they'll do neither, we will come to them,
And make them skirr away, as swift as stones　　　60
Enforcéd from the old Assyrian slings:
Besides, we'll cut the throats of those we have,
And not a man of them that we shall take
Shall taste our mercy....Go and tell them so.
　　　　　　　　　　　　[an English herald obeys

MONTJOY approaches

Exeter. Here comes the herald of the French, my
　　liege.

Gloucester. His eyes are humbler than they used to be.

King Henry. How now, what means this, herald?
　　Know'st thou not
That I have fined these bones of mine for ransom?
Com'st thou again for ransom?

Montjoy.　　　　　　　　　No, great king:

70 I come to thee for charitable licence,
That we may wander o'er this bloody field,
To book our dead, and then to bury them,
To sort our nobles from our common men.
For many of our princes—woe the while!—
Lie drowned and soaked in mercenary blood:
So do our vulgar drench their peasant limbs
In blood of princes, and their wounded steeds
Fret fetlock deep in gore, and with wild rage
Yerk out their arméd heels at their dead masters,
80 Killing them twice....O, give us leave, great king,
To view the field in safety, and dispose
Of their dead bodies.

   King Henry.   I tell thee truly, herald,
I know not if the day be ours or no,
For yet a many of your horsemen peer,
And gallop o'er the field.

   Montjoy.   The day is yours.

   King Henry. Praiséd be God, and not our strength,
     for it!
What is this castle called that stands hard by?

   Montjoy. They call it Agincourt.

   King Henry. Then call we this the field of Agincourt,
90 Fought on the day of Crispin Crispianus.

   Fluellen. Your grandfather of famous memory, an't
please your majesty, and your great-uncle Edward the
Plack Prince of Wales, as I have read in the chronicles,
fought a most prave pattle here in France.

   King Henry. They did, Fluellen.

   Fluellen. Your majesty says very true: if your majesties
is remembered of it, the Welshmen did good service in
a garden where leeks did grow, wearing leeks in their
Monmouth caps, which your majesty know to this hour
100 is an honourable badge of the service: and I do believe

your majesty takes no scorn to wear the leek upon Saint
Tavy's day.

King Henry. I wear it for a memorable honour:
For I am Welsh, you know, good countryman.

Fluellen. All the water in Wye cannot wash your
majesty's Welsh plood out of your pody, I can tell you
that: God pless it, and preserve it, as long as it pleases
his grace, and his majesty too!

King Henry. Thanks, good my countryman.

Fluellen. By Jeshu, I am your majesty's countryman, 110
I care not who know it: I will confess it to all the 'orld,
I need not to be ashamed of your majesty, praised be
God, so long as your majesty is an honest man.

King Henry. God keep me so! Our heralds go
        with him,
Bring me just notice of the numbers dead
On both our parts....[*heralds depart with Montjoy*
        Call yonder fellow hither.. [*he points to Williams*
Exeter. Soldier, you must come to the king.

King Henry. Soldier, why wear'st thou that glove in
thy cap?

Williams. An't please your majesty, 'tis the gage of 120
one that I should fight withal, if he be alive.

King Henry. An Englishman?

Williams. An't please your majesty, a rascal that
swaggered with me last night: who, if a' live and ever
dare to challenge this glove, I have sworn to take him
a box o'th'ear: or if I can see my glove in his cap—which
he swore, as he was a soldier, he would wear if alive—
I will strike it out soundly.

King Henry. What think you, Captain Fluellen, is it
fit this soldier keep his oath?   130

Fluellen. He is a craven and a villain else, an't please
your majesty, in my conscience.

King Henry. It may be his enemy is a gentleman of great sort, quite from the answer of his degree.

Fluellen. Though he be as good a gentleman as the devil is, as Lucifer and Belzebub himself, it is necessary, look your grace, that he keep his vow and his oath: if he be perjured, see you now, his reputation is as arrant a villain and a Jack-sauce as ever his black shoe trod upon
140 God's ground and his earth, in my conscience, la!

King Henry. Then keep thy vow, sirrah, when thou meet'st the fellow.

Williams. So I will, my liege, as I live.

King Henry. Who serv'st thou under?

Williams. Under Captain Gower, my liege.

Fluellen. Gower is a good captain, and is good knowledge and literatured in the wars.

King Henry. Call him hither to me, soldier.

Williams. I will, my liege.   [*he goes*
150 *King Henry.* Here, Fluellen, wear thou this favour for me, and stick it in thy cap: when Alençon and myself were down together, I plucked this glove from his helm: if any man challenge this, he is a friend to Alençon, and an enemy to our person; if thou encounter any such, apprehend him, an thou dost me love.

Fluellen. Your grace does me as great honours as can be desired in the hearts of his subjects: I would fain see the man that has but two legs that shall find himself aggriefed at this glove; that is all: but I would fain
160 see it once, an please God of his grace that I might see.

King Henry. Know'st thou Gower?

Fluellen. He is my dear friend, an please you.

King Henry. Pray thee, go seek him, and bring him to my tent.

Fluellen. I will fetch him.   [*he goes*

King Henry. My Lord of Warwick, and my
        brother Gloucester,
Follow Fluellen closely at the heels.
The glove which I have given him for a favour
May haply purchase him a box o'th'ear.   170
It is the soldier's: I by bargain should
Wear it myself. Follow, good cousin Warwick:
If that the soldier strike him, as I judge
By his blunt bearing he will keep his word,
Some sudden mischief may arise of it:
For I do know Fluellen valiant,
And, touched with choler, hot as gunpowder,
And quickly will return an injury.
Follow, and see there be no harm between them....
Go you with me, uncle of Exeter.   180
        [*Gloucester and Warwick hasten after Fluellen;
                the King, Exeter and the rest following*

[4. 8.]   *Before King Henry's pavilion*

GOWER *and* WILLIAMS *in conversation*

Williams. I warrant it is to knight you, captain.

FLUELLEN *is seen approaching*

Fluellen. [*hails Gower*] God's will, and his pleasure,
captain, I beseech you now, come apace to the king:
there is more good toward you, peradventure, than is in
your knowledge to dream of. [*Williams confronts him*
  Williams. [*points to his own bonnet*] Sir, know you
this glove?
  Fluellen. Know the glove? I know the glove is a glove.
  Williams. [*points to Fluellen's cap*] I know this, and
        thus I challenge it.   ['*strikes him*' 10

Fluellen. 'Sblood, an arrant traitor as any's in the universal world, or in France, or in England.

Gower. How now, sir? you villain!

Williams. Do you think I'll be forsworn?

Fluellen. Stand away, Captain Gower, I will give treason his payment into plows, I warrant you.

Williams. I am no traitor.

Fluellen. That's a lie in thy throat. I charge you in his majesty's name, apprehend him, he's a friend of the
20 Duke Alençon's.

WARWICK and GLOUCESTER hurry up, with the King and Exeter following

Warwick. How now, how now, what's the matter?

Fluellen. My Lord of Warwick, here is, praised be God for it, a most contagious treason come to light, look you, as you shall desire in a summer's day....Here is his majesty.

King Henry. Now now, what's the matter?

Fluellen. My liege, here is a villain and a traitor, that, look your grace, has struck the glove which your majesty is take out of the helmet of Alençon.

30 *Williams.* My liege, this was my glove, here is the fellow of it: and he that I gave it to in change promised to wear it in his cap: I promised to strike him, if he did: I met this man with my glove in his cap, and I have been as good as my word.

Fluellen. Your majesty, hear now, saving your majesty's manhood, what an arrant, rascally, beggarly, lousy knave it is: I hope your majesty is pear me testimony and witness, and will avouchment, that this is the glove of Alençon, that your majesty is give me, in your conscience now.

40 *King Henry.* Give me thy glove, soldier; look, here is the fellow of it:

'Twas I indeed thou promised'st to strike,
And thou hast given me most bitter terms.

Fluellen. An please your majesty, let his neck answer
for it, if there is any martial law in the world.

King Henry. How canst thou make me satisfaction?

Williams. All offences, my lord, come from the heart:
never came any from mine that might offend your
majesty.

King Henry. It was ourself thou didst abuse.　　　50

Williams. Your majesty came not like yourself: you
appeared to me but as a common man; witness the night,
your garments, your lowliness: and what your highness
suffered under that shape, I beseech you take it for your
own fault, and not mine: for had you been as I took you
for, I made no offence; therefore I beseech your highness
pardon me.

King Henry. Here, uncle Exeter, fill this glove
　　　with crowns,
And give it to this fellow. Keep it, fellow,
And wear it for an honour in thy cap,　　　60
Till I do challenge it. Give him the crowns:
And, captain, you must needs be friends with him.

Fluellen. By this day and this light, the fellow has
mettle enough in his belly... [*takes a shilling from his
poke*] Hold, there is twelve-pence for you, and I pray
you to serve God, and keep you out of prawls and
prabbles, and quarrels and dissensions, and I warrant
you it is the better for you.

Williams. I will none of your money.

Fluellen. It is with a good will: I can tell you it will 70
serve you to mend your shoes: come, wherefore should
you be so pashful? your shoes is not so good: 'tis a good
silling, I warrant you, or I will change it.

An English HERALD *returns from the battlefield*

King Henry. Now, herald, are the dead numbered?
Herald. Here is the number of the slaughtered French.
　　　　　　　　　　　　　　　　　[*he delivers a paper*
King Henry. What prisoners of good sort are
　　taken, uncle?
Exeter. Charles Duke of Orleans, nephew to the king,
John Duke of Bourbon, and Lord Bouciqualt:
Of other lords and barons, knights and squires,
80 Full fifteen hundred, besides common men.
　　King Henry. This note doth tell me of ten
　　　　thousand French
That in the field lie slain: of princes, in this number,
And nobles bearing banners, there lie dead
One hundred twenty-six: added to these,
Of knights, esquires, and gallant gentlemen,
Eight thousand and four hundred: of the which,
Five hundred were but yesterday dubbed knights.
So that, in these ten thousand they have lost,
There are but sixteen hundred mercenaries:
90 The rest are princes, barons, lords, knights, squires,
And gentlemen of blood and quality.
The names of those their nobles that lie dead:—
Charles Delabreth, high constable of France,
Jaques of Chatillon, admiral of France,
The master of the cross-bows, Lord Rambures,
Great Master of France, the brave
　　　　Sir Guichard Dolphin,
John Duke of Alençon, Anthony Duke of Brabant,
The brother to the Duke of Burgundy,
And Edward Duke of Bar: of lusty earls,
100 Grandpré and Roussi, Faulconbridge and Foix,
Beaumont and Marle, Vaudemont and Lestrake.

Here was a royal fellowship of death!
Where is the number of our English dead?

[the herald presents another paper

Edward the Duke of York, the Earl of Suffolk,
Sir Richard Kikely, Davy Gam, esquire;
None else of name: and, of all other men,
But five and twenty....O God, thy arm was here:
And not to us, but to thy arm alone,
Ascribe we all: when, without stratagem,
But in plain shock, and even play of battle,　　　110
Was ever known so great and little loss,
On one part and on th'other? Take it, God,
For it is none but thine!

　Exeter.　　　'Tis wonderful!

　King Henry. Come, go we in procession to the village:
And be it death proclaiméd through our host
To boast of this or take that praise from God
Which is his only.

　Fluellen. Is it not lawful, an please your majesty, to
tell how many is killed?

　King Henry. Yes, captain: but with
　　　this acknowledgement,　　　120
That God fought for us.

　Fluellen. Yes, my conscience, he did us great good.

　King Henry. Do we all holy rites:
Let there be sung 'Non nobis' and 'Te Deum',
The dead with charity enclosed in clay:
And then to Calais, and to England then,
Where ne'er from France arrived more happy men.

[they move on towards the village

[5. Prologue]

'Enter CHORUS'

Chorus. Vouchsafe to those that have not read the story,
That I may prompt them: and of such as have,
I humbly pray them to admit th'excuse
Of time, of numbers, and due course of things,
Which cannot in their huge and proper life
Be here presented....Now we bear the king
Toward Calais: grant him there; there seen,
Heave him away upon your wingéd thoughts,
Athwart the sea: behold the English beach
10 Pales in the flood with men, with wives, and boys,
Whose shouts and claps out-voice the deep-mouthed sea,
Which like a mighty whiffler 'fore the king
Seems to prepare his way: so let him land,
And solemnly see him set on to London.
So swift a pace hath thought, that even now
You may imagine him upon Blackheath:
Where that his lords desire him to have borne
His bruiséd helmet, and his bended sword
Before him through the city: he forbids it,
20 Being free from vainness and self-glorious pride;
Giving full trophy, signal, and ostent,
Quite from himself, to God....But now behold,
In the quick forge and working-house of thought,
How London doth pour out her citizens—
The mayor and all his brethren in best sort,
Like to the senators of th'antique Rome,
With the plebeians swarming at their heels,
Go forth and fetch their conqu'ring Cæsar in:
As, by a lower but loving likelihood,
30 Were now the general of our gracious empress,

As in good time he may, from Ireland coming,
Bringing rebellion broachéd on his sword,
How many would the peaceful city quit,
To welcome him! much more, and much more cause,
Did they this Harry....Now in London place him—
As yet the lamentation of the French
Invites the King of England's stay at home:
The emperor's coming in behalf of France,
To order peace between them—and omit
All the occurrences, whatever chanced,   40
Till Harry's back-return again to France:
There must we bring him; and myself have played
The interim, by rememb'ring you 'tis past.
Then brook abridgement, and your eyes advance,
After your thoughts, straight back again to France.

['*Exit*'

[5. 1.]   *France. The English camp*

GOWER *and* FLUELLEN (*a leek in his cap and
a cudgel beneath his arm*)

Gower. Nay, that's right...But why wear you your
leek to-day? Saint Davy's day is past.

Fluellen. There is occasions and causes why and
wherefore in all things: I will tell you, ass my friend,
Captain Gower; the rascally, scauld, beggarly, lousy,
pragging knave Pistol, which you and yourself, and all
the world, know to be no petter than a fellow, look you
now, of no merits—he is come to me, and prings me
pread and salt yesterday, look you, and bid me eat my
leek: it was in a place where I could not breed no   10
contention with him; but I will be so bold as to wear it
in my cap till I see him once again, and then I will tell
him a little piece of my desires.

PISTOL is seen strutting towards them

Gower. Why, here he comes, swelling like a turkey-
cock.

Fluellen. 'Tis no matter for his swellings, nor his
turkey-cocks....God pless you, Ancient Pistol! you
scurvy lousy knave, God pless you.

Pistol. Ha! art thou bedlam? Dost thou thirst,
        base Trojan,
20 To have me fold up Parca's fatal web?
Hence! I am qualmish at the smell of leek.

Fluellen. I peseech you heartily, scurvy lousy knave,
at my desires, and my requests, and my petitions, to eat,
look you, this leek; because, look you, you do not love
it, nor your affections, and your appetites and your
disgestions does not agree with it, I would desire you to
eat it.

Pistol. Not for Cadwallader and all his goats.

Fluellen. There is one goat for you. ['*strikes him*']
30 Will you be so good, scauld knave, as eat it?

Pistol. Base Trojan, thou shalt die. [*draws his sword*
Fluellen. You say very true, scauld knave, when God's
will is: I will desire you to live in the mean time, and
eat your victuals: come, there is sauce for it....[*striking
him again*] You called me yesterday mountain-squire,
but I will make you to-day 'a squire of low degree'....
[*he knocks him down*] I pray you fall to—if you can mock
a leek, you can eat a leek.

Gower. Enough, captain, you have astonished him.

40 *Fluellen.* [*kneels upon him*] I say, I will make him eat
some part of my leek, or I will peat his pate four days:
bite, I pray you, it is good for your green wound, and
your ploody coxcomb.

                    [*he thrusts the leek between his teeth*

Pistol. Must I bite?

Fluellen. Yes certainly, and out of doubt and out of question too, and ambiguities.   [*he cudgels him*

Pistol. [*roaring in pain*] By this leek, I will most horribly revenge I eat and eat I swear.

Fluellen. Eat, I pray you, will you have some more sauce to your leek? there is not enough leek to swear by. 50
                                        [*he beats him again*

Pistol. [*whimpers*] Quiet thy cudgel, thou dost see I eat.

Fluellen. Much good do you, scauld knave, heartily....
[*he releases Pistol*] Nay, pray you throw none away, the skin is good for your broken coxcomb; when you take occasions to see leeks hereafter, I pray you mock at 'em, that is all.

Pistol. Good.

Fluellen. Ay, leeks is good...Hold you, there is a groat to heal your pate.

Pistol. Me a groat!   60

Fluellen. Yes verily, and in truth you shall take it, or I have another leek in my pocket, which you shall eat.

Pistol. I take thy groat in earnest of revenge.

Fluellen. If I owe you any thing, I will pay you in cudgels; you shall be a woodmonger, and buy nothing of me but cudgels...God bye you, and keep you, and heal your pate.   [*he goes*

Pistol. All hell shall stir for this.

Gower. Go, go, you are a counterfeit cowardly knave—will you mock at an ancient tradition, began upon an 70 honourable respect, and worn as a memorable trophy of predeceased valour, and dare not avouch in your deeds any of your words? I have seen you gleeking and galling at this gentleman twice or thrice. You thought, because he could not speak English in the native garb, he could not therefore handle an English cudgel: you find it

otherwise, and henceforth let a Welsh correction teach
you a good English condition—fare ye well.   [*he goes*
   Pistol. Doth Fortune play the huswife with me now?
80 News have I that †my Doll is dead i'th'spital
O' malady of France,
And there my rendezvous is quite cut off...
Old I do wax, and from my weary limbs
Honour is cudgelled....Well, bawd I'll turn,
And something lean to cutpurse of quick hand:
To England will I steal, and there I'll steal:
And patches will I get unto these cudgelled scars,
And swear I got them in the Gallia wars.

                          [*he hobbles away*

[5. 2.]   *France. A royal palace*

'*Enter, at one door, King* HENRY, EXETER, BEDFORD,
WARWICK', GLOUCESTER, WESTMORELAND, '*and other
Lords; at another, Queen* ISABEL, *the*' FRENCH '*KING*',
the Princess KATHARINE, ALICE, *and other Ladies,* '*the
Duke of* BURGUNDY, *and other French*'

   King Henry. Peace to this meeting, wherefore we
      are met!
Unto our brother France, and to our sister,
Health and fair time of day: joy and good wishes
To our most fair and princely cousin Katharine:
And, as a branch and member of this royalty,
By whom this great assembly is contrived,
We do salute you, Duke of Burgundy;
And, princes French, and peers, health to you all!
   French King. Right joyous are we to behold your face,
10 Most worthy brother England, fairly met—
So are you, princes English, every one.

Queen Isabel. So happy be the issue, brother England,
Of this good day, and of this gracious meeting,
As we are now glad to behold your eyes,
Your eyes which hitherto have borne in them
Against the French, that met them in their bent,
The fatal balls of murdering basilisks.
The venom of such looks, we fairly hope,
Have lost their quality, and that this day
Shall change all griefs and quarrels into love.   20
    King Henry. To cry amen to that, thus we appear.
    Queen Isabel. You English princes all, I do salute you.
    Burgundy. My duty to you both, on equal love....
Great kings of France and England: that I
          have laboured
With all my wits, my pains, and strong endeavours,
To bring your most imperial majesties
Unto this bar and royal interview,
Your mightiness on both parts best can witness....
Since then my office hath so far prevailed,
That face to face, and royal eye to eye,   30
You have congreeted: let it not disgrace me,
If I demand before this royal view,
What rub, or what impediment there is,
Why that the naked, poor, and mangled Peace,
Dear nurse of arts, plenties, and joyful births,
Should not in this best garden of the world,
Our fertile France, put up her lovely visage?
Alas, she hath from France too long been chased,
And all her husbandry doth lie on heaps,
Corrupting in it own fertility.   40
Her vine, the merry cheerer of the heart,
Unprunéd, dies: her hedges even-pleached,
Like prisoners wildly over-grown with hair,
Put forth disordered twigs: her fallow leas

The darnel, hemlock, and rank fumitory
Doth root upon; while that the coulter rusts,
That should deracinate such savagery:
The even mead, that erst brought sweetly forth
The freckled cowslip, burnet, and green clover,
50 Wanting the scythe, all uncorrected, rank,
Conceives by idleness, and nothing teems
But hateful docks, rough thistles, kecksies, burs,
Losing both beauty and utility;
And as our vineyards, fallows, meads, and hedges,
Defective in their natures, grow to wildness,
Even so our houses, and ourselves, and children,
Have lost, or do not learn, for want of time,
The sciences that should become our country;
But grow like savages, as soldiers will,
60 That nothing do but meditate on blood,
To swearing, and stern looks, diffused attire,
And every thing that seems unnatural.
Which to reduce into our former favour,
You are assembled: and my speech entreats,
That I may know the let, why gentle Peace
Should not expel these inconveniences,
And bless us with her former qualities.

   King Henry. If, Duke of Burgundy, you would
      the peace,
Whose want gives growth to th'imperfections
70 Which you have cited, you must buy that peace
With full accord to all our just demands,
Whose tenours and particular effects
You have, enscheduled briefly, in your hands.

   Burgundy. The king hath heard them: to the which,
      as yet,
There is no answer made.

   King Henry. Well then: the peace, which you
      before so urged,

Lies in his answer.

French King. I have but with a †cursitory eye
O'erglanced the articles: pleaseth your grace
To appoint some of your council presently　　80
To sit with us once more, with better heed
To re-survey them; we will suddenly
Pass our accept and peremptory answer.

King Henry. Brother, we shall....Go, uncle
　　Exeter,
And brother Clarence, and you, brother Gloucester,
Warwick, and Huntingdon, go with the king,
And take with you free power, to ratify,
Augment, or alter, as your wisdoms best
Shall see advantageable for our dignity,
Any thing in or out of our demands,　　90
And we'll consign thereto....Will you, fair sister,
Go with the princes, or stay here with us?

Queen Isabel. Our gracious brother, I will go
　　with them:
Haply a woman's voice may do some good,
When articles too nicely urged be stood on.

King Henry. Yet leave our cousin Katharine here
　　with us,
She is our capital demand, comprised
Within the fore-rank of our articles.

Queen Isabel. She hath good leave.

　　　　　　[*All depart but King Henry, Katharine,
　　　　　　　　　　　and her Gentlewoman*

King Henry.　　　　　Fair Katharine, and most fair,
Will you vouchsafe to teach a soldier terms,　　100
Such as will enter at a lady's ear,
And plead his love-suit to her gentle heart?

Katharine. Your majesty shall mock at me, I cannot
speak your England.

King Henry. O fair Katharine, if you will love me

soundly with your French heart, I will be glad to hear
you confess it brokenly with your English tongue. Do
you like me, Kate?

Katharine. Pardonnez moi, I cannot tell vat is 'like
110 me'.

King Henry. An angel is like you, Kate, and you are
like an angel.

Katharine. Que dit-il? que je suis semblable à les
anges?

Alice. Oui, vraiment, sauf votre grace, ainsi dit-il.

King Henry. I said so, dear Katharine, and I must not
blush to affirm it.

Katharine. O bon Dieu! les langues des hommes sont
pleines de tromperies.

120 *King Henry.* What says she, fair one? that the tongues
of men are full of deceits?

Alice. Oui, dat de tongues of de mans is be full of
deceits: dat is de princess.

King Henry. The princess is the better English-
woman...I'faith, Kate, my wooing is fit for thy understanding; I am glad thou canst speak no better English,
for, if thou couldst, thou wouldst find me such a plain
king, that thou wouldst think I had sold my farm to buy
my crown.... I know no ways to mince it in love, but
130 directly to say "I love you"; then if you urge me farther
than to say "Do you in faith?" I wear out my suit...
Give me your answer, i'faith do, and so clap hands,
and a bargain: how say you, lady?

Katharine. Sauf votre honneur, me understand vell.

King Henry. Marry, if you would put me to verses,
or to dance for your sake, Kate, why, you undid me:
for the one, I have neither words nor measure; and for
the other, I have no strength in measure, yet a reasonable
measure in strength. If I could win a lady at leap-frog,

or by vaulting into my saddle with my armour on my 140
back, under the correction of bragging be it spoken,
I should quickly leap into a wife: or if I might buffet
for my love, or bound my horse for her favours, I could
lay on like a butcher, and sit like a jack-an-apes, never
off. But before God, Kate, I cannot look greenly, nor
gasp out my eloquence, nor I have no cunning in pro-
testation; only downright oaths, which I never use till
urged, nor never break for urging. If thou canst love
a fellow of this temper, Kate, whose face is not worth
sun-burning, that never looks in his glass for love of any 150
thing he sees there, let thine eye be thy cook. I speak to
thee plain soldier: if thou canst love me for this, take
me; if not, to say to thee that I shall die is true; but for
thy love, by the Lord, no: yet I love thee too. And
while thou liv'st, dear Kate, take a fellow of plain and
uncoined constancy, for he perforce must do thee right,
because he hath not the gift to woo in other places: for
these fellows of infinite tongue, that can rhyme themselves into ladies' favours, they do always reason themselves out again. What! a speaker is but a prater, a rhyme 160
is but a ballad; a good leg will fall, a straight back will
stoop, a black beard will turn white, a curled pate will
grow bald, a fair face will wither, a full eye will wax
hollow: but a good heart, Kate, is the sun and the moon,
or rather the sun and not the moon; for it shines bright,
and never changes, but keeps his course truly. If thou
would have such a one, take me! And take me, take a
soldier: take a soldier, take a king. And what say'st
thou then to my love? speak, my fair, and fairly, I pray
thee.   170

Katharine. Is it possible dat I should love de enemy of
France?

King Henry. No, it is not possible you should love the

K.H.V.—9

enemy of France, Kate; but, in loving me, you should love the friend of France: for I love France so well that I will not part with a village of it; I will have it all mine: and, Kate, when France is mine, and I am yours, then yours is France, and you are mine.

Katharine. I cannot tell vat is dat.

180 *King Henry.* No, Kate? I will tell thee in French, which I am sure will hang upon my tongue like a new-married wife about her husband's neck, hardly to be shook off...Je quand sur le possession de France, et quand vous avez le possession de moi,—let me see, what then? Saint Dennis be my speed!—donc votre est France, et vous êtes mienne. It is as easy for me, Kate, to conquer the kingdom, as to speak so much more French: I shall never move thee in French, unless it be to laugh at me.

190 *Katharine.* Sauf votre honneur, le Français que vous parlez, il est meilleur que l'Anglais lequel je parle.

King Henry. No, faith, is't not, Kate: but thy speaking of my tongue, and I thine, most truly falsely, must needs be granted to be much at one. But, Kate, dost thou understand thus much English? Canst thou love me?

Katharine. I cannot tell.

King Henry. Can any of your neighbours tell, Kate? I'll ask them....Come, I know thou lovest me: and at night, when you come into your closet, you'll question 200 this gentlewoman about me; and I know, Kate, you will to her dispraise those parts in me that you love with your heart: but, good Kate, mock me mercifully, the rather, gentle princess, because I love thee cruelly. If ever thou beest mine, Kate, as I have a saving faith within me tells me thou shalt, I get thee with scambling, and thou must therefore needs prove a good soldier-breeder: shall not thou and I, between Saint Dennis and

Saint George, compound a boy, half French half
English, that shall go to Constantinople, and take the
Turk by the beard? shall we not? what say'st thou, my 210
fair flower-de-luce?

Katharine. I do not know dat.

King Henry. No: 'tis hereafter to know, but now to
promise: do but now promise, Kate, you will endeavour
for your French part of such a boy; and, for my English
moiety, take the word of a king and a bachelor. How
answer you, la plus belle Katharine du monde, mon très
cher et devin déesse?

Katharine. Your majestee 'ave fause French enough
to deceive de most sage demoiselle dat is en France.   220

King Henry. Now fie upon my false French! By mine
honour, in true English, I love thee, Kate; by which
honour, I dare not swear thou lovest me, yet my blood
begins to flatter me that thou dost; notwithstanding the
poor and untempering effect of my visage. Now beshrew
my father's ambition! he was thinking of civil wars
when he got me, therefore was I created with a stubborn
outside, with an aspect of iron, that when I come to woo
ladies, I fright them: but in faith, Kate, the elder I wax,
the better I shall appear. My comfort is, that old age, 230
that ill layer up of beauty, can do no more spoil upon
my face. Thou hast me, if thou hast me, at the worst;
and thou shalt wear me, if thou wear me, better and
better: and therefore tell me, most fair Katharine, will
you have me? Put off your maiden blushes, avouch the
thoughts of your heart with the looks of an empress, take
me by the hand, and say "Harry of England, I am
thine": which word thou shalt no sooner bless mine ear
withal, but I will tell thee aloud "England is thine,
Ireland is thine, France is thine, and Henry Plantagenet 240
is thine"; who, though I speak it before his face, if he

be not fellow with the best king, thou shalt find the best
king of good fellows....Come, your answer in broken
music; for thy voice is music, and thy English broken:
therefore, queen of all, Katharine, break thy mind to me
in broken English; wilt thou have me?

Katharine. Dat is as it sall please de roi mon père.

King Henry. Nay, it will please him well, Kate; it
shall please him, Kate.

250 *Katharine.* Den it sall also content me.

King Henry. Upon that I kiss your hand, and I call
you my queen.

Katharine. Laissez, mon seigneur, laissez, laissez: ma
foi, je ne veux point que vous abaissiez votre grandeur
en baisant la main d'une de votre seigneurie indigne
serviteur; excusez-moi, je vous supplie, mon très-
puissant seigneur.

King Henry. Then I will kiss your lips, Kate.

Katharine. Les dames et demoiselles pour être baisées
260 devant leur noces, il n'est pas la coutume de France.

King Henry. Madam my interpreter, what says she?

Alice. Dat it is not be de fashon pour les ladies of
France,—I cannot tell vat is baiser en Anglish.

King Henry. To kiss.

Alice. Your majestee entendre bettre que moi.

King Henry. It is not a fashion for the maids in France
to kiss before they are married, would she say?

Alice. Oui, vraiment.

King Henry. O, Kate, nice customs curtsy to great
270 kings. Dear Kate, you and I cannot be confined within
the weak list of a country's fashion: we are the makers
of manners, Kate; and the liberty that follows our places
stops the mouth of all find-faults, as I will do yours, for
upholding the nice fashion of your country, in denying
me a kiss: therefore patiently, and yielding. [*kissing her*]

You have witchcraft in your lips, Kate: there is more
eloquence in a sugar touch of them than in the tongues
of the French council; and they should sooner persuade
Harry of England than a general petition of monarchs....
Here comes your father.   280

The FRENCH KING and QUEEN return with BURGUNDY,
EXETER, WESTMORELAND, and other French and English
Lords; the ladies talk apart

Burgundy. God save your majesty! my royal cousin,
teach you our princess English?

King Henry. I would have her learn, my fair cousin,
how perfectly I love her, and that is good English.

Burgundy. Is she not apt?

King Henry. Our tongue is rough, coz, and my condition is not smooth: so that, having neither the voice
nor the heart of flattery about me, I cannot so conjure
up the spirit of love in her, that he will appear in his
true likeness.   290

Burgundy. Pardon the frankness of my mirth, if I
answer you for that. If you would conjure in her, you
must make a circle: if conjure up love in her in his true
likeness, he must appear naked, and blind. Can you
blame her then, being a maid yet rosed over with the
virgin crimson of modesty, if she deny the appearance
of a naked blind boy in her naked seeing self? It were,
my lord, a hard condition for a maid to consign to.

King Henry. Yet they do wink and yield, as love is
blind and enforces.   300

Burgundy. They are then excused, my lord, when they
see not what they do.

King Henry. Then, good my lord, teach your cousin
to consent winking.

Burgundy. I will wink on her to consent, my lord, if

you will teach her to know my meaning: for maids, well summered and warm kept, are like flies at Bartholomew-tide, blind, though they have their eyes, and then they will endure handling, which before would not abide
310 looking on.

King Henry. This moral ties me over to time, and a hot summer; and so I shall catch the fly, your cousin, in the latter end, and she must be blind too.

Burgundy. As love is, my lord, before it loves.

King Henry. It is so: and you may, some of you, thank love for my blindness, who cannot see many a fair French city for one fair French maid that stands in my way.

French King. Yes, my lord, you see them perspectively:
320 the cities turned into a maid; for they are all girdled with maiden walls, that war hath never entered.

King Henry. Shall Kate be my wife?

French King. So please you.

King Henry. I am content, so the maiden cities you talk of may wait on her: so the maid that stood in the way for my wish shall show me the way to my will.

French King. We have consented to all terms of reason.

King Henry. Is't so, my lords of England?
330 *Westmoreland.* The king hath granted every article:
His daughter first; and then in sequel all,
According to their firm proposéd natures.

Exeter. Only he hath not yet subscribéd this:
Where your majesty demands that the King of France,
having any occasion to write for matter of grant, shall
name your highness in this form, and with this addition,
in French: Notre très-cher fils Henri, Roi d'Angleterre,
Héritier de France: and thus in Latin; Præclarissimus
filius noster Henricus, Rex Angliæ, et hæres Franciæ.

French King. Nor this I have not, brother, so denied, 340
But your request shall make me let it pass.
  King Henry. I pray you then, in love and dear alliance,
Let that one article rank with the rest,
And thereupon give me your daughter.
  French King. Take her, fair son, and from her blood
      raise up
Issue to me, that the contending kingdoms
Of France and England, whose very shores look pale
With envy of each other's happiness,
May cease their hatred; and this dear conjunction
Plant neighbourhood and Christian-like accord   350
In their sweet bosoms: that never war advance
His bleeding sword 'twixt England and fair France.
  All. Amen!
  King Henry Now welcome, Kate: and bear me
      witness all,
That here I kiss her as my sovereign queen.
                                        ['*Flourish*'
  Queen Isabel. God, the best maker of all marriages,
Combine your hearts in one, your realms in one!
As man and wife, being two, are one in love,
So be there 'twixt your kingdoms such a spousal,
That never may ill office, or fell jealousy,   360
Which troubles oft the bed of blessèd marriage,
Thrust in between the paction of these kingdoms,
To make divorce of their incorporate league:
That English may as French, French Englishmen,
Receive each other....God speak this Amen!
  All. Amen!
  King Henry. Prepare we for our marriage: on which
      day,
My Lord of Burgundy, we'll take your oath,
And all the peers', for surety of our leagues.

370 Then shall I swear to Kate, and you to me,
   And may our oaths well kept and prosp'rous be!
         [*A trumpet sounds as King Henry leads Katharine
                 forth, the rest following in procession*

[Epilogue]

'*Enter* CHORUS'

Chorus. Thus far, with rough and all-unable pen,
   Our bending author hath pursued the story,
In little room confining mighty men,
   Mangling by starts the full course of their glory.
Small time: but, in that small, most greatly lived
   This star of England. Fortune made his sword;
By which the world's best garden he achieved:
   And of it left his son imperial lord.
Henry the Sixth, in infant bands crowned King
10   Of France and England, did this king succeed:
Whose state so many had the managing,
   That they lost France, and made his England bleed:
Which oft our stage hath shown; and, for their sake,
In your fair minds let this acceptance take.   [*Exit*

THE TEXT OF *HENRY V*

I. The Copy for *Henry V*, 1623, and for the Quarto of 1600

As already stated, two texts of Shakespeare's *Henry V* have come down to us: that included in the First Folio of 1623, and a 'bad' Quarto published in 1600. It is now coming to be agreed that the folio text was set up from a manuscript in Shakespeare's hand, probably the draft, or, as the phrase then was, the foul papers, from which the acting copy was prepared under the prompter's direction[1]. The absence of act and scene divisions (for the folio act-headings have obviously been clumsily inserted by some editorial or publisher's scribe), the carelessness in regard to names or places (v. notes 3 Prol. 4; 3. 2. 45; 4. 1. 94; 5. 2. 12), the characteristic spellings (v. notes 2. 3. 24, 30, 33; 3. 2. 131; 4. 1. 3, 177; 4. 2. 11; 4. 8. 123; 5. 2. 139), the very misprints, many of which can readily be explained as misreadings of Shakespearian script (v. notes 2. 1. 23; 2. 2. 139; 2. 4. 107; 3. 1. 32; 3. 4. 10; 3. 7. 12; 4 Prol. 16; 4. 2. 60; 4. 4. 67; 4. 8. 100)—all point to Shakespeare's pen. Yet his papers cannot have been very 'foul' inasmuch as the text is a comparatively clean one and its punctuation quite surprisingly good. It is in fact the best and most fully pointed text I have yet encountered in this edition; and if A. W. Pollard is right in accounting for the light and scanty punctuation of Q. *Richard II*, by supposing that it was printed from a manuscript which Shakespeare wrote 'at top speed[2]', perhaps the mood in which he composed *Henry V* was more deliberate.

[1] Cf. my Introd. to *Henry V* ('Folio Facsimiles'), 1931; Greg, *Editorial Problem in Shakespeare* (1942), pp. 68–9.
[2] *King Richard II. A New Quarto* (1916), p. 98.

The date of the manuscript is fixed by the reference
in 5 Prologue to the triumphant return of Essex, which
must have been written after March 1599 and excised
from the prompt-book and the 'part' of Chorus after
the summer of that year[1]. The hostile reference to
Scotland at 1. 2. 136 ff. must likewise have disappeared
from the prompt-book after the accession of James I
in 1603. Some have imagined that the more favourable
tone, evident in the portrait of Jamy, who enters in
3. 2 with Gower, Fluellen and Macmorris as the
fourth representative of the British Isles, was a later
insertion for the sake of the monarch who 'two-fold
balls and treble sceptres' carried. Yet it is difficult to
believe that His Majesty King James, with his broad
Lowland speech, could have taken much pleasure in
hearing a Scot called Jamy ridiculed for his pronunciation of English[2]. Except, then, for the act divisions
and some purging of the text for profanity, both probably the work of a scribe in 1622 or 1623, the Folio
Henry V represents, I believe, the manuscript exactly
as Shakespeare handed it to his company soon after the
departure of Essex for Ireland in 1599.

On the subject of the Quarto text there is fortunately
by now also fairly general agreement, viz. that it is a
'reported' version, probably supplied by traitor-actors,
of performances—perhaps in a shortened form for
provincial audiences—of the play as acted by Shakespeare's company[3]. It follows that textual agreement,
in any particular reading, between F. and Q. affords
practical proof that the word or phrase was spoken on
the stage. It follows also that we can occasionally turn

---

[1] v. Introd. p. x.

[2] Cf. H. T. Price, *The Text of Henry V*, pp. 26–7;
Chambers, *William Shakespeare*, I. pp. 392–3.

[3] v. Duthie, *The 'Bad' Quarto of 'Hamlet'*, 1941,
pp. 29–32, and Greg, *The Editorial Problem in Shakespeare*,
pp. 69–70, for the latest statement of the theory.

to Q. to correct corruption or misprint in F. On the other hand, it is certain that previous editors, unable to guess at the true nature of Q., have been too ready to rely upon it.

II. THE DEATH OF FALSTAFF

Yet, though the probable character of both surviving texts is now recognized, and that of F. is eminently satisfactory from an editor's point of view, much history had gone to the making of the 1599 manuscript, from which it was printed. In the first place, there are indications that Shakespeare, having written the play in one form, changed his intentions and adapted certain scenes accordingly. It has long been noticed that 2 Prologue, the main purpose of which was clearly to prepare the audience for a change of scene from London to Southampton, is oddly followed by a scene still in London, Southampton not being reached until 2. 2; and in Pope's edition the Prologue is accordingly actually placed after 2. 1. But it was, I think, Mr Lionel Jacob who first perceived that the lame couplet with which it concludes, viz.

> But till the king come forth, and not till then,
> Unto Southampton do we shift our scene,

following as it does upon another couplet of the usual terminal character, must have been an afterthought added to explain this strange return to London before passing on to Southampton. He communicated the point to Alfred Pollard, who was at the time with me trying out ideas, later abandoned, on the origin of the 'bad' Shakespearian quartos; and we concluded that scene 2. 1 and scene 2. 3, which is closely connected with it, were both later additions to the text[1]. Sir

---

[1] v. *Times Literary Supplement*, 13 March, 1919, 'The "Stolne and surreptitious" Shakespearian texts'.

Edmund Chambers in his turn, while accepting Jacob's interpretation of the second couplet, thought it 'may be due to' a 'Folio editor', who, he suggested, 'may have had the choruses on loose scrolls, and should have inserted this one, and begun Act II, a scene later[1]'. This ingenious revival of Pope's theory will not, however, work, since, as Dr Duthie points out to me, it ignores the fact that 2 Prologue not only states 'the scene is now transported to Southampton' but promises that the audience shall be conveyed 'thence to France', whereas though they find themselves in Southampton after 2. 1 they pass from thence, not to France but back to London once more in 2. 3. There is really no way out of it: when 2 Prologue was first written, the play lacked both the final couplet and scenes 2. 1 and 2. 3, as we have them now.

And when it is observed that 2. 1 introduces us to Bardolph, Nym and Pistol, and that from l. 81 onwards we are being prepared for the famous description of Falstaff's death, which is the main business of 2. 3, it is difficult to avoid the conclusion that the death of Falstaff was the big afterthought which occasioned these minor ones, an episode hastily inserted into a play, not originally designed for it, in order to provide a dramatic excuse for Shakespeare's failure to keep the promise made in the Epilogue of *2 Henry IV* to 'continue the story with Sir John in it'.

These conclusions of Dr Duthie's, which tally with theories of my own, independently arrived at and stated in *The Fortunes of Falstaff*[2], receive strong support from yet another anomaly in the text of *Henry V*, which seems to show, beyond a doubt, that the living Falstaff was once a character in the play, and (shocking though

[1] Chambers, *op. cit.* i. 393.
[2] v. pp. 123-5.

it may sound to his adorers) actually underwent the
ordeal of the leek in place of Pistol.

> News have I that my Doll is dead i'th' spital
> Of malady of France

says the latter at the end of 5. 1, to the standing per-
plexity of editors, most of whom, following Capell,
have shamelessly altered 'Doll' to 'Nell', the name of
mine Hostess, Mistress Pistol, quondam Quickly. But
since Q. also reads 'Doll' it is certain that Shakespeare
wrote the word, and since Pistol himself tells us (2. 1.
74–7) that Doll Tearsheet had gone to 'the spital'
it is also certain that Shakespeare did not write it in
error. And yet, apart from 'Nell's' prior claims, everything that Pistol says of or to Mistress Tearsheet in
2 Henry IV or *Henry V* shows that he hates her, so
that it is absurd for him to call her 'my Doll' here.
Only one person in fact is entitled to do so and that is
Falstaff. She is clearly his in the great second Boar's
Head scene, and when at *2 Henry IV* 5. 5. 33–4 Pistol
informs him outside the Abbey

> Thy Doll, and Helen of thy noble thoughts,
> Is in base durance and contagious prison,

Falstaff does not question the association.

There can, I think, be no doubt about it: Falstaff
once larded the sodden field of Agincourt, had been
cut out of the play (owing, as I have suggested, to the
desertion or expulsion of Will Kempe), and such of
his dramatic effects as could be salvaged by the unhappy
dramatist, including, by an oversight, Doll, had then
been transferred to Pistol. It must have been a con-
siderable operation and one that meant enlarging the
serious as well as curtailing the comic section of the
play. One such enlargement may well be the Jamy-
Macmorris episode (3. 2. 63–end) already noticed,
which is dramatically self-contained, and consisting as

it does of some 70 lines of prose might have been written
on one side of a foolscap sheet. A more patent addition,
again pointed out by Dr Duthie, is the 250 lines that
separate the exit of Erpingham at 4. 1. 34 from the
beginning of Henry's prayer at l. 285. Dr Duthie
notes (i) that Henry's words at ll. 31–2:

> I and my bosom must debate awhile,
> And then I would no other company,

which are obviously intended to prepare the audience
for a soliloquy, if not a prayer, are nevertheless followed
by an encounter with Pistol, a brief dialogue, which
Henry overhears, between Gower and Fluellen, and
a very long dialogue between three soldiers and their
disguised King; (ii) that when at l. 226 we at last reach
a soliloquy it is one that arises directly out of the pre-
ceding conversation and is itself most awkwardly followed, after an interval of only four lines, by a second
soliloquy, the prayer for the army; (iii) that the purpose
of these intervening four lines is to repeat to Erpingham,
who now returns, the very command already given to
the royal dukes at ll. 24–7; and, summing up, (iv) that
the soliloquy at ll. 285 ff. in an earlier version must
have stood immediately after l. 34, and ll. 35–284 have
been inserted by Shakespeare during a revision.

III. The Origins of *HENRY V*
(and perhaps of Fluellen)

And there is more behind. I have elsewhere[1] shown
reasons for thinking that Shakespeare's *Henry IV* and
Henry V are based upon two Queen's Company plays,
written in the eighties, a highly abridged and much
degraded version of which was later reported from
memory and published, in 1594 or 1598, as *The Famous
Victories of Henry V*.

[1] *The Library*, June, 1945.

The thesis has still to be worked out, especially as regards *Henry V*, but some of the links between this play and the second half of *The Famous Victories* will be brought out in the Notes below, where also a good deal of space has been given to the closely related question of sources; and I may conclude this excursus with a brief summary of my tentative conclusions on what the play owes to the various chronicles.

Holinshed, though of course the main source, is far from being the only one. Hall is several times drawn upon (v. notes 1. 2. 45, 52, 138, 256; 3. 7. 147–53; 4. 1. 287) and the fact that the Archbishop's speech (1. 2. 33 ff.), which is palpably a mere versification of Holinshed, should contain a misspelling that can be traced to a misprint in Hall, seems eloquent on the problem of joint-authorship. Fabyan (v. note 4. 1. 294–8), *The Brut* (v. note 1. 2. 282–3), Monstrelet (v. notes 4. 1. 10; 4. 6. 5) and Tito Livio, whom I usually cite from a contemporary English translation (v. notes 3. 7. 1 ff.; 4. 2. 60; 5 Prol. 18, 20) were also probably used. But my most interesting find is the connection between *Henry V* and the *Gesta Henrici Quinti*, an account of the campaign written by one of the royal chaplains, which chronicle, Kingsford tells us, was little known in the fifteenth and sixteenth centuries, both Stow and Holinshed being ignorant of it[1]. Here are some of the dramatic details that seem to derive from hints therein: the storming of the breach at Harfleur, Henry's speech (based on Deut. xx. 10–14) demanding the surrender of the town (v. note 3. 3. 1–43), the fact that the stolen pax or pix was 'of

---

[1] Cf. p. 49, Kingsford, *Eng. Hist. Lit.* Wylie, ii. 87, says the *Gesta* was used by Stow, but gives no evidence. Wylie and Kingsford attribute it to Thomas of Elmham, but V. H. Galbraith shows this to be unlikely (see his *St Albans Chronicle, 1406–1420*, p. xxiii, n. 2).

little price' (v. note 3. 6. 44), the drenching rain that preceded the battle of Agincourt, some of the numbers named for troops on either side, and above all perhaps a character, Fluellen himself! Twice the *Gesta* refers to a Magister Aegidius, once in criticism of the English mining operations, and even might seem to give the impression to an Elizabethan reader that he was present with the army[1], though he had actually died in 1314. This is Aegidius Romanus, who was a pupil of St Thomas Aquinas and a well-known authority on the 'disciplines of wars', in particular of ancient wars, being author of *De re militari veterum*, a section of his best known book *De regimine principum*, of which an English translation by Hoccleve, addressed to Henry himself, survives in copies at the British Museum and the Bodleian[2]. Is it too hazardous a guess that a Master Giles figured in the old *Henry V*, and that Shakespeare made a Welshman out of him to commemorate a more recent student of war, Sir Roger Williams?[3]. Certainly it is not the first time that we seem to have discovered a diligent student of the Chronicles at the back of Shakespeare's history-plays[4].

[1] Cf. pp. 16–17, 24–5, *Gesta Henrici Quinti*, ed. B. Williams, Eng. Hist. Soc. 1850, and below, note 3. 2. 57–8.

[2] *Ibid.* p. 16 n. 2. I am indebted to Prof. Galbraith for some of these particulars.

[3] Cf. Introduction (above), p. ix, and note 3. 2. 58.

[4] Cf. Introductions, *King John*, p. xli, *Richard II*, pp. xxxviii ff.

P.S. [1955]. J. H. Walter anticipated some of the foregoing argument in *M.L.R.*, July 1946. See also his edition (1954) and a note by A. Wilkinson in *R.E.S.* Oct. 1950. In the Notes below, "W. M. T. Dodds" refers to a review by her in *M.L.R.* Oct. 1947, and "J. C. Maxwell" to private communications.

NOTES

All significant departures from F. are recorded; the name of the text or edition in which the accepted reading first appeared being placed in brackets and when it comes from Q. the edition which first adopted it therefrom being noted also. Line-numeration for references to plays not yet issued in this edition is that found in Bartlett's *Concordance* and the *Globe Shakespeare*.

Q. stands for the 'bad' Quarto of *Henry V* (1600); F. for the First Folio (1623); G. for Glossary; O.E.D. for *The Oxford English Dictionary*; S.D. for stage-direction; Sh. for Shakespeare; MSH. for *The Manuscript of Sh.'s 'Hamlet'* by J. Dover Wilson, 1934; Hol. for Holinshed; common words (e.g. prob.= probably), together with names of characters and of well-known editors, are also abbreviated where convenient.

The following is a list of other books cited with abridged titles: Apperson=*English Proverbs and Proverbial Phrases* by G. L. Apperson, 1929; Arden=the ed. by H. A. Evans (Arden Sh.); Bond=*Works of John Lyly* ed. R. W. Bond, 1902; Camb.=*The Cambridge Sh.* ed. W. A. Wright, 1891; Cap.=the ed. by Edward Capell, 1768; Chambers, *Eliz. St.*=*The Elizabethan Stage* by E. K. Chambers, 1923; Chambers, *Med. St.*=*The Medieval Stage* by E. K. Chambers, 1903; Clar.=the ed. by W. A. Wright (the Clarendon Sh.); Creizenach=*The English Drama in the Age of Sh.* by W. Creizenach, 1916; E.E.T.S.=The Early English Text Society; *Ed. III.*=*K. Edward the Third*, 1596 (text as in Tucker Brooke, *Sh. Apocrypha*, 1908); Elmham=*Liber Metricus de Henrico Quinto* (ed. C. A. Cole, *Memorials of Henry V*, 1858); *F.V.*=*The Famous*

Victories of Henry V, 1598, ed. P. A. Daniel (Griggs-Praetorius facsimile, 1887); *First Life*=*The First English Life of Henry V* (1513), ed. C. L. Kingsford, 1911; *Fortunes*=*The Fortunes of Falstaff* by J. Dover Wilson, 1943; Franz=*Die Sprache Shakespeares* (4th ed.) by W. Franz, 1939; *Gesta*=*Gesta Henrici Quinti, Regis Angliae* (ed. B. Williams, Eng. Hist. Soc. 1850), v. also Nicholas; Greg= *Principles of Emendation in Sh.* by W. W. Greg (v. *Aspects of Sh.*, British Academy, 1933); Hall=*Hall's Chronicle*, 1548, reprinted 1809; Hol.=Holinshed, *Historie of England*, vol. iii (ed. ii), 1587; J.=the ed. by Samuel Johnson, 1765; Kingsford=*First Life*; M.S.=the ed. by G. C. Moore Smith, 1896 (Warwick Sh.); Mal.=Malone's Variorum ed. of 1821; McKerrow=*The Works of Thomas Nashe*, ed. R. B. McKerrow, 1904–10; Monstrelet=*Les Chroniques d'E. de Monstrelet* trans. by T. Johnes, 1810, vol. iv; Morgan=*Some Problems of Sh.'s 'Henry IV'* by A. E. Morgan, 1924 (Sh. Association); Nicholas=*The Battle of Agincourt* by N. H. Nicholas, 1827 [a valuable collection of contemporary accounts, including an English trans. of *Gesta* (q.v.)]; Onions= *Sh. Glossary* by C. T. Onions, 1919; Price=*The Text of Henry V* by H. T. Price, 1920; *R.E.S.*=*Review of English Studies*; Ridley=ed. by M. R. Ridley (New Temple Sh.); Schmidt=*Sh.-Lexicon* by A. Schmidt (3rd ed. rev. by G. Sarrazin), 1902; *Sh. Eng.*=*Sh.'s England*, Oxford, 1917; *Sh.'s Hand*=*Sh.'s Hand in 'Sir Th. More'* by A. W. Pollard, etc. 1923; Steev.= the ed. by George Steevens, 1773; Stone=*Sh.'s Holinshed* by W. G. Boswell-Stone, 1907; Stow= Stow's *Annals* (cited from ed. 1615); *T.L.S.*=*Times Literary Supplement*; Theo.=the ed. by Lewis Theobald, 1734; Tito Livio=*Vita Henrici Quinti* by Titus Livius (Tito Livio da Forlì) c. 1437, cited from the Eng. trans. in *First Life* (q.v.); Verity=the ed. by A. W. Verity, 1900 (Pitt Press Sh.); Warb.=the ed.

by William Warburton, 1747; Wylie= *The Reign of Henry V*, by T. H. Wylie, 3 vols., 1914–29.

Names of the Characters. List first given by Rowe. For *Pistol* v. note 2. 1. 56. *Duke of Exeter*, so created 18 Nov. 1416; before then Earl of Dorset. For the other historical characters v. G. R. French, *Shakespeareana Genealogica*, 1869, and Stokes, *Sh. Dictionary of Characters and Proper Names*, 1924.

Acts and Scenes. The scene divisions were first introduced by Pope, there being none in F. Act divisions are found in F. but were clearly inserted by some scribe without authority or understanding of the play, 'Actus Secundus' appearing before 3 Prologue, 'Actus Tertius' before 4 Prologue and 'Actus Quartus', with extreme absurdity, before 4. 7, i.e. in the middle of the battle of Agincourt. The five acts, which are clearly marked by the five prologues, were first regularised by Pope and Johnson.

Punctuation. Cf. p. 111. I have as usual had to make pretty free with commas, have added a few exclamation marks and have occasionally substituted three dots for colons, and dashes for commas (v. 'To the Reader', p. lvii); but otherwise F. has been followed closely, with the exception only of a handful of emendations noted at 1. 2. 281; 2. 2. 9, 54; 3. 3. 54; 3. 6. 73; 4 Prol. 46–7; 4. 1. 137; 4. 3. 49; 4. 6. 14–15; 5 Prol. 10.

Stage-directions. Only those in F. that call for special comment have been noted. For the rest see my facsimile of the F. text (Faber's 'Folio Facsimiles') and Greg, *Editorial Problem*, 1942.

1 Prologue

S.D. F. 'Enter Prologue'. The Prologue wore a wreath and a long black velvet cloak (Creizenach, pp. 275–6). For 'Chorus' v. l. 32 and for its function cf. ll. 23–31, 5 Prol. 1–6, and Introd. pp. xiii–xv. Creizenach (p. 276) notes that the Choruses in *Hen. V* have no parallel elsewhere in Eliz. drama.

1. *fire* loftiest and most etherial of the four elements; cf. 3. 7. 20–1.

5. *like himself*='worthy of so great a king and hero as Henry' (H. T. Price, art. in *R.E.S.* xvi. 178–81).

7. *Famine, Sword, and Fire* Cf. Hol. p. 567 (Stone, pp. 165–6). Henry 'declared' to the people of Rouen, 'that the goddesse of battell, called Bellona, had three handmaidens, euer of necessitie attending vpon hir, as blood, fire, and famine' [Steev.]. Cf. *1 Hen. VI*, 4. 2. 11. A 'leash'=three dogs; cf. *1 Hen. IV*, 2. 4. 6, and *Caes.* 3. 1. 273.

9. *flat unraiséd spirits* Including the playwright himself.

spirits…hath Cf. Franz, p. 158, and below, 1. 2. 27–8, 119, 244. A sing. vb. with plur. subject, or vice versa, is often found in Sh.

13. *this wooden O* i.e. this tiny wooden circle; v. G. 'O'. Prob. the Curtain Theatre, not the Globe, which (begun in Jan. or Feb. 1599 and taking about 28 weeks to build) can hardly have been completed before Aug. or Sept., whereas the 5th Prol. must have been written before June; cf. Introd. p. x, and Chambers, *Eliz. Stage*, ii. 415.

15. *crooked* curved, like a naught, which in the lowest (i.e. the unit's) place may convert 100,000 into 1,000,000. Cf. G. 'place', Peele's *Ed. I* (Mal. Soc.), ll. 204–5, "'Tis but a Cipher in Agrum [=a cipher in algorism or arithmetic=0], And it hath made of 10000 pounds, 100000 pounds', and *Wint.* 1. 2. 6–9.

17. *to this...accompt* in comparison with this great (*a*) sum total, (*b*) story. Cf. p. xiv.

18. *imaginary forces* powers of imagination.

21. *high...abutting fronts* i.e. the cliffs of Dover and Calais.

25. *puissance* A trisyllable.

28. *deck* v. G.

29. *jumping o'er times* The hist. period covered is 1414–20.

33. *prologue-like* Prologues 'usually addressed' the audience 'in flattering terms and asked [them] to grant an indulgent hearing' (Creizenach, pp. 275–6).

I. I.

For the substance of this scene cf. Introd. pp. xviii ff.

S.D. from Camb. Pope 'London'. Theo. 'An Antechamber in the English Court at Kenilworth'. In Hol. the Archb. delivers his speech at Leicester (v. Introd. p. xx) and the King receives the tennis balls at Kenilworth. Sh., who (like *F.V.*) combines them in one court scene, suggests no locality.

1–2. *that self bill...reign* Cf. Hol. p. 545 (Stone, p. 167). The bill was moved by the Lollard knights in the parl. of 1410; v. Kingsford, *Henry V* (Heroes of the Nations), pp. 66–7.

9–19. *For all...the bill* Closely follows Hol.

15. *age,* (Cap.) F. 'age'. The three classes correspond with those mentioned by Hol. [Clar.].

25–7. *The breath...too* Cf. *2 Hen. IV*, 5. 2. 123–4. Cf. Nowell's *Largest Catechism* (1570): 'By the force of Christ's death our old man is, after a certain manner, crucified and mortified, and the corruptness of our nature is, as it were, buried' [Baldwin, *Petty School*, p. 183].

28–31. *like an angel...spirits* Cf. Genesis iii. 23–4. 'Eden was identified with Paradise, the abode of the blessed' (M.S.).

33–4. *a flood...faults* Alluding to the cleansing of the Augean stables. 'Hercules is still in our author's head when he mentions the Hydra' (J.).

36. *seat* throne, sovereignty; cf. l. 88.

—*and...once*— F. '; and...once;'.

44. *rendered...in music* i.e. he understands war so well that he can see order and harmony even behind the chaos and discord of a battle.

45. *cause of policy* political problem.

48. *chartered libertine* one licensed to go where he pleases. Cf. *A.Y.L.* 2. 7. 47–8.

49. *wonder* i.e. wonderer (which perhaps Sh. wrote). Staunton conj. 'wand'rer'. Cf. *Tw.Nt.* 1. 1. 5–7, where the wind steals odours.

51–2. *the art...theoric* action and experience must have taught him theory. Cf. G. 'art', 'mistress'.

53. *grace* majesty. A title no longer given to monarchs.

59. *haunts...popularity* Cf. G. and *1 Hen. IV*, 3. 2. 69.

60–2. *The strawberry* Those from Ely Place were famous; cf. *Ric. III*, 3. 4. 34.

Eliz. gardeners believed that a plant derived from its neighbours the good or evil qualities they possessed: but the strawberry was an exception. Although it crept along the ground exposed to every sort of contamination, yet no evil companionship could taint its purity. (Prothero, *Sh. Eng.* i. 373.)

67. *miracles are ceased* Cf. *All's Well*, 2. 3. 1. A protestant doctrine.

68. *the means* i.e. a natural cause.

75–81. *an offer...withal* closely follows Hol. p. 546 (Stone, pp. 171–2).

86. *severals* v. G. Pope read 'several' (qualifying 'passages' balancing 'generally', l. 88).

1. 2.

For the substance of this scene v. Introd. pp. xviii–xxiv.

S.D. based on Camb., which derives from Theo. F. and Q. include Clarence with the entries; edd. omit.

4. *cousin* By marriage.

15. *understanding* i.e. knowing the truth to be otherwise.

16. *right* title, claim.

27. *wrongs gives* 27–8. *swords…makes* Cf. note 1 Prol. 9.

32. *as sin* i.e. as original sin is washed away.

33 ff. *Then hear me* etc. Follows Hol. almost word for word; cf. Stone, pp. 169–71, for parallel texts. N.B. neither Hol. nor Sh. mention Isabella, the peg upon which Henry's whole case hangs (cf. Introd. p. xxiii); but *F.V.* and Hall do.

36. *make against* v. G. [1955].

38. *succedant* (F 2) F. 'ſuccedaul'.

45, 52. *Elbe* (Cap.) F. 'Elue' (Hol. 'Elbe'). The error derives from a misprint in Hall (v. p. 50).

49. *dishonest* v. G. Hol. gives 'dishonest' (ed. ii), 'unhonest' (ed. i).

53. *Meisen* Mod. Meissen.

57–64. *Until four…five*. Dates and arithmetic from Hol.

66. *heir general* v. G.

72. *find* Many read 'fine' (Q.); but v. G. 'find'.

74. *Lingare* Hol. 'Lingard' (orig. German 'Luitgard'). Poss. an *e* : *d* error (MSH. p. 109). Q. 'Inger' suggests that 'Lingare' was spoken on the stage. Cf. note l. 82.

75. *Charlemain* Historically Charles the Bald; the error is Hol.'s and Hall's.

77. *the tenth* Hol.'s error for 'the ninth' (St Louis) which Hall reads correctly.

82. *Ermengare* Hol. 'Ermengard'. Cf. note l. 74.

93. *a net* The tissue of contradiction is pictured as a criss-cross.

94. *imbare* (Warb.'s conj. adopted by Theo., J., Mal.; Rowe reads 'make bare') F. 'imbarre'. F3 'imbar' which most mod. edd. follow, though disputing the meaning. Cf. O.E.D. *em-* 1 *a* for 'embare'=make bare (1615). To paraphrase ll. 93–4: they prefer to hide themselves in a transparent network of contradictions than to expose to the world at large the rottenness of their own titles. This emphasizes the main point of the speech, which is the muddle-headedness of these glozing French lawyers. Cf. Introd. p. xxiii.

98. *Numbers* xxvii. 8. Sh. inadvertently omits 'without a son', which Hol. reads.

101. *bloody flag* Cf. *Cor.* 2. 1. 84; *Caes.* 5. 1. 14.

106. *a tragedy* The battle of Crécy, 1346.

108. *on a hill* Hol. p. 372 (Stone, p. 171) relates that at Crécy Ed. III 'stood aloft on a windmill hill'.

112. *half* Actually two-thirds.

120. *youth* In fact Henry was 27.

125. *cause...might* Cf. Introd. p. xxviii n. 1.

126. *hath* Accented.

131. *With blood...fire* Follows Hol.
blood (F3) F. 'Bloods'.

132–5. *In aid...ancestors* Cf. Introd. p. xxii and Wylie (i. 434) who shows the sum was nothing extraordinary.

137. *proportions to defend* Cf. 2. 4. 45 and G.

138 ff. *Against the Scot* etc. This seems to go back to Hall, who gives much more space to Scotland here than Hol., though the 'saying' at ll. 167–8 comes from Hol. [Price, p. 38].

139. *With all advantages* with everything in their favour.

150. *brim fulness* (F.) Cf. 'brimme full' at *2 Hen. IV*, 3. 1. 67 (Q.), *Temp.* 5. 1. 14 (F.). Orig. written as two words (v. O.E.D. 'brimful').

160. *impounded...stray* Contemptuous; v. G. 'stray'.

161. *the King of Scots* David II, taken at Neville's Cross in 1346.

send to France A link with the play *Ed. III* (pub. 1596); in Hol. David's captor goes to France without him [Clar.].

163. *her* (Johnson) F. 'their.' Poss. 'her' was misread 'ther' (a common sp.). Price (p. 45) and Greg (*Aspects*, p. 174) propose 'your'; but after 'her' in ll. 156, 157, 158, 'her' is expected once again.

164. *ooze and bottom* Hendiadys. Cf. *Ric. III*, act 1, sc. 4.

165. *wrack* (F.). Theo. and subs. edd. 'wreck'. Cf. Greg, p. 174.

166–73. *But there's a saying* etc. F. prefix followed. Cap. transferred to West. (following Hol.) and all mod. edd. do likewise. Q. heads the corresponding speech 'Lord' and *F.V.* 'Cant.'.

168. *begin:* F. 'begin'.

169. *in prey* v. G. 'prey'.

173. *'tame* Aphetic form of 'attame'=broach, break into (O.E.D. 'tame' v^2), which exactly describes the habits of the weasel. Rowe (ii) read 'tear' and all edd. follow. The restoration is Greg's (p. 171). The conj. 'tarre' ('Folio Facsimiles') is withdrawn.

174. *then* F. 'there'.

180 ff. *For government* etc. Sh. sets this discourse on good government in the forefront of his portrait of 'the mirror of all Christian kings' as he sets Ulysses's on Discord early in *Troil.* (1. 3. 84–134). Both are based on Bk. i, chs. 1 and 2 of Elyot's *Governour*, 1531 (cf. Kellett, *Reconsiderations*, pp. 42–3), from Bk. ii,

ch. 6 of which Sh. took the story of the L.C. Justice
and Prince Hal (cf. *Library*, xxvi, no. 1, pp. 7–9).
Elyot also writes of bees (v. note ll. 188–9).

180. *high...lower* Cf. Elyot, Bk. i, ch. 1. Order
is not order 'except it do contain in it degrees high
and base'.

181–3. *Put into parts...music* Cf. G. 'parts',
'consent' (concent), 'congreeing', 'close', all with two
meanings, 'congreeing' being a word invented to suit
both government and music. Elyot does not refer to
music, but the analogy is as old as Pythagoras; cf. my
art. on 'Sh.'s Universe' in *Univ. of Edin. Journal*,
1942.

184. *the state of man* 'The estate of mankind'
(Elyot), i.e. the State, not, I think, the 'little kingdom'
of man's person, as *Jul. Caes.* 2. 1. 67.

185. *Setting...motion* 'So that there should be a
continual stimulus to effort' (M.S.)—one of Elyot's
main points.

186–7. *To which.. Obedience* 'The end of all
being obedience' (M.S.). Cf. Elyot, end of i, ch. 1.

187–204. *for so work the honey-bees...drone* Speaking
of bees Elyot refers to Pliny (*Nat. Hist.* xi. 5–20) and
Virgil's *Georgics* (iv), and taking the hint, it seems,
Sh. drew on his memories of both these, though more
upon his own invention.

188–9. *Creatures...kingdom* An obvious paraphrase of Elyot, i. ch. 2: 'the Bee is lefte to man by
nature, or it semeth, a perpetuall figure of a iuste
gouernaunce or rule.'

rule in nature instinctive polity.

act v. G.

190 ff. *they...officers...some* etc. Cf. Pliny (tr.
Ph. Holland, 1601), xi. 10, 'They have their several
officers within. Some' etc.

190. *sorts* v. G.

193–5. *like soldiers...home* Pliny, *op. cit.* (xi. 8)

writes of spies sent to forage for honey-flowers; a
point not in the abridgement of Pliny's account in
Euphues (Bond, ii. 44–6), usually considered Sh.'s
source. Cf. also Pliny xi. 10, 'marching abroad'.

196. *the tent-royal* etc. Cf. *Georgics*, iv. 75, 'et
circa regem atque ipsa ad praetoria densae'.

197. *busied in his majesty, surveys* Cf. Pliny, xi. 17,
'when all his people are busie in labor, himselfe (as a
right good captaine) ouerseeth their workes'.

majesty (Rowe) F. 'Maiefties'.

198. *building* Cf. Pliny, xi. 10, 'building'.

200–4. *the poor...drone* Cf. *Georgics*, iv. 165–8.

205–6. *having full...consent* all related to a common purpose.

207–9. *As many arrows...town* F. 'As many
Arrowes...wayes/Come...marke: as many wayes...
towne' Q. 'As many Arrowes...wayes, flye to...
marke:/As many feueral/wayes meet in one towne'
Q. surely preserves the right metre; and 'many' and
'several', first separate and then combined, surely also
show the poet's hand; while the F. compositor would
have a strong temptation to omit 'several', since to
include it in the long line 'come to...one towne'
would have overrun the column. Cap. adopted both
'several' and 'fly' from Q.

213. *End* (Q., Pope) F. 'And'.

borne v. G. 'bear'.

222. *Dauphin* F. 'Dolphin' *et passim*.

225. *ours* i.e. by right

to our awe to our obedience.

229. *urn* grave, v. G.

230. *tombless* without monument.

234. *worshipped* honoured.

with...epitaph with an epitaph in wax, still less
one in brass or stone. Q. 'with a paper Epitaph'.

S.D. Hol. reports three Fr. missions, the first from
the Dauphin with tennis-balls, the last (headed by the

Archb. of Burges and M. Cole the Fr. K.'s secretary) in answer to Henry's claim to the Fr. crown. In *F.V.* Burges and Cole deliver the tennis-balls in 'a gilded tun'.

240. *sparingly...far off* Cf. *Ric. III*, 3. 5. 93.

241. *meaning* F. 'meauing'.

243. *grace* v. G.

244. *is* Cf. note 1. 2. 27–8.

251–4. *Says...dukedoms there* The Dauphin shows little knowledge of Prince Hal's youth! Cf. Introd. p. xlii.

252. *advised there* (Camb.) F. 'aduis'd: There's—which conveys the Camb. interpretation [J. C. Maxwell, 1955].

256. *tun* Hall and *F.V.* use this word; Hol. p. 545 (Stone, p. 173) speaks of 'a barrell of Parris balles'.

259. *Tennis-balls* This story, though prob. a fable, was believed in by Henry's contemporaries (v. Wylie, i. 425–30). *F.V.* reads 'a Carpet and a Tunne of Tennis-balles'—'Meaning', the ambassador explains, 'you are more fitter for a Tennis court then a field, and more fitter for a Carpet then the Camp'. Cf. Kingsford, *First Life*, p. xliii.

259–67. *Tennis* was fashionable in the late sixteenth and early seventeenth centuries. Of Fr. origin: name prob. from 'tenez' (= take!); balls, of white leather stuffed with hair, called 'Paris-balls' (v. G.); 'rackets' of string; walls surrounded the 'court', 'hazards' being openings in these, and a ball struck into a hazard being unplayable; a 'chase' = lit. the second bound of the ball, but here used for any point of the game. Cf. *Sh. Eng.* ii. 459–62.

263. *in France* Perhaps part of the tennis-court was called 'France.' Dekker (*Gull's Hornbook*, 1609, ch. v) calls sweating in the tennis-court 'sweting... in Fraunce'. Cf. *F.V.* ix. 157, 'Such balles as neuer were tost in France'.

265. *wrangler* (*a*) opponent, (*b*) disputant (the 'chase' being the most arguable point in tennis).

270. *We never valued* etc. Ironical, leading up to ll. 274–6.

271. *hence* away from this 'seat of England', i.e. the court.

274. *keep my state* v. G. 'state'.

275. *sail* v. G., and *Son.* 86.

277–8. *For that...days* 'To qualify myself for this undertaking, I have descended from my station and studied the arts of life in a lower character' (J.). Cf. Introd. p. xliii.

for working-days=during working days (i.e. not forgetting the day of rest coming) [M.S.].

279–81. *I will rise...look on us* The sun-image of majesty; cf. Introd. *Ric. II*, pp. xii–xiii, and *History*, vol. xxvi, pp. 238–9.

281. *on us.* F. 'on vs,'.

282–3. *this mock...gun-stones* Hol. does not mention 'gun-stones'. But Henry actually used them (v. Wylie, i. 448), and with them breached the walls of Harfleur (*ibid.* ii. 34). Clar. (Preface, pp. xiii–xiv) quotes from *The Brut*:

And whanne the King hadde herde...the answere of the Dolfyne, he was wondir sore agrevyd,...and anon lette make tenysballis for the Dolfyn in alle the haste that thay myghte be maad, and that thei were harde and grete gune-stonys, for the Dolfyn to play with-alle. (Part II, p. 375, ed. F. W. D. Brie, E.E.T.S.)

304. *that run before* i.e. whatever he undertakes is preceded by prayer.

308. *God before* God leading us; cf. l. 304.

2 Prologue

Pope placed this after 2. 1; cf. p. 113. F. gives no act-division; cf. p. 111.

2. *silken dalliance* Cf. *Cor.* 1. 9. 45 and *Ed. III*, 2. 2. 94, 'Away, loose silkes of wauering vanitie!'

6. *mirror...kings* Cf. Hall, 'mirror of Christen-

dom' (cited Introd. p. xviii), a phrase not in Hol.;
v. G. 'mirror'.

7. *English Mercuries* Cf. *1 Hen. IV*, 4. 1. 106.

9–10. *a sword...coronets* Prob. suggested by a
woodcut of Ed. III holding a sword encircled by
two crowns (England and France) found in Hol. (ed. i)
p. 885 and in Rastell's *Pastyme of People* (cf. note on
frontispiece to my *K. John*). For 'hilts' v. G.

12. *intelligence* secret service.

16. *model* v. G.

19. *kind and natural* loving and filial.

20. *see, thy fault France* (F.) Cap., Camb. etc. 'see
thy fault! France'.
France= the Fr. king.

21. *nest* haunt or breeding-place.

22–5. *three corrupted men* As these are to appear in
one scene (2. 2) only, the audience needs preparatory
information.

26. *gilt...guilt* An irresistible pun to Sh.; cf.
2 Hen. IV, 4. 5. 128, etc.

28. *grace of kings* i.e. 'who does most honour to
the title'. Taken perhaps from Chapman's *Iliad*,
bk. i (1598 text): 'the grace of kings, wise Ithacus'
[Steev.]. Cf. *Ham.* 3. 4. 98, 'vice of kings'.

31–2. *Linger...play* The words fit awkwardly into
the context. Perhaps Sh. meant to delete them.
digest...distance A playful allusion to the Unities:
stomach the sin against the unity of place.

32. *force* stuff, cram full; a culinary word, following close upon 'digest'. Spelt 'farce' at 4. 1. 259
and 'force' at *Troil.* 2. 3. 233 (F. and Q.), 5. 1. 64
(F. 'forced'; Q. 'faced'). Hitherto explained 'produce
a play by *compelling* many circumstances into a narrow
compass' (Steev.).

38. *charming* v. G.

40. *offend one stomach* (*a*) make any one seasick,
(*b*) offend any one's taste; cf. note ll. 31–2.

41–2. *But till...scene* Cf. pp. 113–14.

2. 1.

2. *Lieutenant* Bard. is a corporal in *2 Hen. IV* (2. 4. 148) and again at 3. 2. 3 below.

5–10. *For my part...end.* Nym sulkily agrees to be friends, some day, perhaps; but Pist. had called him a coward and he is full of dark hints.

5. *I say little* Cf. the Boy's comment, 3. 2. 36 ff.

9. *toast cheese* Cf. *K. John*, 4. 3. 99.
will endure cold i.e. does not mind being naked.

10. *there's an end* that's all there is to it.

12. *sworn brothers* v. G. A fraternity of rogues.

14–16. *Faith...of it* Pist. had evidently been threatening him. Cf. G. 'rest', 'rendezvous'.

19. *troth-plight* v. G.

23–4. *though...plod* Cf. Apperson, p. 485, 'Patience is a good nag, but she'll bolt'—which confirms the conj. 'mare'.

23. *mare* (Q., Theo.) F. 'name'; cf. MSH. pp. 106–8.

25. S.D. I follow Mal.'s S.D., and agree with Duthie that Nym is the aggressor. Camb. and mod. edd. read 'Nym & Pistol draw'.

28. *How...host Pistol!* F. continues this to Bard.; but Q. gives the corresponding salute 'How do you my Hoste?' to Nym. As Clar. notes, 'Bard. has no motive for picking a quarrel with Pist., and Pist.'s vapouring is all directed against Nym'.

36–7. *if he be not hewn now, we* (F.) Hanmer, 'if he be not drawn now! we'—which Camb. and most mod. edd. read. But 'hewn'=cut down (v. G.); and as Nym draws, Quickly screams to her bridegroom to cut the villain down, lest the worst befall.

38. *lieutenant* Bard. seeks to placate Pist. Cf. note 3. 6. 12 and G. 'ancient'. The 'corporal' is of course Nym.

41–2. *Iceland...Iceland* F. 'Iſland...Iſland'.

41. *Iceland dog* a long-haired lap-dog, v. G.

45. *Will you.. solus* i.e. Let's settle this privately (away from the lady). 'Solus' is theatre Latin.

S.D. Malone, 'sheathing his sword'.

46–53. '*Solus*'...*follow*. Pist., ignorant of Latin, takes 'solus' as an insult. F. prints his speeches as prose.

47. *marvellous* (F3) F. 'meruailous' is prob. a Sh. spelling; cf. 'maruailes' *M.N.D.* (Q.), 3. 1. 3; 4. 1. 23; *2 Hen. IV* (Q.), 5. 1. 32.

50. *nasty* v. G.

52. *take* A quibble; v. G.

cock lever.

up i.e. for firing.

54. *I am...conjure me* i.e. I am no fiend to be exorcised by big words, but a mortal foe.

56. *foul...scour* Quibbles, v. G. Nym's rapier will clean the foul pistol like a ramrod. Mal. notes (on 3. 6. 77):

Pist.'s character seems to have been formed on that of Basilisco, a cowardly braggart in *Solyman and Perseda,* which was performed before 1592. A basilisk was the name of a great gun.

57–9. *in fair terms...in good terms...that's the humour of it.* Nym lards his speech, often nonsensically, with fashionable clichés; the third being the very latest thing, cf. Chapman, *Humourous Day's Mirth,* 1597, Jonson, *Every Man in his Humour,* 1598, and G. 'terms.'

60. *braggart vile* Good, from Pistol! Nym is feline, not 'furious'.

61. *doth gape...doting* eagerly desires...amorous; cf. *2 Hen. IV,* 5. 5. 54.

62. *exhale!* i.e. let swords flash forth (like meteors)! cf. G.

S.D. Q. 'They drawe'. The two men are, I think

intended to draw (and at l. 66, sheathe) their swords sharply and simultaneously, in ludicrous fashion. The second S.D. derives from Collier (ed. ii).

67. *fore-foot* i.e. fore-paw; cf. ll. 41, 73.

71–9. *Couple...enough.* F. prints as prose.

71. *'Couple a gorge'* Cf. 4. 4. 33–8. Pist. airs his (comic) French tag, acquired for the coming campaign.

72. *I thee defy* (Q.) F. 'I defie thee'—compositor's transposition.

73. *hound of Crete* Cf. Golding's trans. of Ovid's *Metamorphoses*, (1565) iii, 247, 'hound of Crete', iii, 267, 'And shaggie Rugge with other twaine that had a syre of Crete'. Nym's hair is clearly a prominent feature; cf. note l. 41.

76. *the lazar...kind* Stock phrase for a whore. Cf. Gascoigne, *Dan Bartholomew*, 1577, l. 69, 'kits of Cressides kind' and O.E.D. 'kit' sb. 4₂. In Henry-son's *Testament* Cresseid becomes 'lyke ane lazarous' (343) and dwells 'at the Spittail hous' (391), as a divine punishment for her infidelity to Troilus.

kit (F4) F. 'kite'. Cf. previous note. Short for 'Katherine', but suggesting claws.

77. *Doll Tearsheet* Cf. *2 Hen. IV*, 2. 4, 5. 4, where she is being haled to prison, 5. 1. 80 (below), and p. 115.

79. *only* v. G.

79–80. *enough. Go to* (Pope) F. 'enough to go to'.

82. *and you,* (Hanmer) F. 'and your'; cf. Greg in *Aspects*, p. 169.

83. *thy face* Cf. *1 Hen. IV*, 3. 3. 24–51.

86. *he'll* i.e. the Boy.

yield...pudding make crow's-meat on the gallows. A proverbial phrase; cf. Apperson, 'crow' 10, and G. 'pudding'.

87. *killed his heart* By the rejection in *2 Hen. IV*, 5. 5. 48 ff. Cf. *Fortunes*, pp. 123–6.

92. *Let floods...howl on!* Let evil (or riot) have its

way and the Devil wait for his prey a little longer. Cf. Spurgeon, *Sh.'s Imagery*, pp. 92–4.

95. *Base...pays* Perhaps proverb. or another tag. Steev. cites Heywood, *Fair Maid of the West* (acted 1617), 'My motto shall be, "Base is the man that pays"' (Works, ed. Pearson, ii. 416) which is perhaps an echo from Pist.

97. *As...compound* As men settle such accounts.

100–1. *Sword...course* Cf. l. 66. For 'sword is an oath' cf. *Ham.* 1. 5. 147 (add. note).

102. *Corporal* (F2) F. 'Coporall'.

104. *put up* sheathe.

105–6. *I shall...betting* (Q., Cap.) F. omits this speech, but Q. prob. gives the sense of it.

107–13. *A noble...hand* (Pope) F. prints as prose.

107–11. *a noble* = 6s. 8d. The 1s. 4d. difference is discount for cash ('present pay'), and there are to be free drinks and pickings from the army catering business as well (v. G. 'sutler').

109. *combine* With 'us' understood.

110. *live by Nym* Quibble on 'nim' = thieve.

116. *that's* (F2) F. 'that'.

117. *come of* (F.) Imperfect tense in south. and mid. dialects. Cf. O.E.D. 'come' col. i, p. 651. Q., F2 'came of' which most edd. read.

118. *Ah* F. 'a'. *shaked* Not a solecism; cf. *Troil.* 1. 3. 101.

119. *quotidian tertian* 'The quotidian and the tertian were intermittent fevers, the paroxysm of the one recurring every day, of the other every other day' (*Sh. Eng.* i. 435). She refers apparently, confusedly, to ague, though some think the 'sweating-sickness' is implied, for which v. Creighton, *History of Epidemics in Britain* (i. 237–64, ii. 310, 311 n. 1). If the latter, Sh. may be slyly fulfilling, in part, the promise of the Epil. to *2 Hen. IV*: 'where (for anything I know) Falstaff shall die of a sweat.' But neither ague nor 'sweat' has anything to do with a broken heart.

121. *run bad humours* = 'vented his ill humour' (M.S.). Cf. *Wives*, 1. 1. 156, 'run the nuthook's humour on me'.

123–4. *Nym...corroborate* (Capell) F. prints as prose.

124. *fracted and corroborate* 'fracted' is as ridiculous as 'fractured' would be in mod. English, and 'corroborate', grand as it sounds, means just the opposite of broken.

126. *passes...careers* = indulges in passions and lets himself go in them. Cf. *2 Hen. IV*, 4. 4. 33–5, but also above, 1. 2. 242–4; v. G. 'pass', 'career'.

127–8. *Let us...will live* = Let's go and sympathize with him, my lambs, for *we* are going to have a good time [after Verity].

2. 2.

Based on Hol. But the irony of the traitors' professions of loyalty and of their advice in the case of the drunkard who railed against the K.'s person, together with the device of the pretended commissions, are Sh.'s additions. No such sc. in *F.V.*

S.D. 'Southampton' (Pope). 'A council-chamber' (Mal.). Cf. 2 Prol. 30, 35, 42 and also l. 91 below.

4. *sat* F. 'sate'.

8. *his bedfellow* i.e. Scroop, cf. Hol., upon whose account of him Sh.'s at ll. 94 ff. is based.

9. *dulled* bored.

favours— F. 'fauours;'.

10. *for a foreign purse* The motive traditionally given, endorsed by Hall and Hol. For the actual motive v. note, ll. 155–7.

11. S.D. 'Trumpets sound' F. 'Sound Trumpets'.

22. *grows...consent* Cf. G. and 1. 2. 181.

30. *galls* Cf. *Lucr.* 889.

33. *forget...hand* Cf. Ps. cxxxvii. 5.

43. *on his more advice* 'when he had come to his senses' (W. M. T. Dodds) [1955]. *his* here and in l. 46

is an objective genitive. Cf. Franz, pp. 289–90 and above, 1. 2. 225, 'to our awe'.

44. *security* v. G.

46. *by his sufferance* 'by neglecting to punish him' (Onions).

49. *Sir* F. prints with l. 50.

53. *heavy orisons* weighty pleas.

54. *faults,* F. 'faults'.

distemper i.e. intoxication; cf. *Ham.* 3. 2. 300–4.

55. *how...eye* how shall we stare.

58. *dear* Ironical and equivocal, v. G.

61. *late* lately appointed.

63. *it* the commission. The K. has pretended to put the government into commission during his absence.

67. *knight,* F. 'Knight:'.

76. *out of appearance* out of sight.

83. *As dogs...masters* Like Actaeon's hounds [Clar.]. Cf. 'monsters' l. 85; Actaeon was transformed into a stag.

87. *him* (F 2) F. omits.

100. *May* can.

102. *might* could

104. *black on white* (J. C. Maxwell) F. 'blacke and white'. Sh.'s sp. 'one' for 'on' misread 'and' [1955].

106. *yoke-devils* Cf. G. 'yoke-fellow'.

107–8. *so grossly...at them* so palpably in a cause natural to them that they excited no surprise. Cf. *A.Y.L.* 3. 2. 193.

111–25. *And whatsoever...Englishman's* Perhaps Sh.'s most vivid glimpse into the infernal regions.

112. *preposterously* v. G. Antithetical to 'in a natural cause' (l. 107).

113. *voice* vote.

114. *All* (Hanmer) F. 'And'.

115–17. *Do botch...piety* 'They tempt a man to commit a damnable deed by patching it up as best they can with the radiant outward shows of piety'

(M.S., who compares 'being fetched' with *1 Hen. IV*, I. 3. 49, 'smarting with my wounds being cold').

118. *tempered thee* 'rendered thee pliable to his will' (Steev.). Cf. *2 Hen. IV*, 4. 3. 127, 'I have him tempering between my finger and my thumb'.

stand up=rebel. Cf. *Lear*, 3. 7. 80; *Caes.* 2. 1. 167 and O.E.D. Stand 103, n. (W. M. T. Dodds) [1955].

120. *Unless...traitor* Unless it was to offer you the title of 'Sir Traitor'.

122. *his lion gait* Cf. 1 Peter v. 8, 'Your adversary the devil, as a roaring lion, walketh about, seeking whom he may devour'. A fine instance of Sh.'s allusive use of the Bible.

123. *vasty Tartar* limitless Tartarus.

124. *the legions* Cf. Mark v. 9.

126. *jealousy infected* suspicion tainted.

134. *complement* v. G.

135. *Not...ear* i.e. listening as well as looking. Cf. *M.V.* 2. 9. 26–8; 3. 2. 63–101 for the fallibility of the eye.

137. *finely bolted* like bread of the finest flour; v. G. 'bolted'.

139. *mark the* (Theo. 'mark'; Pope 'the') F. 'make thee'. A minim-error; cf. MSH. pp. 106–8. The emendation is accepted by most (cf. *Cymb.* 3. 4. 63–6).

147. *Henry* (Q., Theo.) F. 'Thomas'. Prob. caught by the compositor's eye from l. 149.

148. *Masham* (Rowe) F. 'Marſham'.

155–7. *For me...intended* A hint of the real motive of the plot (mentioned as a poss. alternative to Fr. gold by Hall and Hol.; cf. Wylie, i. 513–25), viz. the supplanting of the murdered Henry by Edmund Mortimer, Earl of March, heir of Lionel, Duke of Clarence, who as elder to John of Gaunt was in the direct line from Ed. III (cf. *1 Hen. IV*, table, p. 129 and 1. 3. 80 note); since Mortimer, being childless, would be succeeded by the children of Cambridge, his brother-in-law. As this marks the beginning of the Yorkist claim to the throne, which is the main topic of *Henry VI*, it seems odd that Sh. did not make it more explicit, until we remember that he must avoid anything that casts doubts on the legitimacy of Henry V. Cf. 2. 4. 88 ff.

156. *motive* v. G.

159. *I* (F2) F. omits.

sufferance= suffering.

rejoice i.e. rejoice at.

176. *you have* (Q., Knight) F. 'you' F2 'you three'—which may be right.

178. *wretches* condemned criminals; cf. 1. 2. 244; 2. 2. 53.

181. *dear* v. G.

183. *like* alike.

190. *puissance* A trisyllable.

192. *the signs...advance* raise the standards (Lat. 'signa').

2. 3.

S.D. From Cap.

2. *Staines* i.e. Staines bridge, the first stage on the Southampton road [Clar.].

3, 6. *earn* F. 'erne' F3 'yern'. Edd. read 'yearn', which suggests a misleading sense to mod. readers; cf. 4. 3. 26, and G.

3–6. *No...therefore* (Pope) F. prints as prose. Pist. affects a forced cheerfulness.

4. *vaunting veins* exultant spirit.

7. *wheresome'er* often found in Sh.

9. *Arthur's bosom* For 'Abraham's bosom' v. Luke xvi. 22; *Ric. III*, 4. 3. 38. She fancies perhaps that her knight has joined others at the Round Table.

11. *finer* i.e. 'too fine an end to be now in hell' (Verity).

13. *at the...tide* Acc. to popular belief, as old as Aristotle, persons near the sea died at the turn of the

tide. Cf. *David Copperfield* (death of Mr Barkis). The tide meant very much more to Shakespeare's London than it has since the embanking of the Thames in 1866.

13–16. *fumble...a pen* Traditionally accepted signs. Cf. Lupton, *Thousand Notable Things*, 1578, bk. ix: 'If the foreheade of the sicke waxe redde—and his nose waxe sharpe—if he pull strawes, or the cloathes of his bedde—these are most certain tokens of death.'

15. *finger's end* (Duthie) F. 'fingers end' Q. (and most edd. since Cap.) 'fingers' end'.

16. *as sharp as a pen* i.e. as a goose-quill (dead white) lying point downwards, the 'nib' or 'neb' (=beak) being the nostrils.

and...green fields (Theo.) F. 'and a Table of greene fields'. See Greg, *Emendation* (*Aspects*, pp. 129, 172) for the graphical evidence. The Q. 'and talk of floures', through a perversion of the F. 'and play with flowers', was prob. also influenced by 'babbled'. H. Bradley (O.E.D. 'field' 14) suggested the alternative 'on a table of green field' (=on the green cloth of a counting-house table), continuing the pen-image. I prefer Theobald. Perhaps Sh. wished to hint that Fal. babbled of 'green pastures', i.e. repeated in his delirium the 23rd psalm (got by heart in the days when he ruined his voice in 'singing of anthems') as Ophelia repeated 'old lauds' in hers. Cf. note ll. 36–7.

22–5. *I put my hand...stone* Cf. Plato's account of the death of Socrates in the *Phaedo* (Jowett, 2nd ed., i. 498):

And the man who gave him the poison...pressed his foot hard, and asked him if he could feel; and he said No; and then his leg, and so upwards and upwards, and showed us that he was cold and stiff.

24. *felt to his knees* After this Q. repeats 'and they were as cold as any stone', which Cap. and later edd. follow, unnecessarily. Cf. Greg (p. 172).

up'ard and up'ard F. 'vp-peer'd, and vpward'; the second I take to be normalizing by the compositor.

26. *cry out of sack* v. G. 'cry out of'. A death-bed repentance.

30. *devils* F. 'Deules'. 33. *devil* F. 'Deule'. A Sh. spelling; cf. MSH. p. 116.

36. *rheumatic* She 'prob. means lunatic' (Malone).

36–7. *the whore of Babylon* Can this be a recollection of a babbling of Ps. cxxxvii? Cf. note l. 16.

40. *hell* (F.). All edd. since Cap. read 'hell-fire' with Q. 'I do not think they were justified', Greg (p. 142).

41–2. *the fuel...fire* Cf. *1 Hen. IV*, 3. 3. 43–7.

45–54. *Come, let's away* etc. F. prints as prose. Cap. divided as verse.

47. *Let senses rule* Keep your wits about you [M.S.].
the word...pay our motto is 'cash down'. Cf. G. 'word', 'pitch and pay', and Apperson, p. 498.
word (Q 1, Rowe ii) F. 'world'.

49. *men's...cakes* i.e. promises are like pie-crust; cf. Apperson, 'promise' 3.

50. *hold-fast...dog* Cf. Apperson, p. 63: 'Brag is a good dog, but Hold fast is a better.'

51. *Caveto* v. G. Q. 'Cophetua' (!).

52. *clear thy crystals* Pistolic diction for 'wipe your eyes'.

53–4. *Let us...suck* Cf. 2. 1. 110–12.

55. *And that's...they say* Cf. A. Boorde, *Dyetary*, 1542 (E.E.T.S. extra 10), p. 276: 'The blode of all beestes & fowles is not praysed, for it is hard of digestyon.'

59. *Let...keep close* Be thrifty and don't gad about (or 'keep the house locked up'; cf. *Merch.* 2. 5. 52–5).

2. 4.

S.D. 'The French King's Palace' (Theo.) Rowe added Constable to F. entries and Camb. changed 'Berry' (F.) to 'Berri'. Q. reads 'Bourbon' for F. 'Britaine,' perhaps to save an actor. The historical D. of Brittany played fast and loose with the Fr. King and did not turn up until after Agincourt, v. Wylie, ii. 121–3. The historical Fr. King was subject to fits of madness; but Sh. shows no consciousness of this.

1 *comes the English* Cf. note, 1 Prol. 9.

2–3. *more...defences* it is vitally important that we should put up a first-class defence.

10. *gulf* whirlpool.

12. *late examples* Crécy and Poitiers; cf. ll. 53–62.

13. *fatal and neglected*= fatally despised.

18–19. *But that...collected* The verbs refer to their respective nouns in order.

25. *Whitsun morris-dance* 'The summer feast held usually on May 1 or at Whitsuntide' (Chambers, *Med. Stage*. i. 172–3). Cf. *Wint.* 4. 4. 134 (note); *Two Gent.* 4. 4. 156–66; *All's Well*, 2. 2. 23; and G. 'morris-dance'.

29. *fear...not* she has no terrors in her train.

34. *in exception* when he took exception.

37. *Brutus* (=stupid) He feigned madness when planning to free Rome from the Tarquin tyranny. Cf. *Lucrece*, 1807–17.

45. *So...are filled* 'In this way the forces necessary for defence are fully made up' (M.S.).

46. *Which*=defence.

of a...projection if planned on a weak or niggardly scale.

51. *that bloody strain* that breed of bloodhounds; cf. 'fleshed' (50) and 'haunted' (52).

54. *Cressy...struck* Cf. Hol. p. 551: 'At length

the King approched the river Seine, and...came...
where his great grandfather King Edward the third
a little before had stricken the battell of Cressie' [Clar.].

57. *mountain sire* 'Of more than human proportions'; cf. the Dragon in *F.Q.* 1, xi, 4: 'Where stretcht
he lay uppon the sunny side | Of a great hill, himselfe
like a great hill' [Steev.].

64. *The native...fate* The destiny he inherits.

68–71. *this chase...before them* Continues the
metaphor begun with 'fleshed' (50).

69. *Turn head* v. G. and cf. *1 Hen. VI*, 4. 2. 45 ff.,
esp. 'desperate stags | Turn on the bloody hounds
with heads of steel | And make the cowards stand
aloof at bay'.

79–80. *glories...'longs* Cf. note, 1 Prol. 9.

83. *ordinance of times* usage of past ages, v. G.

85. *awkward* v. G.

86–7. *Picked...raked* v. G. 'pick'. Suggesting (1)
selection, (2) search.

from the worm-holes...oblivion i.e. like the Salic
laws. Nashe has a close verbal parallel (*Pierce Penni-
lesse*, 1592; McKerrow, i. 212) in which he speaks
of plays, a *Henry V* in particular, as being

borrowed out of our English Chronicles, wherein our fore-
fathers valiant acts (that haue line long buried in rustic
brasse and worme-eaten bookes) are reuiued, and they
themselues raised from the Graue of Oblivion, and brought
to pleade their aged Honours in open presence.

88. *memorable line* noteworthy pedigree.

96–7. *what...constraint* Cf. *K. John*, 1. 1. 16–18.

102. *in the bowels of the Lord* A phrase from Hol.
p. 548 (Stone, p. 178).

107. *pining* (Q., Pope and most edd.) F. 'priuy'.
Had F. stood alone Schmidt's explanation, 'the secret
groans of maidens', would be accepted. But 'priuy'
is graphically so close to the Q. 'pining', that it must

yield to the easier reading. Cf. *Tw. Nt.* 2. 4. 112, 'She pined in thought' and Greg, p. 168.

112. *too* (Q., F2) F. 'to'. Cf. MSH. p. 116.

117. *defiance,* (F.) Capell and mod. edd. 'defiance;'. But this is to impede the torrent of scorn that breaks from Ex.'s lips, and to mark a more precise syntactical arrangement than was in Sh.'s mind.

126. *second accent* = echo.

ordinance = ordnance; v. G.

127. *Say:* A significant pause.

129–30. *Nothing...vanity* (Rowe) F. ends l. 129 at 'England'.

131. *Paris-balls* The old word for tennis-balls. Cf. note, 1. 2. 256, and Elmham, *Liber Metricus,* 'pilae Parisianae'.

132–3. *He'll make...Europe* Cf. note 1. 2. 282–3, and Hol. p. 548 (Stone, p. 173):

the K. wrote to him that yer ought long he would tosse him some London balles that perchance should shake the walles of the best court in France.

140. S.D. Dyce transferred 'Flourish' to the end of the sc. and most edd. follow. But Cap. justifies the position in F. by suggesting 'that the Fr. King rises at this point, as dismissing the embassy' and that Exeter 'will not be dismissed' [Duthie].

3 Prologue

F. heads this 'Actus Secundus', v. p. 121.

1–3. *Thus...thought* Cf. *2 Hen. IV,* 4. 3. 33–4; *Ham.* 1. 5. 30; v. G. 'imagined'.

2–3. *In motion...seen* (Rowe's arr.) F. 'In motion...Thought | Suppofe...feene'.

4. *Hampton* (Theo.) F. 'Douer'. Cf. 2 Prol. 30, 35, 42. Theo. blames 'the indolence of a transcriber

or a compositor'; a more probable cause is Sh.'s inadvertence. Cf. note 3. 2. 45.

6. *the young Phœbus fanning* i.e. seen fluttering against the rising sun. Sh. images the fleet 'fanning the hot face of a god' (M.S.). Cf. *Macb.* 1. 2. 49–50.

fanning (Rowe) F. 'fayning'—the word misread 'faining'. Cf. MSH. pp. 106–9.

9. *whistle* i.e. the ship-master's; cf. *Temp.* 1. 1. 6–7. *order* A quibble.

16. *fleet majestical* Of about 1400 ships (*Gesta,* p. 13).

18. *Grapple* As if they were ships.

26. *ordinance* ordnance; cf. note 2. 4. 126.

32. *nimble* Suggests quick firing.

33. S.D. *chambers* v. G.

35. *eche* Cf. Q., *Pericles* 3 Prol. 13 (where it rhymes with 'speech') and Q. *Merch.* 3. 2. 23.

3. 1.

S.D. 'France...Harfleur' (Rowe). F. 'Enter the King, Exeter, Bedford, and Gloucefter. | Alarum: Scaling ladders at Harflew'. Cf. G. 'alarum'.

1. *Once more* etc. (Pope) As two lines in F.

the breach No mention in Hall or Hol. But *Gesta* (pp. 22 ff.) describes the making of the breach in a bulwark specially erected to defend one of the gates and speaks of many assaults being launched upon it. Cf. p. 117.

7. *conjure* (Walter) F. 'commune'. A better conj. than Rowe's 'summon' hitherto accepted. [1955.]

8. *fair nature* kindly feeling; cf. G. 'nature'.

12–13. *as fearfully...base* as dreadfully as the worn rock overhangs and projects beyond its ruined base.

15. *nostril* F. 'Nosthrill'.

16. *bend up* v. G.

17. *noblest English* (F2) F. 'Noblifh Englifh'. Henry addresses the gentry first.

18. *of war-proof* tested in war. Another allusion to the wars of Ed. III; cf. 1. 2. 106 ff.

19. *Alexanders* Sighing for more worlds to conquer.

21. *argument* i.e. foes to fight with; v. G. and cf. 4. 2. 23.

22. *Dishonour* etc. Do not cast doubts on your paternity by playing the coward.

24. *men* (F4) F. 'me'.

25. *yeomen* v. G. They supplied the longbowmen, which proved irresistible at Crécy, Poitiers and Agincourt; cf. Trevelyan, *Hist. of Eng.* pp. 226–9.

27. *the mettle...pasture* 'the quality of your rearing' (M.S.). Referring to the grazing of sheep and cattle.

31. *greyhounds in the slips* Cf. Sh.'s Addition to *Sir Thomas More*, l. 122, 'slip him like a hound'.

32. *straining* (Rowe) F. 'straying'. Cf. MSH. pp. 106–9; note, 3 Prol. 6.

33. *follow your spirit* Cf. 1. 2. 128–9.
upon this charge when you make this charge.

33–4. *charge...George!* Note the rhyme.

3. 2.

4. *case* set, v. G.

5. *plain-song* i.e. simple truth, v. G.

6–10, 13–19. F. prints as prose; Capell arr. as verse. Generally supposed to be snatches of ballads, now lost.

8–10. *sword and shield...Doth* Cf. note, 1 Prol. 9.

18. *truly*= (*a*) honourably, (*b*) in tune.

19. S.D. For Fluellen v. pp. 116 ff.

22–5. *Be...sweet chuck!* (Pope) F. as prose.

22. *men of mould* 'poor mortal men' (J.); cf. 'clayman', *2 Hen. IV*, 1. 2. 7.

25. *bawcock...chuck* Characteristic bathos after 'great duke' [Duthie].

26–7. *These...bad humours* Nym addresses Pist. first and then Flu. ('your honour').

29–32. *all they three...to a man* the three of them together, even if they were my servants instead of my being theirs, could not be as much of a man as I am (with a quibble on 'man'=servant); for indeed three such scarecrows don't equal one man.

34–5. *a killing...sword* Cf. *2 Hen. IV*, 2. 4. 92 ff.

35. *breaks words*=(*a*) exchanges words (cf. *Err.* 3. 1. 75), (*b*) breaks promises.

37. *best* bravest.

42. *purchase* v. G.

45. *Calais* How Nym and Bard. had come from Calais, towards which they would soon be marching (cf. 3. 3. 56), we are not told. Perhaps Sh.'s inadvertence; cf. note, 3 Prol. 4, and pp. 114–16.

46. *service* i.e. military service; cf. *2 Hen. IV*, 1. 2. 146, 'Your day's service at Shrewsbury'.

would carry coals would prove cowards, v. G. 'carry coals'.

50. *pocketing up of wrongs*=(*a*) appropriating ill-gotten goods, (*b*) submitting to insults.

53. *cast it up*=throw it up (in two senses).

57–8. *the mines is...war* Cf. p. 118 and *Gesta*, pp. 24–5, 'Sed opus hoc, contra doctrinam magistri Aegidii, in conspectu hostium...inchoatum' etc.

58. *the disciplines of the war* Cf. ll. 70, 79, 94, 98, 126, 135. Cf. the *De re militari veterum* of Master Giles (v. p. 118) and *A Briefe Discourse of Warre* (1590) by Sir Roger Williams, which is chiefly concerned with military discipline and tactical theory (v. pp. ix, 118).

60–1. *is digt...counter-mines* i.e. in Flu.'s peculiar dialect, 'the enemy has digged himself *counter-mines* four yards under the *mines*' (J.).

62. *plow...better* F. is not consistent with Flu.'s b's and p's. 'The poet thought it sufficient to mark his diction a little and in certain places only' (Cap.);

relying no doubt on the actor to do the rest. Cf. note
4. 1. 70.

63–4. *The Duke...given* Cf. Hol. p. 549; Stone,
p. 180: 'The duke of Glocester, to whom the order
of the siege was committed.'

66. *It is Captain Macmorris* etc. From here to the
end of the sc. Flu.'s speeches are headed 'Welch' to
correspond with 'Irish' and 'Scot' for Macmorris and
Jamy. Cf. p. 115.

69. *verify* prove.

in his beard to his face.

75. *expedition* v. G. A term in rhetoric.

76. *ancient* F. 'aunchiant'. This and 'aunchient'
which F. gives at 3. 6. 12, 17, 29, 49, 51 and 4. 1. 67,
and edd. retain, are almost certainly Sh.'s spellings. Cf.
'auncient' *M.N.D.* (Q.) 1. 1. 42 etc. and 'aunchentry'
Ado (Q.), 2. 1. 69.

77. *directions* i.e. the pedantic instructions he gives
his troops.

100. *gud* An amusing word in a Scot's mouth,
four times spoken [M.S.].

101. *quit you* 'requite you, that is, answer you, or
interpose my arguments' (J.).

105–7. *it is no time...nothing* (F. punct.) Mod.
edd. (except Ridley) 'it is no time to discourse. The
town is besieged, and...the breach; and we...do
nothing'.

106. *beseeched*= besieged.

109. *an* F. 'and'—the usual spelling [Duthie].

110. *Chrish* F. 'Christ'. Cf. note l. 62.

111. *these* F. 'theise'. A normal MS. sp. (not a
dialect pron.). Cf. *Sh.'s Hand*, pp. 125–6.

112–13. *ay'll...ay'll...ay'll* F. 'ayle...Ile...
Ile'. Cf. note l. 62.

115. *hear* (Camb.) F. 'heard' ('heare'. Cf. MSH.
p. 109).

119. *nation!* Note this display of national touchiness.

124–5. *as in discretion* A veiled threat! [Duthie].
use=treat.

127. *the derivation* Cf. Earle, *Microcosmographie*,
1628 [A Herald]. 'In Wales...they are born with
Heraldry in their mouths, and each name is a pedigree'
[Verity].

130. *you will* you are determined to.

131. *Ah!* F. 'A', Sh.'s usual spelling.

134. *required*=acquired [Duthie].

3. 3.

S.D. F. gives Gov. an entry at l. 43; perhaps because
he 'doubled' with a character in 3. 2. Cap. reads
'Governor and others, upon the walls; below, the
English Forces. Flourish. Enter' etc.

1–43. *How yet resolves* etc. Nothing corr. to this
speech in Hall, Hol. or Stow. Clearly based on *Gesta*,
p. 21 (trans. Nicholas, p. 106):

Our King who sought peace, not war, in order that he
might further arm the cause in which he was engaged
with the shield of justice, according to the law of Deuteronomy, chap. xx, offered peace to the besieged, if they
would open the gates to him.

And later *Gesta* (pp. 29–30; Nicholas, pp. 122–3)
relates that the town surrendered partly through fear
of 'the penalties of the law of Deuteronomy'. Now
Henry's speech is merely an elaboration of Deut. xx.
10–14, which ordains 'how to use the cities that
accept or refuse the proclamation of peace', while,
though dreadful to modern ears, it no doubt reflects
the fate of besieged towns in Sh.'s own day. Cf.
Wylie, ii. 59.

4. *proud of destruction* 'elated with the thought of
death' (M.S.).

10. *the gates...shut up* Cf. 'Open Thy gate of

mercy, gracious God' (*3 Hen. VI*, 1. 4. 177). Gray echoes this in l. 68 of the *Elegy*: 'And shut the gates of mercy on mankind.'

12. *liberty* licence.

13. *wide* (*a*) loose, (*b*) gaping, v. G.

16–18. *Arrayed...desolation?* Cf. 'hellish Pyrrhus' (*Ham*. 2. 2. 456–67), a development of the present passage.

18. *Enlinked...desolation?* 'concomitant to the sack of cities' (J.).

25. *in their spoil* in the act of sacking.

26–7. *As...ashore* (Rowe) F. divides 'aſhore | Therefore'.

26. *precépts* Not the same as 'précepts'; v. G. Cf. Job xli. 1–4.

32. *heady* (F 3) F. 'headly'.

34. *blind* v. G. and 5. 2. 300.

35. *defile* (Rowe ii) F. 'deſire'.

40. *break* pierce.

54. *all. For us* (Pope) F. 'all for vs,'.

55. *sickness* 'The number of his people was much minished by the flix [flux] and other feuers' (Hol. p. 550), being actually reduced to under 6000 (*Gesta*, p. 36).

56. *retire to Calais* Cf. Hol. p. 550 (Stone, pp. 181–2), who explains that to return home might 'of slanderous toongs be named as running away'. Cf. also Wylie, ii. 73–5.

3. 4.

S.D. 'Rouen...palace' (Mal.) F. 'Enter Katherine and an old Gentlewoman'.

The scene is...mean enough, when it is read; but the grimaces of two French women, and the odd accent with which they uttered the English made it divert upon the stage. (J.)

No doubt too the boys, who were making a contemporary success of *A.Y.L.* in the parts of Rosalind and Celia, would play it well. In the French, which here and in later scenes has been 'set right or nearly so by successive' editors, I follow Camb. on the whole and omit, except a selection for illustrative purposes, the F. readings. If we allow for Sh.'s handwriting, for the F. compositor's ignorance of Fr., for phonetic spellings to help the boy players, and for the occurrence of early mod. Fr. forms, it is doubtful whether there was orig. very much wrong with Sh.'s Fr. except the genders. But cf. notes on 3. 4. 39; 3. 7. 14; 4. 4. 54.

1. *été* F. 'este'. Early mod. Fr.; cf. 'escholier' (l. 13), 'vistement' (l. 14), 'escoute' (l. 16), 'dict' (l. 18), 'apprins' (l. 24) etc.

7. *La main...de hand* F. 'Le main il & appelle de Hand'. Poss. 'est' written 'et' phonetically and set up '&' in error as at 5. 2. 191; 'appelle' intended to be trisyllabic; and 'de'=a Fr. pronunciation of 'the'.

8. *Et les doigts?* F. gives this to Alice, ll. 9–11 to Kath., and ll. 12–13 (as far as 'écolier') to Alice. Theobald rectified.

10. *souviendrai* F. 'souememeray'. Poss. < sovendray (minim+e : d misreading).

13. *gagné* F. 'gaynie'. Obvious phonetic sp.; cf. F. 'desia' for 'déjà' (l. 39).

15. *nailès* F. 'Nayles'; cf. note l. 42.

39. *N'avez...déjà* F. 'N'aue vos y desia'. What the 'y' denotes is hard to say.

42. *mailès* F. 'Maylees'. Here F. clearly denotes a disyllabic pron., a natural error for Fr. speakers. Hence we may assume that F. 'nailes' (ll. 15–17, etc.) should be so also [Duthie].

45. *Sauf votre honneur* F. 'Sans vostre honeus'—'vostre'=sixteenth cent. Fr.; 'sans' and 'honeus' obvious misprints.

49. *foot* cf. 'foutre' (*2 Hen. IV*, 5. 3. 101, 118).

50. *ils* F. 'il'.

3. 5.

S.D. F. 'Enter the King of France, the Dolphin, the Conſtable of France, and others'. Q. gives entry for 'Burbon' which Theo., Camb., etc. follow, and acc. give speeches ll. 10, 32, headed 'Brit.' in F., to 'Bour.'. But Q.'s 'Burbon' is the pirate's substitution for 'Britain' (cf. S.D. 2. 4). Hol. names 'Berrie and Britaine' (not 'Bourbon') among those of the Fr. K.'s council (v. Hol. p. 552; Stone, p. 182) [Duthie]. The attitude of the Fr., here represented, is true to history; cf. Wylie, ii. 123–4.

1. *passed the river Somme* On his hurried march to Calais, v. 3. 3. 55–6.

5. *sprays of us* i.e. bastards, begotten by Norman French on the 'wild and savage' Anglo-Saxon stock.

6. *emptying...luxury* v. G.

7. *savage* v. G.

9. *grafters* v. G.

11. *Mort Dieu!* (Greg) F. 'Mort du' Q. 'Mor deu'. Cf. note 4. 5. 3.

12. *Unfought withal* From Hol. [Price, p. 32].

14. *nook-shotten* 'running out into corners or angles' (O.E.D.). Cf. letter by Allen Mawer (*T.L.S.* 25/7/'35) for a field with nine corners at Stoneleigh, Warwickshire, called 'Nookshotten Close' down to 1830. A term of contempt, denoting shapelessness, while 'shotten' (cf. G. *1 Hen. IV*) implies worthlessness.

15. *where*=whence.

17. *whom* 'They' (antecedent) understood.

18–19. *sodden...broth* The wine-drinking Frenchman's idea of beer, which, like the mash given to overdriven horses, is largely composed of malt. Cf. Const.'s reference to 'stale drinke' (note 3. 7. 147–53). For 'sur-reined jades' cf. 'ouer-ridden jades' (*Ed. III, 3. 3. 162*), cited in the same note.

23. *roping* Cf. 'down-roping', 4. 2. 48.

26. *Poor...lords* i.e. if we do, then the fields are not rich but poor in the mettle of their pasture (cf. 3. 1. 26–7).

may (F2) F. omits. I conj. 'must we' for 'we may'.

32. *They bid...schools* They bid us go and teach dancing to the English.

35. *lofty* stylish, v. G.

39. *hie* (F4) F. 'high'.

40–5. *Charles...Charolois* All but two of these are taken from Hol.'s list of the 'cheefest nobilitie' slain at Agincourt; the exceptions (Berri and Charolois) occur elsewhere in his account of the battle.

Delabreth=D'Albret.

44. *Faulconbridge* (F.) Cf. 4. 8. 100. Cap. substitutes 'Fauconberg' from Hol.'s list (v. note ll. 40–5), but Hol. himself spells the name 'Fauconbridge' a page before, and Sh. has that form in *L.L.L.* (2. 1. 42, 203), *K. John*, 1. 1. 52 etc.

45. *Foix* (Cap.) F. 'Loys'. Hol. 'Fois'.

Lestrake (Hol.) F. 'Leſtrale'.

46. *Knights* (Pope and Theob.) F. 'Kings'.

52. *The Alps...upon* Cf. 'Juppiter hibernas cana nive conspuit Alpes', an absurd line burlesqued by Horace (*Sat*. ii. 5. 41) [Steev.]. J. says: 'The poet has here defeated himself by passing too soon from one image to another' and speaks of 'the grossness' of this line. But is not the image (borrowed from the line laughed at by Horace) deliberately placed in the Fr. K.'s mouth to render him ridiculous?

his the Alps taken as sing.

54. *chariot captive* (P. A. Daniel) F. 'Captiue Chariot'. Cf. Hol. p. 554 (Stone, p. 182): 'The noble man had deuised a chariot wherein they might triumphantlie conueie the king captiue to the citie of Paris.' Something of the Mussolini touch.

60. *for achievement* instead of victory (cf. O.E.D.

'achievement' 2) W. M. T. Dodds (*M.L.R.* 1947, p. 500) interprets 'in order to bring the war to an end' [1955].

64–6. *Prince...with us* Cf. Hol. p. 552. Sh. evidently forgets this when he brings the Dauphin to Agincourt; v. 3. 7. S.D. (note).

3. 6.

S.D.F. 'Enter Captaines, Englifh, and Welch, Gower and Fluellen'. Mod. edd., after Cap. and Mal., head the sc. 'The English camp in Picardy'. Cf. note l. 2.

2. *the bridge* Over the Ternoise. Cf. Stone, p. 183. An English patrol seized this bridge on 23 Oct. Henry and his army crossed it on 24 Oct., the night before Agincourt. The scene takes place between these events.

5. *Exeter* Left behind by Sh. at Harfleur (3. 3. 51–3); but, as Hol. explains, Ex. left Sir John Fastolfe in charge and himself took part in the battle at Agincourt. For obvious reasons, Sh. did not wish to mention 'Fastolfe'. [Cf. Price, pp. 32–3.]

12. *ancient lieutenant* Usually thought an error; but v. G. and note, 2. 1. 38.

20–1. *Captain,*etc. F. prints Pist.'s speeches throughout the sc. as prose; Cap. arranged as verse.

25. *buxom* v. G.

30–1. *painted blind...is blind* (F., Q.) The agreement confirms the repetition.

37. *moral* v. G.

38. *Fortune...on him* Ref. to the ballad 'Fortune, my foe! Why dost then frown on me' [Staunton]. Cf. *Wives,* 3. 3. 60–1.

39. *pax* (F., Q. 'packs') Agreement of F. and Q. proves that 'pax' was spoken on the stage. Prob. an error of Sh.'s. Cf. Wylie, ii. 116–17 and Hol. p. 552 (Stone, p. 184): 'a souldier took a pix out of a church, for which he was apprehended, &...strangled.' Pix=a box of consecrated wafers; pax, v. G.

44. *pax of little price* Clearly derived from *Gesta*, p. 41:

Et adductus est regi in campo illo quidam praedo Anglicus, qui contra Deum et edictum regium pixidem de cupro deaurato, *quam forte credebat auream,* in qua erat reconditum corpus Dominicum, ab ecclesia delatam repertam in manica rapuisset [italics mine].

47. *With edge...cord* The penny cord serves for the shears of Atropos.

50. *Why...therefore* A Pistolic cliché; cf. *2 Hen. IV,* 5. 3. 111.

57. S.D. Cf. G. 'fig' and *Rom.* 1. 1. 48–58.

58. *Very good* (F.) Q. 'Captain Gour, cannot you hear it lighten & thunder?'—perhaps actor's gag.

69. *services* Cf. l. 3 and G.

71. *came off* Cf. G. and *2 Hen. IV,* 2. 4. 48.

72. *what terms...on* how the enemy was situated.

73. *war, which* F. 'Warre; which'.

74. *new-tuned* v. G.

75. *horrid suit* Cf. 'diffused attire', 5. 2. 61.

81. *find...coat*=catch him out, cf. G. 'hole'.

83. *from*=about.

S.D. 'his poor soldiers', i.e. Sh. directs that the audience shall see for themselves how 'sick and famished' (3. 5. 57) and ill-clad (v. 4. 8. 72) is the 'ruined band' (4 Prol. 29) that Henry leads towards Agincourt. Yet all edd. omit 'poor'! Did the 'scarecrows' that Fal. led to Shrewsbury return to the stage? Q. gives an entry for Gloucester, who speaks at l. 166.

100. *flames afire* F. 'flames a fire'.

102. *his nose is executed* i.e. slit as he stood in the pillory, before being hanged.

102–3. *his fire*=its fire.

105–10. *we give...winner* Cf. Hol. p. 552, and Introd. p. xxxiii.

109. *lenity* (Q., Rowe) F. 'Leuitie'.

111. *habit* i.e. his herald's tabard coat.

120. *bruise an injury* squeeze out an abscess; v. G.

121. *upon our cue* i.e. it's our turn to take part in this dialogue!

122. *England* i.e. Henry.

123. *admire our sufferance* wonder at our forbearance.

126–7. *in weight...under* 'fully to compensate would be too much for his small resources' (M.S.).

135–6. *What is...Montjoy.* Montjoy is not a name, as Sh. implies, but the title of the chief herald of France (in fact, a 'quality'), borrowed from 'Montjoy St Denis!' the French K.'s war-cry (Wylie, ii. 178 n. 4).

138–60. *And tell...Discolour* An expansion of Hol. p. 552 (Stone, p. 185):

Mine intent is to doo as it pleaseth God: *I will not seeke* your maister at this time; but, if he or his seeke me, I will meet with them, God willing. If anie of your nation attempt once to stop me in my iournie now towards Calis, at their ieopardie be it; and yet wish I not anie of you so vnaduised, as to be the occasion that I die *your tawnie ground with your red blood* [italics mine].

142. *of craft and vantage* who has cunning and the initiative in his favour.

156. *there's for thy labour* 'He gaue him a princelie reward' (Hol.).

166–7. *I hope...theirs* Cf. Introd. p. xxxix.

3. 7.

S.D. Theobald and mod. edd. 'The French camp near Agincourt'. Sh. has no support in history, chronicle or *F.V.* for the Dauphin's presence, which is moreover contradicted by 3. 5. 64–6. T. Johnes (trans. Monstrelet, iv. pp. 410–11) conj. that the mention by Hol. (pp. 553, 555) of Sir Guichard Dauphin among the Fr. nobles at Agincourt gave rise to this confusion; cf. P. A. Daniel, Introd. to *Parallel Texts of Hen. V* (1877), p. xiii. But as Price (p. 34) notes Sh. was obliged for dramatic reasons to humiliate the braggart of the tennis-balls at Agincourt.

1 ff. *the best armour of the world* etc. This French bragging about armour and horses, which has no counterpart in Hol. or Hall, seems to reflect the following words of Tito Livio:

> The Frenchmen had so much…confidence in the great multitude of theire people, in theire shyning armor and beauteous, and in there great and mightie horses, that manie of theire greate Princes and Lords leauinge behinde them there seruants and souldiers…came towards the Englishmen in right greate hast, as if they had bin assured of victorie. (Eng. trans. in *First Life*, p. 55.) Cf. note 4. 2. 60.

12. *pasterns* (F 2) F. 'poftures'. Prob. *a* : *o* + minim missp. > 'pasturnes'.

13. *Ça, ha!* (Theo.) F. 'ch' ha'.

13–14. *as if…hairs* i.e. as if he were a tennis-ball, stuffed with hair [Warb.].

14–15. *chez…feu* = with fiery nostrils. Sh.n French.

17. *the pipe of Hermes* v. G. 'Hermes'.

20. *pure…fire* Cf. *Ant.* 5. 2. 292 and above, note, 1 Prol. 1.

23. *beasts* Mal. explains: 'The general term for quadrupeds may suffice for all other horses.'

26. *palfreys* v. G. An error, unless we are to suppose the effeminate Dauphin riding a lady's horse into battle.

31. *lodging* v. G.

vary v. G. and *L.L.L.* 4. 2. 8–9, 'the epithets are sweetly varied'.

32–3. *fluent as the sea* Cf. *Ant.* 1. 4. 46, 'the varying tide'.

35. *reason* discourse.

36. *the world* all humanity.

39. *"Wonder of nature"* So Rollo addresses Edith in Fletcher's *Bloody Brother*, 5. 2. 36 (Mr Percy Simpson, privately).

44. *bears well* carries her riders well. For the jesting that follows, cf. *2 Hen. IV*, 2. 4. 57 (note), *Shrew*, 2. 1. 200 ff. and next two notes.

52. *rode* Cf. *2 Hen. IV*, 2.1.78–9; 2.2. 165, 166–7 (notes).

52–3. *Your French hose…strossers.* Cf. G. 'The Irish strait trossers… being made extremely tight, Sh. has here employed the words in an equivocal sense' (Mal.).

59–60. *wears his own hair* Cf. *Merch.* 3. 2. 92–6.

63–4. *Le chien…bourbier* 2 Pet. ii. 22 (The French is from the Huguenot Bible).

la truie (Rowe) F. 'la leuye'.

64–5. *thou…thing* you will say anything to score a point.

69. *to-night*=last night.

stars Cf. Sidney, *Ast. & Stella* (civ): 'If I but stars upon my armour bear' [Steev.].

77. *dismounted*=taken down a peg.

81–2. *faced…way*=put to shame.

83. *about…the English* A more modest hope than the Dauphin's.

84–5. *go to hazard* etc. Cf. 4 Prol. 19 and Hol. p. 554 (Stone, p. 186), 'the soldiers the night before had plaid the Englishmen at dice'.

91. *eat…kills* Cf. *Ado*, 1. 1. 39–42.

94. *tread out* i.e. treat it with the contempt it deserves; cf. O.E.D. 'foot' 33. 98. *doing* v. G.

110. *but his lackey* i.e. he has tried his valour on nobody else; 'he has beaten nobody but his footboy' (J.).

110–11. *'tis a hooded…bate.* I.e. it is never very obvious, and when it does show itself (e.g. 'in the field') it rapidly dwindles. All this is conveyed in a metaphor from falconry: the hawk is hooded before action, and when unhooded 'bates' (=flutters) a little before flight.

112–14. *Ill will...friendship* For these and the other proverbs, v. Apperson, pp. 326, 219, etc.

120. *the better...by how much*=all the better... in that.

122. *over* wide; lit. over the target.

123. *overshot* beaten at a match.

125. *fifteen hundred paces* Hol. says 250 paces; Monstrelet, about 3 bowshots.

132–3. *mope...knowledge* cf. *Temp.* 5. 1. 240, and G.

134. *apprehension* (*a*) intelligence, (*b*) fear.

140. *mastiffs* Famous throughout Europe for bull- or bear-baiting.

147–53. *give them...to fight* Cf. words from the Oration of the Constable (Hall, p. 66; not in Hol.):

Kepe an Englishman one moneth from his warme bed, fat befe and stale drynke [cf. 3. 5. 18–20], and let him that season tast colde and suffre hunger, you then shall se his courage abated.

Also reflected in *Ed. III*, 3. 3. 159 ff.:

Such as, but scant them of their chines of beefe
And take away their downie feather bedes,
And presently they are as resty stiffe,
As twere a many ouer ridden jades.

150–1. *shrewdly out of beef* Historically correct; v. Wylie, ii. 114, 128 (fin.).

4 Prologue

Sh.'s imperishable picture of the two armies on St Crispin's Eve is historically accurate in detail; cf. Wylie, ii. 136–9, and 'The night...was dark and...it poured with rain' (Wylie, ii. 215).

1. *entertain conjecture* imagine.

2. *poring dark* darkness that strains the eyes, v. G.

3. *the wide vessel* Cf. 'that inverted bowl we call the sky' (Fitzgerald's *Omar*).

8. *fire answers fire* Hol. p. 552: 'fiers were made to

giue light on euerie side, as there likewise were in the
French host.'

9. *battle* army.

umbered shadowy, v. G.

13. *rivets* Some rivets were closed after the armour
was on, e.g. that fastening the bottom of the helmet to
the top of the cuirass (Douce, *Illustrations of Sh.* i. 501).

14. *note* (*a*) warning, (*b*) sound.

16. *name* (Tyrwhitt) F. 'nam'd'.

17. *secure* v. G.

19. *Do...dice* Cf. note 3. 7. 84–5.

23. *sacrifices* doomed victims; cf. *1 Hen. IV*,
4. 1. 113.

25. *gesture sad* serious air.

26. *Investing* Many suspect corruption. But =(I
think) 'dignifying' (lit. 'clothing with dignity,' O.E.D.
4); suggested to Sh. by 'sad'=grave, solemn.

27. *Presenteth* (Hanmer) F. 'Preſented'.

the gazing moon Cf. *Ham*. 1. 4. 53.

36. *enrounded* 'Hopelessly enmeshed', Wylie, ii.
132.

38. *all-watchéd* sleepless throughout.

39. *overbears attaint* suppresses the slightest sign
of weariness or exhaustion, v. G. 'attaint'.

46–7. *define,* | *A...night.* (F2) 'define. A...
Night,'.

46. *as may...define* i.e. as I hope my poor pen
and we poor players may be able to make clear in what
follows. Cf. Introd. pp. xiii–xv.

49. *O for pity!* The nearer Sh. draws to the great
battle itself the more he despairs of his capacity to
represent it.

50. *four or five...foils* Cf. Sidney, *Apology* (Gregory
Smith, *Eliz. Crit. Essays*, i, p. 197):

Two Armies flye in represented with foure swords and
bucklers, and then what harde heart will not receiue it
for a pitched fielde?

4. 1.

S.D. Theobald and mod. edd. 'The English camp at Agincourt'.

3. *Good* (F2) F. 'God'.

4. *There is...evil* Playful rather than profoundly serious, as the context shows; yet there is deep feeling in the words.

6. *bad neighbour* i.e. likely to be up to his tricks while we sleep.

7. *husbandry* v. G.

9. *all,* F. 'all;'.

10. *dress us...end* Cf. Monstrelet, p. 170:

The English...notwithstanding they were much fatigued and oppressed by cold, hunger, and other discomforts,...made their peace with God, by confessing their sins with tears, and numbers of them taking the sacrament; for...they looked for certain death on the morrow.

18–23. *'Tis good...legerity* Cf. Introd. p. xxxviii. Perhaps an aside [M.S.].

23. *With casted slough* Cf. *Tw. Nt.* 2. 5. 152–3. The snake is torpid before casting.

31–2. *I and...company* This connects with l. 10 and seems to lead up to a prayer, which we get at ll. 285–301. Cf. p. 116.

34. *God-a-mercy* I thank thee.

35. *Qui va là?* (Rowe) F. 'Che vous la?' Q. 'Ke ve la?' Cf. Greg (p. 169). F. prints Pist.'s speeches as prose; Pope rearranged.

39. *gentleman of a company* v. *1 Hen. IV*, 4. 2. 24, and G.

In those days gentlemen volunteers worked their way up from the ranks, and more than one peer trailed a pike in the regiments of Maurice of Nassau. (Fortescue, *Sh. Eng.* i. 115.)

Infantry consisted of pikemen and musketeers.

45. *imp of Fame*=child of Renown; cf. *2 Hen. IV*, 5. 5. 43.

65. *fewer* (F.) Q. 'lewer' (=missp. 'fewer') Q3 'lower' (=corr. 'lewer'). Mal. and most mod. edd. follow Q3. 'Speak fewer'='Don't talk so much!' And 'all the time it is Flu. who babbles, while Gower can hardly get a word in edgeways' (Greg, pp. 143–4). Cf. Hol. p. 552 (Stone, p. 187): 'Order was taken...that no noise or clamor should be made in the host.'

70. *pibble pabble* (Theo.) F. 'pibble bable'. Cf. note 3. 2. 62.

75. *the enemy is loud* Cf. *Gesta*, p. 48, 'audivimus adversariam hospitatam, et unumquemque, ut moris est, vociferantem' etc. Hol. merely says, the enemy 'made great cheare, and were verie merie, pleasant, and full of game'.

83. *out of fashion* eccentric.

85 ff. *Brother John Bates* etc. Most of this dialogue can be very entertaining on the stage. Hazlitt liked it 'exceedingly', and J. wrote of ll. 146–82: 'the whole argument is well followed, and properly concluded.' For the soldiers' mood, cf. note l. 10.

94. *Thomas* (Theobald) F. 'Iohn'. Yet Sh. has it correctly at l. 24. The inconsistency arises perhaps from the two passages being written at different times. Cf. p. 116.

97–8. *wracked...tide* i.e. doomed to-morrow.

102–3. *the element shows* the sky looks.

104–6. *conditions...ceremonies...affections* v. G.

106–7. *mounted...stoop* Terms of falconry, v. G.

109. *in reason* 'in all fairness' (M.S.).

115–16. *quit here* done with this job.

125. *minds. Methinks* (Rowe) F. 'minds, me thinks'.

129–32. *Ay, or more...us* As Bates is a grouser, Cap. and Mal. would transfer this to Court, who has no speech in F. except ll. 85–6.

132. *us* Emphatic.

137. *place; some* (Rowe) F. 'place, ſome'.

140. *well* i.e. a Christian death.

141. *charitably* 'in good-will to all men' (M.S.).

144. *who* (F.) F 2 'whom'—which most edd. read.

144–5. *against...subjection* entirely contrary to the principles that govern a subject's duties. Cf. 2. 2. 109.

154. *bound to answer* responsible for.

162. *the broken...perjury* Cf. *Meas.* 4. 1. 6, *Son.* 142. 7.

167. *beadle* i.e. chastiser; cf. *2 Hen. IV*, 5. 4. 5.

168. *before* previous. Parallel with 'now' l. 169.

174–5. *Every subject's...own* 'This is a very just distinction' (J.).

177. *mote* (Mal.) F. 'Moth'—Sh. sp. Cf. *L.L.L.* 4. 3. 158 (note).

180–1. *so free an offer* a free-will offering.

187–8. *I myself...ransomed* Cf. Hol. p. 553 (Stone, p. 190 n. 2): 'assuring them that England should neuer be charged with his ransome' (from 'K. Henries oration to his men').

194. *You pay him then!* Well, *you* pay him out then, if he breaks it!

195. *a poor and a private* i.e. of a poor commoner. Cf. ll. 233–4.

221–5. *Indeed...clipper.* Three points here: (i) the Fr. greatly outnumber the English, (ii) a quibble on crowns = (*a*) heads, (*b*) coins (v. G.), which were often clipped by the debasers of coinage, (iii) such 'coining' (cf. *Lear*, 4. 6. 83) came under the law of treason.

226 ff. *Upon the king!* etc. J. comments in a self-revealing note:

There is something very striking and solemn in this soliloquy....Reflection and seriousness rush upon the mind upon the separation of a gay company, and specially after forced and unwilling merriment.

Hen.'s theme had been already developed by his father
at *2 Hen. IV*, 3. 1. 4–31 and by himself as Prince, *ibid.*
4. 5. 21–31. But while 'remorse and fear helped to
drive sleep from Bol.'s eyes', it is an 'overwhelming
sense of responsibility' that keeps Hen. V awake
[Boas, v. *supra*, p. xxxii n. 2.]. Cf. Daniel, *Civil Wars*
(1595), iii. 65, 66, for a close parallel.

227. *careful* v. G.

229–33. *O hard...enjoy!* Lined as by Camb.
F. divides 'We...all; | O...Greatneſſe, | Subiect...
ſence | No...winging. | What...neglect, | That...
enioy?'

232. *wringing*=belly-ache, v. G.

241. *What! Is...adoration?* (W. M. T. Dodds)
F. 'What? is thy Soule of Odoration?' i.e. 'What!
Does thy essence consist merely in being adored?' This
scornful question agrees with the context. See G. 'soul'
and *M.L.R.* xlii. pp. 498–9 [1955].

249. *Thinks* (F.) Rowe and subs. edd. 'Think'st'.
The 't' of the 2nd pers. sing. is often omitted by Sh.
Cf. MSH. p. 291.

249–50. *the fiery...adulation?* that you can blow
out the fires of fever with the windy praises of flattery?
Cf. 'blown', G. and next note.

259. *farcèd title* 'the tumid puffy titles with which
a king's name is always introduced' (J.), v. G.

260–1. *the tide...world* Cf. Introd. p. xlvi. Combines the images in *Son.* 60. 1; 64. 5–6 with that of
'high majesty' (*All's Well*, 2. 1. 113; *Ric. II*, 2. 1.
295, etc.).

262. *ceremony*, F. 'Ceremonie;'; v. G.

266–9. *distressful bread...Sweats* Cf. Gen. iii. 17,
'In sorrow shalt thou eat', and 19, 'In the sweat of
thy face shalt thou eat bread'.

268. *like a lackey* i.e. always on the run; v. G.
O.E.D. cites Munday, *Silvayn's Orator*, 1596, p. 354:
'How manie Noble men doe burst their lacquise
legs with running.'

275. *Winding up*=wholly absorbing, v. G.

276. *Had the fore-hand* Would have the pull of.

277. *member* sharer. Cf. *Oth.* 3. 4. 112.

280. *best advantages* turns to greatest profit; cf. l. 273 and *Ric. III*, 4. 4. 323: 'Advantaging their loan with interest' [Arden].

281. *jealous of* disturbed by.

282–4. *Good...thee* (Pope) F. divides 'Good... together | At...thee'. Perhaps a link-passage in the MS., cf. note ll. 31–2.

285 ff. *O God of battles* etc. For this speech, cf. Introd. *1 Hen. IV*, pp. xxv f., *Hen. V*, p. xl.

287. *reck'ning, or...numbers* (M.S.) F. 'reckning of...numbers:' Camb. and most mod. edd. (Tyrwhitt conj.) 'reckoning, if...numbers'. [Here *or*=ere (cf. O.E.D. 'or' adv., C. 1. b.) with an implied sense of prevention, of a 'so that...not' (see *M.L.R.* xlii. 496) 1955.] This is supported by Q. 'Take from them now the sence of rekconing, | That the apposed multi-tudes which stand before them, | May not appall their courage'. Cf. also the exhortation of Hen. before battle (Hall, p. 67; not in Hol.): 'Let not their multitude feare youre heartes, nor their great nombre abate your courage', which is clearly the source of the lines. I explain F. 'of' as a normalization of 'a', itself a mis-reading of Sh.'s 'or'; cf. MSH. pp. 110–11.

294–8. *Five...soul* Based, not on Hol. or Hall, but Fabyan's *Chronicle* (1516), ed. Ellis, pp. 577, 589 (cited, Stone, p. 188).

296–8. *Toward...do* (Pope) F. divides 'Toward ...blood: | And...Chauntries, | Where...still | For...doe'.

306. *friends* (Q., Theo.) F. 'friend'.

4. 2.

2. *Montez à* (Cap.) F. 'Monte'. For Sh.'s French, cf. head-note 3. 4. *varlet* F. 'verlot'.

5. *via...terre* (Theo. 'les eaux'; Rowe, 'la terre'). F. 'Via les ewes & terre'. Deighton cites *Ant.* 4. 10. 3–4 and explains:

He says to his horse 'Away (over) water and land!' to which Orl. bantering him replies 'Nothing more? not air and fire also?' and the Dauph. answers '(Yes) Heaven!' Cf. 3. 7. 20–1.

6. *le feu* (Rowe) F. 'feu'.

7. *Ciel!* (J.) F. 'Cein'. I suspect a missp. of 'cieu' (for 'cieux').

8. *Hark...neigh* Were there 'noises off' for this in Sh.'s theatre? The sound of galloping could be simulated. Cf. W. J. Lawrence, *Pre-Restor. Stud.* pp. 217–18.

9. *make incision* let blood (with the spur) to cool their ardour.

11. *dout* (Rowe, ii) F. 'doubt'. Cf. F. *Ham.* 4. 7. 192.

courage 'Here synonymous with the blood in which it is supposed to reside' (M.S.).

25. *'gainst* (F2) F. 'againſt'.

26–9. *superfluous...foe* Cf. Wylie, ii. 145.

30. *this mountain's basis* Cf. 4. 7. 56, and Wylie, ii. 130. Hol. p. 552 speaks of a hill near by.

31. *for...speculation* as idle spectators; cf. 1. 2. 108–14; 2. 4. 57 ff.

35. *sonance* (J.) F. 'Sonuance'. 'Tucket' (v. G.) is used as an adj.

36–7. *dare...couch* v. G.

39–52. *Yon island...them all.* Cf. *Ed. III*, 4. 5. 49–51:

Euen so these rauens for the carcases
Of those poore English, that are markt to die,
Houer about.

39. *carrions* cf. 'lank-lean cheeks', 4 Prol. 26, and G. *desperate of* = without hope of saving.

41. *ragged curtains* i.e. tattered banners.

45. *like...candlesticks* Alluding to candlesticks 'fashioned like a man in armour, holding a tilting-staff [the candle] in his hand' (Webster, *White Devil*, 3. 1. 69–70).

49. *gimmaled* (Delius, O.E.D., Arden) F. 'Iymold.' J. and most subs. edd. 'gimmal'. Cf. *Ed. III*, 1. 2. 29, 'their Iacks of Gymould mayle'; v. G.

50. *chawed-grass* (F.) J. and subs. edd. 'chew'd grass'.

still Vaughan conj. 'stiff', which is prob. right.

51. *executors* i.e. 'who are to have the disposal of what they shall leave, their hides and their flesh' (J.).

54. *life* v. G.

56. *They...death* (Camb.) F. divides 'prayers, | And'.

60. *guidon: to* (Rann, Camb., etc.) F. 'Guard: on | To'. A minim misprint. F. is poss. and has defenders, e.g. M.S., but 'guidon' (v. G.) is strongly supported by ll. 61–2 and by Tito Livio, who thus continues the quot. given in note 3. 7. 1 ff.:

Amongest whome the Duke of Brabande wch for hast had left behinde him his banners, tooké from a trumpet his banner of armes, and commaunded it to bee borne before him vppon a speare in steade of his banner. (*First Life*, p. 55.)

Hol. p. 554, is close to this, but does not use the words 'for haste'.

4. 3.

S.D. Theo. 'The English camp'.

3. *three-score thousand* Cf. Hol. p. 552 (citing Mon-strelet): 'threescore thousand horssemen, besides foot-men, wagoners, and other.'

4. *five to one* This would give Henry an army of *c.*12,000. But v. note l. 76. Hall and Hol. 'six to one'.

6. *God bye you* (M.S.). F. 'God buy' you' Rowe and most edd. 'God be wi' you'. Cf. MSH. p. 288, and 5. 1. 66.

11–14. *Farewell, good...of valour* (Thirlby) F. prints ll. 13–14 as part of Bed.'s speech and follows on with l. 12 (*Exe.* Farwell kind...to day). Led astray perhaps by two consecutive lines in Sh.'s MS. beginning 'Farwell', the compositor prob. skipped l. 12 and then inserted it at the wrong place. For a different explanation cf. Greg, p. 143. N.B. Q. supports Thirlby's reading.

14. *framed* v. G.

17. *ten thousand* Hol. gives no number. But cf. *Gesta* (p. 47):

Quidam dominus Walterus Hungyrford miles impraecabatur ad faciem regis, quod habuisset ad illam paucam familiam quam ibi habuit, *decem millia* de melioribus sagittariis Angliae, qui secum desiderarent esse.

Cf. Wylie, ii. 134. Westmoreland was not at Agincourt.

18 ff. *What's he* etc. 'Perhaps the most stirring expression of high courage in the English language' (M.S.). Sh. greatly expands a speech in Hol. p. 553, derived from Tito Livio.

23–4. *God's will...By Jove* 'The king prays like a Christian, and swears like a heathen' (J.). But a scribe prob. substituted 'by Jove' for 'by Heaven' in acc. with the act of 1606 against blasphemy [Arden].

24–7. *By Jove...desires.* Note this evidence as to Henry's character.

26. *earns* F. 'yernes' Cf. note 2. 3. 3, 6 and G.

28–33. *But if...one more* Cf. *Fortunes*, p. 72. Cf. also *1 Hen. IV*, 1. 3. 201–8. Hotspur passionately deprecates any one's sharing in *his* honour; Henry gaily encourages his troops to rejoice in their luck. Cf. ll. 73–7.

37. *crowns for convoy* 'The king provided transport both for the outward and the return voyage', Wylie, i. 464.

38. *die in* Coleridge conj. 'live in', which Hudson reads.

44. *see...live* (F.) Pope 'live...see', which all mod. edd. read. 'Such a transposition is by no means... likely', Greg (pp. 170–1), who conj. 'live t'old age,' with Keightley; but, as Schmidt notes, 'live old age' is a poss. construction.

48. *And say...day* (Q., Mal.) F. omits. Cf. Greg, pp. 170–1.

49–50. *yet all...remember* = yet everything else will be forgotten before he fails to remember. *But* = rather than not [J. C. Maxwell, 1955].

52–5. *his mouth...their...cups* 'His' is the old soldier; 'their' are the neighbours who feast with him.

57–9. *Crispin...remembered* v. G. 'Crispin'. J. notes:

This prediction is not verified; the feast of Crispin passes by without any mention of Agincourt. Late events obliterate the former; the Civil Wars have left in this nation scarcely any tradition of more ancient history.

60. *We few...brothers* The F. pauses, before and after this line, isolate it significantly.

62–3. *vile* = of humble birth.

gentle his condition Nothing of this in Hol. or other chroniclers. But Nicholas (p. 401) notes:

when the King, upon the occasion of another expedition in 1417, found it necessary to restrain the assumption of coats of arms, he specially excepted such as had borne them at Agincourt.

64–5. *And gentlemen...not here* Cf. 'qui secum desiderarent esse' (note l. 17).

69. *bravely* i.e. they 'made a great shew' (Hol. p. 553).

76. *five thousand* i.e. our whole army. This prob. derives from *Gesta* (p. 57):

Erant enim ex eis juxta propriam numerationem eorum plus quam LX millia educentium gladium, ubi nostra paucitas sex millia virorum pugnantium non excessit.

Cf. 4. 3. 3–4 which agrees on the size of the Fr., but not on that of the Eng., army. Wylie, ii. 141–2, gives the varying estimates on both sides and concludes that the English numbered *c*. 6320.

79 ff. *Once more* etc. This second visit by Montjoy is based on Hol., who takes it from Hall. Actually it was Henry who, realizing his hopeless plight, sued for terms, which the Fr. rejected; v. Wylie, ii. 132–3.

86. *retire* = retreat. Sarcastic.

91. *achieve* (*a*) catch, (*b*) kill.

93–4. *sell...lived* Cf. prov. 'To sell the bear's skin before the beast is caught' (Apperson, p. 557).

96. *native* i.e. in England.

98–103. *And those...France* Cf. Introd. p. xli n. Hen. jestingly replies to ll. 85–8: The sun exhales their honour (the fiery element in them; cf. note 1 Prol. 1) like vapour upwards, leaving their 'muddy vesture of decay' (*Merch.* 5. 1. 65) to corrupt the air ('clime') of France.

104. *abounding* (F.) Q. 'abundant'. A pun, cf. ll. 105–6. Theobald read 'a bounding'.

105. *crasing* (F., Q.) F 2 'grazing', which all edd. read. Prob. Sh. intended 'grazing' (= ricochetting), but the agreement of F. and Q. proves that he wrote 'crasing' (= shattering).

107. *relapse of mortality* fatal rebound.

108. *Let...proudly* i.e. leave this jesting.

109. *for the working-day* i.e. we are not here on a holiday.

111. *rainy...field* The English were exposed to drenching rain 'fere per totam noctem' before the battle (*Gesta*, p. 48). Not mentioned by other Eng. chroniclers, but St Remy and Des Ursins also speak of it, the latter describing the battlefield as 'softened by a week of rain' (cf. Nicholas, pp. 186 n., 211–12 n. and Wylie, ii. 128, 136).

115. *in the trim* (*a*) in fine attire, (*b*) fully rigged and ready to sail.

117. *in fresher robes* i.e. in Heaven [Duthie]; cf. Rev. vii. 9.

119. *turn...service* An Eliz. servant wore his master's livery.

121. *Will...labour* (Pope, omitting 'thou') F. divides 'leuyed. | Herauld'.

124. *'em* F. 'vm'.

128–9. *I fear...ransom* (F. as prose) Theo. and most subsequent edd. print verse, reading 'thou wilt' as 'thou'lt.' But 'how much more dramatic that...the K. should fall back into the language of every-day life and pronounce these words with measured irony' (Arden).

130–1. *My lord...vaward* Cf. Hol. p. 553; Stone, p. 191.

132. *Take...away* F. prints in two lines.

133. *And how...day!* Cf. Introd. p. xli.

4. 4.

S.D. Theo. and mod. edd. 'The field of battle'. For 'Alarum. Excursions' v. G. and Chambers, *Eliz. Stage*, iii. 53:

Nothing was more beloved by a popular audience, esp. in an historical play...than an episode of war.... The actual fighting tended to be sketchy and symbolical... the stage was often only on the outskirts of the main battle.

For the French v. 3. 4 head-note. *F.V.* sc. xvii is a comic episode between Derrick, the clown, and a

Fr. soldier, which suggests that Sh. found hints in the old play for this scene and its parallel in *2 Hen. IV*, 4. 3. Cf. also Hol. 'manie on their knees desired to have their liues saued'.

4. *Calen o custure me!* (Mal.) F. 'calmie cuſture me' ('calmie' prob.<'calin o'). The Irish refrain to a popular Eliz. song (v. Clement Robinson's *Handefull of Pleasant Delites*, 1584, ed. H. E. Rollins, 1924, p. 38). Pist. wishes to show that he can talk gibberish as well as this Frenchie; and 'Irish' was in the air, cf. Introd. p. x.

7–11. *O...ransom* (Pope) F. as prose.

14–16. *Moy...blood* (Johnson) F. as prose.

14. *Moy* We need not suppose a real coin referred to.

15. *Or* (Theo.) F. 'for'; cf. the 'or' in l. 40.

19–21. *Brass...brass?* (J.) F. as prose.

20. *mountain*=wild.   *goat* lecher.

23–5. *Say'st...name* (Pope) F. as prose.

28, 29. *Master* (Cap.) F. 'M.'.

29–30. *firk...ferret* v. G.

35. *à vous* F. 'a vous'.

36. *à cette heure* (Theo.) F. 'aſture'—16th c. French.

37. *couper* (F2) F. 'couppes'.

38–40. *Owy...sword* (Camb.) F. as prose.

38. *cuppele gorge* Cf. 'coupele a gorge' 2. 1. 71 (note). The only 'French' he knows thus comes in useful.

49–50. *Tell...take* (J.) F. as prose.

54. *l'avez promis* (Mal.) F. 'layt a promets' (> l'estes promettre).

à vous F. 'a vous'.

la liberté F. 'le liberte'.

57. *remercîments* (F2) F. 'remercious'.

suis tombé (Theo.) F. 'intombe'.

58. *pense* F. 'peuſe'.

59. *distingué* (Cap.) F. 'diſtinie'.

65. *suck blood* Cf. 2. 3. 53–4.

67. *Suivez* (Rowe) F. 'Saaue' (minim-error <
'suiue').

69. *heart* The seat of courage.

69–70. *The empty* etc. Cf. *Euphues* (Bond, i. 194),
'The emptie vessell giueth a greater sownd, then the
full barrell'; Apperson, p. 182 and *2 Hen. IV*, 1. 3.
74–5.

71–2. *roaring...dagger* Cf. *Tw. Nt.* 4. 2. 123–30
(note). The Devil was attacked by the Vice, who sent
him roaring off the stage, the crowning indignity app.
being the paring of his nails.

that...nails = whose nails anyone may pare.

73. *both hanged* The only exit Nym has.

74–7. *I must stay...but boys* This, the Boy's exit,
points on to 4. 7. 5.

4. 5.

S.D. Theo. and mod. edd. 'Another part of the field'.

2. *est perdu...est perdu* (Rowe) F. 'et perdia...
et perdie'.

3. *Mort Dieu!* (Greg, p. 175) F. 'Mor Dieu'.
Mod. edd. 'Mort de'. Cf. note 3. 5. 11.

5. *Sits* Cf. note 1 Prol. 9.

in our plumes At once mocking their fine feathers
(cf. 4. 3. 112) and disdaining them from above; the
latter a common notion with Sh.; cf. *Ric. II*, 3. 2.
160–3, *1 Hen. IV*, 3. 1. 214 (note).

12. *die in harness: once* F. 'dye in once'. Knight,
Camb. and mod. edd. 'die in honour:'. Clearly F. has
dropped a word and a stop after 'in,' and we are left
to mere guesswork. Knight filled the gap with 'honour'
taken from 'Lets dye with honour' in Q. But Greg
(p. 170) notes that '"in honour" is a less natural
phrase than "with honour", and assorts ill with the
"eternal shame" of the line before'. My conj. (cf.
Macb. 5. 5. 52) avoids these difficulties.

15. *pandar* Q. 'leno', which suggests that the pirate had some Latin as he certainly had French. Cf. his curious 'contramuracke' for 'contaminated' in l. 16.

16. *by a slave* (Q., Pope) F. 'a baſe slaue'—the 'baſe' caught from the line above.

gentler = better born.

18. *spoiled* = ruined.

19. *on heaps* Cf. *Gesta*, p. 55: 'tanta crevit congeries occisorum...quod nostrates ascenderunt ipsas congeries, quae creverant ultra altitudinem longitudinis hominis.'

24. S.D. For their future movements v. Introd. p. xxxvii.

4.6.

S.D. Capell added 'Exeter and others'.

5. *I saw him down* Monstrelet (p. 193) alone notes that York is struck down.

11–27. *Suffolk...love* A variation upon the death of the Talbots in *1 Hen. VI*, 4.7. Cf. 'Two Talbots, wingéd through the lither sky' (*ibid.* l. 21).

14–15. *face, And* (Q., Pope) F. 'face. He'. After 'takes' and 'kisses' an 'and' must be intended before 'cries'.

26–7. *And...testament* Cf. Matth. xxvi. 28.

28. *pretty* v. G.

31. *all my mother...eyes* Cf. *Tw. Nt.* 2. 1. 36–8; *Ham.* 4. 7. 188.

32. *And gave...tears* Cf. Milton, *P.L.* xi. 497.

34. *mistful* (Warb.) F. 'mixtfull'. As 'x' and 'ſ' are totally unlike in Sh.'s hand we must invoke printer's correction, perhaps induced by misunderstanding of 'compound' (v. G.), to explain F.

35–8. *But hark!...through* Cf. Hol. p. 554 and Introd. pp. xxxiv f.

4. 7.

F. heads this 'Actus Quartus'. Cf. p. 121. Theo. and mod. edd. 'Another part of the field'.

3. *offert. In* F. 'offert in'.

8–10. *wherefore...throat* Cf. Introd. pp. xxxiv f.

16. *great* (F2) F. 'grear'.

33. *figures* prototypes; v. G.

53. S.D. F. 'Alarum. Enter King Harry and Burbon with prisoners. Flourish'. Cap. (+ Camb. and mod. edd.) added 'Warwick, Gloucester, Exeter and others'; but dropped 'Bourbon with prisoners' at the same time, and thus obliterated an important clue to Sh.'s intentions. Cf. Introd. p. xxxvii.

61. *Assyrian slings* An untraced allusion, since Judith ix. 7 does not help much. 'Sounds like an echo from Marlowe' (Clar.).

65 ff. *Here comes* etc. Hol. times Montjoy's visit 'in the morning' after the battle; otherwise Sh. closely follows him.

68. *fined* v. G. Cf. 4. 3. 91. Before fighting Hen. offered or staked his bones in place of ransom; he has won the game, so the bones remain his own.

77. *and their* (Mal.) F. 'and with'—prob. 'caught' from l. 78.

79. *arméd* spiked.

87. *hard by* Hol. and *F.V.* agree in reading 'neere adioyning' [Price, p. 31].

94. *prave pattle* i.e. Crécy. If Ed. III be meant in l. 91, he should be 'great-grandfather'.

97–100. *Welshmen...service* Flu. seems our sole authority for this. The custom is usually supposed to commemorate a victory over the Saxons on St David's Day, March 1, A.D. 540. For 'Monmouth caps' v. G.

101–2. *your majesty...day* M.S. (privately) cites Francis Osborne, *Works*, 8th ed. (1682), p. 610:

Nor did he [the Earl of Essex] fail to wear a Leek on St David's day, but besides would upon all occasions vindicate the Welch inhabitants, and own them for his Countreymen, as Q. Elizabeth usually was wont, upon the first of March.

108. *and his majesty too!* Added so as not to give God a title lower than that he had just given the K. [M.S.].

109. *countryman* (F2) F. 'Countrymen'.

114. *God* (F3) F. 'Good'. Here F. gives S.D. 'Enter Williams.' Cf. S.D.s ll. 53, 116.

116. S.D. 'Points to Williams' (Mal.).

124. *a' live* (Cap.) F. 'alive'. J., Mal., Craig, and Alexander accept the emendation [1955].

134. *from the answer...degree* too high to give satisfaction to a man of this status.

135–6. *as good...devil* Cf. *Lear*, 3. 4. 148.

151–2. *when Alençon* etc. Cf. Hol. p. 554, Monstrelet, p. 193. In the fight with Alençon the K. is said to have been 'almost felled' and to have received the blows referred to in 5 Prol. 18 (cf. Wylie, ii. 163–5).

177. *touched* Cf. 3 Prol. 33.

4. 8.

S.D. from Theo.; cf. 4. 7. 165.

11. *any is* (F2) F. 'anyes'.

14. *Do...forsworn?* Cf. 4. 7. 137–8.

72. *your shoes is not so good* A hint, with 'war-worn coats' (4 Prol. 26), for dressing the 'poor soldiers' at 3. 6. 83 S.D.

73. S.D. for 'returns' v. 4. 7. 114–16.

74. *the dead* The figures (10,000 French to 29 English) given at ll. 81, 104–6, may be impossible, but are at least not so much exaggerated as one might suppose. 'With such Fr. and Eng. contemporaries as have committed themselves to details the numbers [of Eng. slain] range from 100 to 600', Wylie, ii. 186.

77–107. *Charles...twenty* In the main Hol. versified, like 1. 2. 35 ff. N.B. the list includes 'Sir Guichard Dolphin'; cf. note 3. 7. S.D.

100. *Faulconbridge* F. 'Fauconbridge'. Cf. note 3. 5. 44.

101. *Vaudemont* (F2, Hol.) F. 'Vandemont'.

Lestrake (Hol.) F. 'Leſtrale'—an *l* : *k* error.

105. *Kikely* (Hol.) F. 'Ketley', ? *t* :*k* error < 'Kekely.' Is this the mod. 'Keighley,' Yorks? Wylie (ii. 188) spells it 'Kyghley.'

107–13. *O God...thine!* Cf. l. 124, 5 Prol. 20–2, and Hol. p. 555.

107. *O God*, etc. F. begins a fresh line with this, and indents as if to mark a new paragraph.

109–10. *without stratagem...battle* A point which most mod. historians dispute, yet the truth; cf. Wylie, ii. 210.

111. *loss*, F. 'loſſe?'.

112. *th'other?* F. 'th'other,' Pope rectified.

114. *we* (F2) F. 'me'.

village i.e. Maisoncelles. Hol. p. 555 does not name it.

123. *rites* (Pope) F. 'Rights'. Cf. MSH. p. 116 (foot).

124. *Let...'Te Deum'* Cf. Hol. p. 555.

125. *The dead...clay* App. from Stow's *Annals*, p. 351 *a*. But cf. Laboureur, cited Nicholas, p. 243.

with charity=with due Christian burial; cf. 4. 1. 141. Most of the English dead were burned, those of noble birth being parboiled that their bones might be carried home (Wylie, ii. 217).

5 Prologue

3–4. *admit...Of* excuse us in our treatment of.

9–13. *behold the English beach...way* seems to be based on Stow (p. 351 *b*), who gets it from Tito Livio; nothing about the reception at Dover in Hall, Hol. or *Gesta*.

10. *flood with* (Pope) F. 'flood; with'. For 'pales' cf. *Cymb.* 3. 1. 19.

men, with wives (F 2) F. 'Men, Wiues'.

14. *solemnly*=in state.

17. *Where that*=where.

18. *bruiséd helmet...sword* Hol. p. 556, abridging Tito Livio, mentions the helmet with its 'blowes and dints', but omits 'his other armour that in that cruell battell was sore torne and broken' (v. *First Life*, p. 65).

20. *free...pride* Cf. Tito Livio: 'he eschewed all occasions of vaine glory' (*First Life*, loc. cit.).

23. *forge...thought* Cf. *2 Hen. IV*, 4. 3. 97, 'forgetive'; *Ham.* 4. 7. 88.

29–35. *As, by a...this Harry* This must have been omitted after the performances in the early summer of 1599. Cf. Introd. pp. ix–x.

29. *but loving* (Seymour, Camb.) F. 'but by louing,' i.e. but also lovingly anticipated.

30. *the general* Note the combined skill and caution of this compliment: after the reference to Caesar to call Eliz. 'empress' puts Essex neatly in his place.

35–9. *him—As yet...them—and* F. 'him. As yet ...them: and'. Perhaps Sh. left the passage in a rough state. A reference to the Dauphin's death, which is needed by his absence from 5. 2, might follow l. 37. 'The emperor's coming'=the visit of Sigismund, 1 May, 1416.

5. 1.

S.D. 'France. The English camp' (Theo. and Camb.).

9. *yesterday* i.e. St David's Day.

19–21. *Ha!...leek* (Pope) F. as prose.

20. *fold...web* i.e. end your life. 'Parca' for Parcae, the fates.

28. *Cadwallader* The last British king.

goats Cf. *1 Hen. IV*, 3. 1. 38.

36. '*a squire...degree*' Title of a metrical romance (early 14th century).

39. *astonished* 'stunned' (J.).

42. *green* fresh.

47–8. *By this leek...swear* Punctuated as in F. 'The words come wildly from the victim while he writhes and eats and roars, and the cudgel supplies a very satisfactory punctuation for them' (P. Simpson, *Sh. Punctuation*, p. 12). For the oath under compulsion, cf. Kyd, *Soliman and Perseda*, 1. 3. 160–78.

52. *do*=may it do.   57. *Good*=Very well!

70. *began* (F) Cap.+edd. 'begun'. Cf. Franz §164.

70–1. *upon...respect* =for an honourable reason.

79–86. *Doth...steal* (Pope) F. as prose.

80. *my Doll* (F., Q.) Capell and most subs. edd. 'my Nell.' Cf. pp. 114 f.

81. *O*' (Pope 'Of') F. 'of a'. Sh. prob. wrote 'A' (=O') and the compositor added 'of' [J. C. M., 1955].

malady of France=venereal disease.

5. 2.

S.D. From Camb. and F. Mal. (following Hol.) located at 'Troyes in Champagne'; but Sh. displays no consciousness of this. Exeter, Bedford and Warwick do not speak. Burgundy spelt 'Bourgongne' by F. The add. names introduced by Mal. and Cap. The parallels with *F.V.* show that the courtship of Katherine is based on the old play; nothing of it in Hol.

1. *Peace...met!* 'Peace, for which we are met, be to this meeting' (J.).

7. *Burgundy* (Rowe) F. 'Burgogne', Hol. 'Burgognie'.

11. *princes English*, F. 'Princes (Englifh)'.

12. *England* (F 2) F. 'Ireland'. Perhaps an indication of Sh.'s preoccupation with Irish affairs; cf. Introd. p. x.

15–17. *Your eyes...basilisks* Cf. 3. 1. 9–11, and G. 'bent', 'basilisks'.

15–16. *Your eyes...bent* (F 2) F. divides 'borne| In'.

18–19. *The venom...day* A double change of constr.: (i) 'have' agrees with 'such looks', (ii) 'and that' depends on 'hope', virtually though not actually a main verb.

23. *on equal love* springing from equal love.

24 ff. *that I have laboured* etc. Sh. does not explain the connexion of these efforts with those of the emperor (5 Prol. 38–9).

40. *it* Old genitive.

42. *even-pleached* v. G.

44. *leas* v. G. Contrasted with 'mead' (l. 48).

45. *fumitory* (F 4) F. 'femetary'.

50. *all* (Rowe) F. 'withall'.

51. *Conceives by idleness* i.e. idleness fathers the weeds.

nothing teems brings forth nothing.

54–5. *as...wildness*, (Cap.) F. 'all...wildneffe'. F. makes a kind of sense, but 'Even so' (l. 56) points to a previous 'as.' For 'fallows' v. G.

55. *Defective...natures* Cf. l. 62, 'unnatural'. Believing that the vegetable and animal world degenerated with man at the Fall, med. and Eliz. thought conceived of cultivation, culture, civilization as attempts to restore 'nature' to its pristine excellence and thus more

'natural' than life in its wild state. Since Darwin we have taken the opposite view.

61. *diffused* (F3) F. 'defuſ'd'. Cf. 3. 6. 75.

78. *cursitory* F. 'curſelarie' Q. 'curſenary' Q3 'curſorary'. Pope and mod. edd. follow Q3, a mere emend. of Q. and a word not found elsewhere in English, whereas 'cursitory' or 'cursetory' (of which F. is an obvious missp.) is a recognized seventeenth-century word = cursory.

83. *Pass...answer* = Deliver 'the answer we have accepted or adopted as decisive' (Clar.).

94. *Haply* (F4) F. 'Happily'. Cf. F. 'haply' at 4. 7. 170. The two forms were not distinguished.

95. *When...on* i.e. When men get to quarrelling about straws.

99. S.D. F. 'Exeunt omnes. | Manet King and Katherine'.

109. *vat* (Rowe) F. 'wat'. Also at ll. 179, 263. Cf. note 3. 2. 62. For the French, cf. head-note 3. 4.

123. *dat is de princess* Perhaps F. omits 'say'.

131. *suit* A pun.

132. *clap hands* Cf. *Wint.* 1. 2. 104, and G.

134. *vell* (Cap.) F. 'well'. Cf. note l. 109.

138. *I have...measure* Dancing is not my strong suit.

139. *win...leap-frog* Cf. *2 Hen. IV*, 2. 4. 245 (note).

140. *vaulting* F. 'vawting'.

142. *leap into a wife* Tillyard (*Sh.'s History Plays*, p. 309) detects here a 'stalely indecent double-meaning'. I should call it rather plain dealing, like the rest of his speech; to Elizabethans, frank not indecent.

buffet Free fights for a girl were doubtless common among prentice-boys.

144–5. *sit...never off* A monkey trained to rough riding may have been one of the 'turns' in the shows of 'jugglers' that preceded the modern circus. Cf. the botanical 'jackanapes on horse-back' under 'jacka-napes' 5, O.E.D.

149–50. *not...burning* so ugly that the sun cannot make it more so. Cf. *Troil.* 1. 3. 282.

151. *be thy cook* i.e. dress the dish for you.

155. *while thou liv'st* An adjuration; cf. *Temp.* 3. 2. 111.

156. *uncoined* i.e. of metal (mettle) not current, 'to woo in other places'.

171–2. *Is it...of France?* Cf. *F.V.* xx. 55: 'How should I loue thee, which is my fathers enemy?'

191. *il est meilleur* F. 'il & melieurs'. Cf. 3. 4. 7, n. 2.

194. *at one* = (*a*) alike, (*b*) allied.

205. *I get...scambling* I have scrimmaged for you.

209–10. *go to...beard?* To drive the Turk from Constantinople was, professedly, the dearest wish of all sixteenth-century Christian princes. That the Turk did not capture it until 1453, 31 years after Henry's death, made no odds to Sh., even if he knew it. That the 'boy' turned out to be Henry VI was the point he desired to suggest. Cf. Introd. p. xliv.

225. *untempering* Cf. G. and 2. 2. 118.

231. *that ill layer up* Cf. *2 Hen. IV*, 5. 1. 82, 'like a wet cloak ill laid up.' The image suggests 'wear' (l. 233).

243–4. *broken music* v. G.

247, 250. *sall...sall* F. 'fhall...fall'.

255. *d'une...indigne* (Camb.) F. 'd'une nostre Seigneur indignie'.

260. *noces* (Dyce) F. 'nopcese', early mod. Fr.

263. *baiser* (Hanmer) F. 'buiffe'.

271. *weak list* = 'slight barrier' (Steev.).

272. *follows our places* = belongs to our rank.

278–9. *they should...monarchs* Cf. *F.V.* xviii. 88–90.

292–4. *If you...blind* Cf. *Rom*. 2. 1. 24–6 and
Congreve, *Love for Love*, 2. 1 (Mermaid ed. p. 225).

300. *blind* v. G.

306–7. *well...warm kept* well grazed in a warm
pasture (v. G. 'summer'), i.e. well brought up in a
sheltered home.

307–8. *Bartholomew-tide* Aug. 24, when the
evenings begin to be chilly and flies sleepy.

311–12. *This moral...summer* That means I am
to wait for a hot summer.

313. *too* (F2) F. 'to'.

319. *perspectively* i.e. the cities, viewed in a per-
spective-picture or through a perspective-glass, appear
like a maid; v. G.

321. *never* (Rowe) F. omits. Some such word is
needed.

324–5. *so the...on her* provided she brings the
cities with her. Cf. the last par. of Hudson's comment
quoted p. xlv above, and Palmer (*Pol. Characters of Sh.*
1945, pp. 244), who interprets the wooing as mere
play-acting for political ends and comments on these
words, 'For all his pleasant-spoken ways, he never loses
grip of the next business in hand.' There is no inconsistency between marrying Kate for her own sake and
refusing to 'compromise the dignity of his state'.

331. *then* (F2) F. omits.

335. *for...grant* i.e. a deed conferring lands or titles.

338. *Præclarissimus* Rightly 'præcarissimus'. In
Hall (ed. i) 'præcharissimus'; missp. 'præclarissimus'
in ed. ii, whence Hol. took it and so passed it on to
Sh. 'Ignorance cannot be certainly inferred from
inaccuracy' (J.).

349. *dear conjunction*=solemn union. Here 'dear'
almost=epoch-making. Cf. *1 Hen. IV*, 4. 1. 34.

362. *paction* (Theo.) F. 'Pation'.

368–9. *we'll take...peers'* In *F.V.* Burg. and the
Dauphin take the oath on the stage. In the *Hen. V*

mentioned by Nashe (McKerrow, 1. 213) both the Fr. K. and the Dauphin 'sweare fealty'.

371. S.D. F. 'Senet. Exeunt'. Most edd. follow; but as 'sennet'='a set of notes on the trumpet...app. as a signal for the ceremonial entrance or exit of a body of players' (O.E.D.), it is inappropriate for the Fr. court.

Epilogue

A sonnet. Cf. Prol. to *Rom*.

2. *bending* Cf. *Ham*. 3. 2. 148, 'Here stooping to your clemency' [Steev.] and Introd. p. xiii.

4. *by starts* by fits and starts.

5. *Small time* Referring to Henry's early death.

13. *oft...shown* Testifies to the popularity of *1, 2, 3 Henry VI*.

14. *let...take* let this play meet with your favour.

GLOSSARY

ABSOLUTE, perfect; 3. 7. 24

ABUSE, insult; 4. 8. 50

ACCOMPLISH, equip completely; 4 Prol. 12

ACCORD, agree, consent; 2. 2. 86

ACQUIT OF, pardon (cf. 'quit' l. 166) for; 2. 2. 144

ACT, 'the act of order' = the operation of order; 1. 2. 189

ADDITION, title, style of address; 5. 2. 336

ADMIRATION, astonishment; 2. 2. 108; wonder; 4. 1. 66

ADMIRE, wonder; 1. 1. 39; 3. 6. 123

ADVANCE, raise; 2. 2. 192

ADVANTAGE (sb.), (i) opportunity; 1. 2. 139; 3. 6. 118; (ii) increment (*M.V.* 1. 3. 67); 4. 3. 50

ADVENTURE, 'at all adventures' = whatever be the consequence; 4. 1. 115

ADVISED, (i) cautious; 1. 2. 179, 252; (ii) informed; 2 Prol. 12

AFFECTIONS, desires; 4. 1. 106; 5. 1. 25

ALARUM, trumpet-call to arms; 3. 1. S.D.; 4. 4. S.D.

ALE-WASHED, ale-fuddled (cf. *A. & C.* 2. 7. 105); 3. 6. 76

AMPLE, complete; 1. 2. 150, 227

AMPLY, frankly; 1. 2. 94

ANCIENT, ensign, standard-bearer. The equivalent of sub-lieutenant in mod. times and already recognized as

such (cf. 2. 1. 38; 'ancient lieutenant', 3. 6. 12; *2 Hen. IV,* 5. 5. 90); 2. 1. 3

ANNOY, hurt; 2. 2. 102

ANON, at once, soon; 4. 1. 26

ANSWER (sb.), penalty, satisfaction; 2. 2. 143; 2. 4. 123; 4. 7. 134

ANSWER (vb), answer for; 4. 1. 154; correspond to; 4 Prol. 8

ANTIC, figure of fun. Gen. suggests emaciation in Sh.; 3. 2. 31

ANTIQUE, ancient; 5 Prol. 26

APPROBATION, attestation; 1. 2. 19

ARGUMENT, subject-matter of debate or discourse; 3. 1. 21; 3. 7. 34; business in hand; 4. 1. 142

ART, 'the practice as distinguished from science or theory' (Johnson); 1. 1. 51

ASTONISH, stun; 5. 1. 39

ATTAINT, exhaustion (O.E.D. 7), or lack of freshness (O.E.D. 6); 4 Prol. 39

ATTEND (ON), wait upon, accompany; 2. 2. 24; 2. 4. 29

ATTEST, (i) vouch for; 1 Prol. 16; (ii) prove; 3. 1. 22

AVOUCH, make good; 5. 1. 72

AWKWARD, perverse ('awk' = the wrong way round); 2. 4. 85

BANDS, swaddling-clothes; Ep. 9

BANKROUT, bankrupt; 4. 2. 43

BANNER, properly 'banderole', i.e. 'the little fringed silk flag that hangs on a trumpet' (Johnson's *Dict.*); 4. 2. 61

BAR, court of decision; 5. 2. 27

BARBASON, name of a devil; 2. 1. 54

BASE, low-born, of low rank; 2. 1. 29; 4. 1. 38

BASILISK, (i) fabulous serpent that killed with its look; (ii) large cannon; 5. 2. 17

BATE, flutter; 3. 7. 111

BATTLE, line, battle array; army; 4 Prol. 9; 4. 3. 2, 69

BAWCOCK, fine fellow (from Fr. 'beau coq'); 3. 2. 25; 4. 1. 44

BEAR, perform; 1. 2. 213; (of a horse) carry (v. note for quibble); 3. 7. 44

BECOME, grace, adorn; 1. 2. 8; 4. 2. 40

BEDLAM, mad. Corruption of 'Bethlehem' (i.e. the Hospital of St Mary of Bethlehem, a madhouse); 5. 1. 19

BEND UP, strain to the utmost (cf. *Macb.* 1. 7. 79); 3. 1. 16

BENT, line of (*a*) sight, (*b*) fire; 5. 2. 16

BESTOW (reflex.), take up one's position; 4. 3. 68

BIG, mighty; 4. 2. 43

BLIND, possessed by lust (cf. 'blind-drunk'); 3. 3. 34; 5. 2. 300

BLOWN FROM, (*a*) puffed from, (*b*) inflated by; 4. 1. 250

BLUNT, rude; 4. 7. 174

BOLTED, sifted (like fine flour); 2. 2. 137

BOOK (vb), record; 4. 7. 72

BOOT, booty, 'make boot upon' = plunder; 1. 2. 194

BOTCH UP, contrive clumsily; 2. 2. 115

BOTTOM, ship; 3 Prol. 12

BOUND, make to leap; 5. 2. 143

BOW (vb.), falsify; 1. 2. 14

BOWELS, supposed the seat of compassion; 2. 4. 102

BRAVE, fine, gallant; 3 Prol. 5; 4. 4. 39

BRAVELY, gallantly; 4. 3. 69

BREATH, breathing-time, brief interval (cf. *K. John*, 3. 4. 134); 2. 4. 145

BRED OUT, exhausted, degenerated (cf. *Tim.* 1. 1. 259); 3. 5. 29

BREED (contention), pick a quarrel (cf. *Lear*, 1. 3. 24; *2 Hen. IV*, 2. 4. 248); 5. 1. 10

BRING, accompany (cf. *Gen.* xviii. 16, 'bring them on the way'); 2. 3. 1

BROACHED, spitted; 5 Prol. 32

BROKEN MUSIC. Lit. music arranged in parts; here used punningly; 5. 2. 243–4

BRUISE, squeeze; 3. 6. 120

BUBUKLE. Confusion of 'bubo' (= abscess) and 'carbuncle' (O.E.D.); 3. 6. 99

BULLY, fine fellow; 4. 1. 48

BUXOM, brisk, vigorous; 3. 6. 25

CADWALLADER, last British king (killed A.D. 635); 5. 1. 28

CAPITAL, principal; 5. 2. 97

CAREER, lit. short gallop at full speed, (hence) unbridled behaviour; 2. 1. 126

CAREFUL, anxious; 4. 1. 228

CARRION, wasted corpse or skeleton (cf. *M.V.* 2. 7. 63, 'carrion death'); 4. 2. 39

CARRY COALS, submit tamely to insult (cf. *Rom.* 1. 1. 1); lit. belong to the lowest grade of menial servants; 3. 2. 46

CASE, set (either 'of two', e.g. 'case of pistols' or 'of four', e.g. 'case of viols'); 3. 2. 4

CAUSE, matter, affair; 1. 1. 45, 77; 2. 2. 60

CAVETO, caution! (imperative of Lat. 'caveo', I beware); 2. 3. 51

CEREMONY, accessory or symbol of state; 4. 1. 72, 104, 235 ff.

CHALLENGE, lay claim to; 4. 1. 213; 4. 7. 125

CHALLENGER, one who claims as a right; 2. 4. 95

CHAMBER, 'a small piece [of ordnance]... to fire salutes' (O.E.D.), or for theatre use; 3 Prol. 33 S.D.

CHANGE (vb.), lose colour (cf. *2 Hen. IV*, 4. 5. 6); 2. 2. 73

CHANGE, IN, in exchange; 4.8.31

CHARGE (sb.), post, military duties; 4. 3. 6

CHARM, lay spells upon; 2 Prol. 38

CHARTERED, privileged, licensed; 1. 1. 48

CHASE, or CHACE. See note on *Tennis* at 1. 2. 259–67

CHAW, chew. Now vulgar; 4. 2. 50

CHERISH, favour; 1. 1. 74

CHEWED, ruminated, pondered; 2. 2. 56

CHIVALRY, men-at-arms; 1. 2. 157

CHOICE-DRAWN, selected with care; 3 Prol. 24

CHRISTOM CHILD. A corruption (by association with 'christen') of *chrisom child*, i.e. one who, dying within a month of birth, was buried in its chrisom-cloth or christening robe; 2. 3. 11–12

CHUCK, chick. Term of endearment; 3. 2. 25

CHURLISH, rough, uncomfortable; 4. 1. 15

CIVIL, well-ordered; 1. 2. 199

CLAP HANDS, strike hands in token of a bargain, in particular at a betrothal; 5. 2. 132

CLIPPER, one who pares coins; 4. 1. 225

CLOSE (sb.), (*a*) cadence; (*b*) close union (cf. 1. 2. 211 and O.E.D. sb. 2. 3, 'the close or oneness', 1674); 1. 2. 182

CLOSE (vb), meet, unite; 1. 2. 211

CLOSE (adv.), shut up; 2. 3. 59

COME OFF, acquit oneself; 3. 6. 71

COME OVER, twit, 'get at'; 1. 2. 268

COMING IN, income; 4. 1. 239

COMPANY, companion (cf. *M.N.D.* 1. 1. 219); 1. 1. 55

COMPLEMENT, exterior. Lit. outward polish; cf. *L.L.L.* 1. 1. 168; (Lat. 'complementum' = that which completes); 2. 2. 134

COMPOUND, make terms; 4. 3. 80; 4. 6. 33

CONDITION, (i) quality, disposition, character; 4.1.104; 5. 2. 286; (ii) rank; 4. 3. 63

CONFIRM, ratify; 2 Prol. 27

CONFOUNDED, worn away, ruined, lost; 3. 1. 13; 4. 5. 3

CONGREE, agree together. A verb. poss. coined from the early mod. Fr. 'congréer' (= congréger; cf. Cotgrave) by analogy with 'agree'; 1. 2. 182

CONGREET, greet mutually. Nonce-word; 5. 2. 31

CONJURATION, solemn appeal; 1. 2. 29

CONSCIENCE, real opinion, conviction; 4. 1. 117; 4. 7. 132

CONSENT, (i) (a) unanimity, (b) rightly 'concent', playing or singing together; 1. 2. 181; 2. 2. 22; (ii) concerted plan of action; 1. 2. 206

CONSIDERATION, reflection; 1. 1. 28

CONSIGN, agree; 5. 2. 91, 298

CONTAGIOUS, pestilential; 3. 3. 31; 4. 8. 23

CONTEMPLATION, study of life; 1. 1. 63

CONTROVERSY, struggle; 2. 4. 109

CONVEYED HIMSELF, passed himself off. From Hol.; 1.2. 74

CONVOY, conveyance; 4. 3. 37

COPY, example; 3. 1. 24

CORANTO, quick dance, gallop; 3. 5. 33

CORRECT, inflict punishment; 1. 2. 191

CORRECTION, punishment, thrashing; 2. 2. 51

CORROBORATE, made strong. Used absurdly; 2. 1. 124

COST (upon one's), at one's expense; 4. 3. 25

COUCH, crouch (like a terrified bird). Cf. Lucr. 507 ('coucheth' = makes to crouch); 4. 2. 37

COUPLE A GORGE, Fr. couper la gorge, cut the throat; 2. 1. 71; 'cuppele gorge'; 4. 4. 38

COURSE, course of action; 1. 1. 24

COURSING, marauding; 1. 2. 143

CRASING, shattering. Prob. error for 'grazing' = (ricochetting); 4. 3. 105

CREATE, created (cf. Franz, p. 159); 2. 2. 31

CRESCIVE, growing; 1. 1. 66

CRESSID (v. note); 2. 1. 76

CRISPIN CRISPIAN, Oct. 25. SS. Crispinus and Crispianus (brothers) were martyred at Soissons, c. A.D. 287; 4. 3. 57

CROOKED, false; 1. 2. 94

CROWN, v. French crown; 4. 1. 224

CRUSHED, 'subdued and overpowered by contrary reasons' (J.); 1. 2. 175

CRY OUT OF, complain loudly or vehemently of (O.E.D.); 2. 3. 26

CULLED, 'hand-picked'; 3 Prol. 24

CULLION, base fellow; 3. 2. 21

CURRANCE, current (Onions); not in O.E.D. Clar. suggests a nonce-word, derived from Fr. 'courrance' = 'the flux, or laxativenesse of the bodie' (Cotgrave); 1. 1. 34

CURSITORY (v. note), wandering, cursory (cf. 'cursitor' = vagabond; O.E.D.); 5. 2. 78

CURTLE-AXE, broad-sword. Perversion of 'cutlass', Fr. 'coutelas'; 4. 2. 21

DARE, 'paralyse, or render [birds] helpless with the sight of something' (O.E.D.). A term in fowling; cf. Hen. VIII, 3. 2. 282, 'And dare us...like larks'; 4. 2. 36

DEAR, (i) (a) deeply felt, (b) dire; 2. 2. 58; (ii) heavy, grievous; 2. 2. 181

DECK, equip, fit out (cf. *Ric. II*, 1. 4. 62); 1 Prol. 28

DECOCT, warm up; 3. 5. 20

DEFEAT (sb.), disaster; 1. 2. 107, 214

DEFEAT (vb), cheat; 4. 1. 165

DEFENSIBLE, capable of defending ourselves; 3. 3. 50

DEFINE, describe (cf. *Ham.* 5. 2. 117); 4 Prol. 46

DELICATE, exquisite; 2. 4. 40

DEMAND, enquire (O.E.D. 3); 5. 2. 32

DERACINATE, root up (cf. *Troil.* 1. 3. 99); 5. 2. 47

DESPERATE, reckless (cf. *Tw. Nt.* 5. 1. 67); 4. 2. 39

DESPITE, contempt; 3. 5. 17

DIFFUSED, disorderly; 5. 2. 61

DIGEST, put up with, swallow, get over (cf. *L.L.L.* 5. 2. 289); 2 Prol. 31; 3. 6. 126

DISCUSS, declare (comic misuse); 3. 2. 60; 4. 4. 5, 30

DISHONEST, unchaste; 1. 2. 49

DISPOSE, handle, manage; 4 Prol. 51

DOING, copulation (Schmidt 'do' 5); 3. 7. 98

DOUT, put out; 4. 2. 11

DOWN-ROPING, v. *roping*; 4. 2. 48

DRENCH, draught of medicine for animals; 3. 5. 19

DRESS, prepare; 4. 1. 10

EARN, grieve (cf. *Caes.* 2. 2. 129); 2. 3. 3, 6; 4. 3. 26

EGREGIOUS, surpassing all others of its kind (Lat. *egregius*); 2. 1. 46; 4. 4. 11

ELDER-GUN, popgun; 4. 1. 195

ELEMENT, sky; 4. 1. 103

EMBASSY, mission; 1. 1. 95

EMBRACE, welcome joyfully; 4. 1. 203

EMPERY, absolute dominion; 1. 2. 227

EMPTYING. Poss. = dregs (v. O.E.D. 2); 3. 5. 6

ENDING, death; 4. 1. 154

ENGLUTTED, swallowed up; 4. 3. 83

ENROUND, surround; 4 Prol. 36

ENTERTAIN, engage; 1. 2. 111

ESTATE, situation; 4. 1. 96

ESTIMATION, reputation; 3. 6. 14

EVEN, (i) unruffled; 2. 2. 3; (ii) straightforward (cf. *Ham.* 2. 2. 291); 4. 8. 110; (iii) 'the even of it' = the plain truth of it; 2. 1. 122

EVENLY, 'directly, without any interruptions in the straight line of descent'. Cf. 'crooked titles', 1. 2. 94 (Clar.); 2. 4. 91

EVEN-PLEACHED, made of boughs evenly trimmed and intertwined (cf. *Ado*, 1. 2. 8); 5. 2. 42

EXCEPTION, objection; 2. 4. 34; 4. 2. 25

EXCURSION, lit. sortie; here, sally from the tiring-room; 4. 4. S.D.

EXECÚTORS, executioners; 1. 2. 203

EXÉCUTORS, legal executors; 4. 2. 51

EXHALE! draw sword! Lit. 'exhale' = draw forth meteors, as the sun was supposed to do (cf. *Rom.* 3. 5. 13); 2. 1. 62

EXHIBITER, presenter of a bill (cf. *Wives*, 2. 1. 24); 1. 1. 74

EXPEDIENCE, speed; 4. 3. 70

EXPEDITION, (i) enterprise; 1. 2. 302; (ii) speedy motion; 2. 2. 191; (iii) readiness in argument (rhet., v. O.E.D. 6); 3. 2. 75

FACE (OUT), brazen out; 3. 2. 33; shame; 3. 7. 81–2

FACULTY, innate power; 1. 1. 66

FAIRLY, in seemly fashion; 4. 1. 10

FALLOW, ploughed field (O.E.D. sb. 1); 5. 2. 54

FARCE, stuff, cram full. A culinary word; here = pad out with pompous phrases (cf. *force*); 4. 1. 259

FAT-BRAINED, dull, stupid; 3. 7. 132

FAVOUR, (i) token worn in hat or helmet (cf. *1 Hen. IV*, G.); 4. 7. 150; (ii) appearance; 5. 2. 63

FEAR, frighten; 1. 2. 155

FEEL, test, sound; 4. 1. 124

FERRET, worry like a ferret; 4. 4. 30, 31

FET, fetched; 3. 1. 18

FIGO or FIG OF SPAIN, 'contemptuous gesture in which the thumb is thrust between two of the closed fingers, or into the mouth' (O.E.D.); 3. 6. 55, 57; 4. 1. 60

FIGURE, emblem, type (O.E.D. 12); 4. 7. 33, 43

FIND, (i) provide, furnish (O.E.D. 18); 1. 2. 72; (ii) find out; 4. 1. 255

FINE, lit. pay as a fine or penalty; here, 'fix as the sum to be paid' (Schmidt); 4. 7. 68

FIRK, beat; 4. 4. 29, 32

FIT, befit; 2. 4. 11

FLAT, stupid, dull (cf. *Ham.* 1. 2. 133); 1 Prol. 9

FLESHED, trained or inured to the taste of blood; 2. 4. 50; 3. 3. 11

FLEXURE, obsequious bowing; 4. 1. 251

FLOWER-DE-LUCE, fleur-de-lys; 5. 2. 211

FLUENT, copious; 3. 7. 32

FOOT, 'be footed' = have a foothold (O.E.D. 4); 2. 4. 143

FORAGE, raven, glut oneself; 1. 2. 110

FORCE, stuff out, cram full. A variant of *farce* (q.v.); 2 Prol. 32

FORE-HAND, upper hand, advantage; 4. 1. 276

FORESPENT, past; 2. 4. 36

FORM, good order; 4. 1. 242

FOUL, (a) foul-mouthed, abusive, (b) dirty (of a pistol); 2. 1. 56

FOX, sword; 4. 4. 9

FRACTED, broken; 2. 1. 124

FRAME, build (as carpenters built an oaken framework for a house); 4. 3. 14

FREELY, frankly; 1. 2. 239

FRENCH CROWN, the French gold coin (*écu*), bearing a shield surmounted by a crown. Worth 6s. in Eliz.'s time; 4. 1. 222, 224

FRENCH HOSE, the fashionable Eliz. loose wide breeches, of 'mid-thigh length, shaped like pumpkins' (Linthicum); 3. 7. 52

FULL-FRAUGHT, lit. fully laden, hence (of a man) complete, all-round; 2. 2. 139

GALL (vb), (i) harass, chafe;
1. 2. 151; 3. 1. 12; (ii) scoff
(at); 5. 1. 73

GALLIARD, 'a quick and lively
dance in triple time'
(O.E.D.); 1. 2. 253

GAMESTER, one who plays for
stakes; 3. 6. 110

GAPE, desire eagerly (cf. *Rom.*
2 Chor. 2); 2. 1. 61

GENERAL, public; 4. 1. 235

GENTLE (vb), make of gentleman's rank; 4. 3. 63

GENTLEMAN OF A COMPANY,
gentleman volunteer in the
ranks (v. note); 4. 1. 39

GESTURE, bearing, deportment;
4 Prol. 25

GIDDY, uncertain, fickle; 1. 2.
145; 2. 4. 28; 3. 6. 26

GILT, 'fine trappings'; cf.
Tim. 4. 3. 302 (M.S.); 4. 3.
110

GIMMALED, 'consisting of two
similar parts hinged to-
gether' (O.E.D.); 4. 2. 49

GIPE, gibe, jape; 4. 7. 48

GIRD, besiege; 3 Prol. 27

GLEANED, stripped of de-
fenders; 1. 2. 151

GLEEK (vb), gibe; 5. 1. 73

GLOZE, interpret speciously;
1. 2. 40

GO ABOUT, make it one's
object; 4. 1. 196

GO TO! An expression of contempt; (in mod. slang) 'get
along with you'; 2. 1. 80

GOD-A-MERCY! Thank you!, lit.
'God reward you'; 4. 1. 34

GOD BYE YOU, God be with
you; 4. 3. 6; 5. 1. 66

GOD-DEN, good evening; 3. 2.
82

GRACE (sb.), (i) gracious disposition, mercy; 1. 1. 22;

1. 2. 243; 3. 3. 30; (ii)
ornament; 2 Prol. 28

GRACE (himself), gain credit;
3. 6. 66

GRAFTER, 'original tree from
which a scion has been taken
for grafting' (O.E.D.); 3.
5. 9

GREAT-BELLY DOUBLET, doublet
with 'belly' (= lower part)
stuffed out with bombast (cf.
L.L.L. 3. 1. 18, 'thin-belly
doublet'); 4. 7. 47

GREENLY. Not 'unskilfully,
foolishly' (*Ham.* 4. 5. 82),
but 'love-sick' (cf. O.E.D.
'green' 3 and *Tw. Nt.* 2. 4.
113); 5. 2. 145

GROSS, (i) glaring, flagrant;
2. 2. 103; (ii) excessive;
2. 2. 132; (iii) coarse,
ignoble; 3. 1. 24; (iv) dull,
stupid; 4. 1. 278

GROSSLY, glaringly; 2. 2. 107

GROW, live; 2. 2. 22

GUIDON, standard, used by
generals or kings, v. Segar,
Honor, military & civill
1602 (cited O.E.D.); 4. 2.
60

GULF, whirlpool; 2. 4. 10;
4. 3. 82

GULL (sb.), simpleton (or
poss. = fraud, v. O.E.D. 2,
3); 3. 6. 65

GULL (vb), dupe (cf. *Son.* 86.
10); 2. 2. 121

GUN-STONE, cannon-ball (formerly often made of stone);
1. 2. 283

HAGGLED OVER, hacked about;
4. 6. 11

HANDLE, treat of; 2. 3. 35

HAPPY, fortunate, favourable;
1. 2. 215, 301

HARD-FAVOURED, ugly (v. *favour*, ii); 3. 1. 8

HAUNT (sb.), public resort; 1. 1. 59

HAUNT (vb), follow persistently; 2. 4. 52

HAZARD, (i) v. note on *tennis* at 1. 2. 259–67; 1. 2. 264; (ii) game at dice; 3. 7. 84–6

HEAD, (i) 'in head', as an organized armed force (cf. *1 Hen. IV*, 4. 4. 25); 2. 2. 18; (ii) v. *turn head*; 2. 4. 69

HEADY, headstrong; 1. 1. 34; 3. 3. 32

HEAP, 'on heaps' = in a body, in a prostrate and disorderly mass; 4. 5. 18; 5. 2. 39

HEIR GENERAL, 'heir at law, whether descent be through the male or the female' (M.S.); 1. 2. 66

HERMES, Mercury, who invented the pipe and lulled to sleep with it Argus of the hundred eyes; 3. 7. 17

HEW, cut down, fell (O.E.D. 4); 2. 1. 36

HILDING, sorry, mean; 4. 2. 29

HILTS. For sing. 'hilt'; 2 Prol. 9; 2. 1. 65

HOLD, hold good; 1. 2. 89

HOLE, 'find a hole in his coat' = catch him out. The phrase 'pick a hole' = find a fault, is more common (v. O.E.D. 'hole' 8); 3. 6. 81

HONOUR-OWING, honourable, lit. honour-possessing; 4. 6. 9

HOOP, whoop, shout with astonishment; 2. 2. 108

HORRID, hideous, horrible; 3. 6. 75; 4 Prol. 28; 4. 1. 267

HOUSEWIFERY, thrift, domestic economy; 2. 3. 59

HUMOROUS, capricious, featherbrained; 2. 4. 28

HUMOUR, (i) fancy, mood; 2. 1. 55, 121, 126; 3. 2. 6, 26, 27; (ii) 'that's the humour of it' = (vaguely) that's the way; 2. 1. 59, 96, 116

HUSBANDRY, (i) housekeeping, farm-management; 4. 1. 7; (ii) crops; 5. 2. 39

HUSWIFE (cf. *A. & C.* 4. 15. 44), hussy; 5. 1. 79

HYDRA, the mythological beast with nine heads, which grew two for every one cut off; 1. 1. 35

ICELAND DOG, lap-dog, 'curled and rough all over, which by reason of the length of their hair show neither of face nor of body', Topsell, *Four-footed beasts* (ed. 1607), p. 178. A term of contempt; 2. 1. 41

IDLY, foolishly, frivolously; 2. 4. 26

ILL-DISPOSED, v. *dispose*; 4 Prol. 51

IMAGINED, of imagination (cf. *Merch.* 3. 4. 52); 3 Prol. 1

IMBARE, expose (v.note); 1.2.94

IMP, child; 4. 1. 45

IMPAWN, pledge, hazard; 1.2.21

IMPEACHMENT, hindrance; 3. 6. 140

IMPUTATION, responsibility. Theol. term (v. O.E.D. 'impute' 2); 4. 1. 148

INDIFFERENTLY, tolerably; 2. 1. 55

INDIRECTLY, unjustly (cf. *Oth.* 1. 3. 111); 2. 4. 94

INFECT, taint; 2. 2. 126

INJURY, (*a*) sore, (*b*) mod. sense (O.E.D. 3*b*); 3. 6. 120

INLAND, the heart of the country (cf. *A.Y.L.* 2. 7. 96; 2. 3. 340, where as adv. and adj. it means 'cultured, refined'); 1. 2. 142

INLY, inwardly; 4 Prol. 24

INSTANCE, motive (cf. *Ric. III*, 3. 2. 25); 2. 2. 119

INTELLIGENCE, espionage; 2 Prol. 12

INTENDMENT, purpose, project; 1. 2. 144

INTERTISSUED, i.e. woven of twisted gold-thread, thus doubly rich (v. Linthicum, *Costume in Eliz. Drama*, pp. 117–18); 4. 1. 258

INVENTION, poetic creation or imagination; 1 Prol. 2

INVEST, give dignity to (v. note); 4 Prol. 26

INWARD, secret (cf. O.E.D. 4 and *L.L.L.* G.); 1. 1. 39

IRRECONCILED, not atoned for; 4. 1. 151–2

ISSUE, shed tears; 4. 6. 34

JACK-AN-APES, monkey (? trained to rough-riding; v. note); 5. 2. 144

JACK-SAUCE, saucy Jack; 4. 7. 139

JEALOUS, apprehensive; 4. 1. 281

JEALOUSY, suspicion; 2. 2. 126

JUST, (i) just so; 3. 7. 145; (ii) exact; 4. 7. 115

KECKSY, hemlock or cow parsnip; 5. 2. 52

KERN, Irish soldier (cf. *Macb.* 1. 2. 13); 3. 7. 52

KIT, loose woman (v. note); 2. 1. 76

KNOWLEDGE (OUT OF), (a) unconsciously; cf. *mope*; (b) beyond his ken; 3. 7. 133

LACKEY, a running footman; 3. 7. 110; 4. 1. 268

LADY. An apostrophe of the Virgin Mary (cf. 'marry'); 2. 1. 36

LAMBKIN. A term of endearment; 2. 1. 127

LARD, enrich with blood (cf. *Ric. II*, 4. 1. 137; *1 Hen. IV*, 2. 2. 106); 4. 6. 8

LARGE, (AT), in full; 1. 1. 78; 2. 4. 121

LATE, (i) recently appointed; 2. 2. 61; (ii) recent; 2. 4. 12

LAVOLTA, 'a lively dance for two persons, consisting a good deal in high and active bounds' (O.E.D.); 3. 5. 33

LAY DOWN, calculate (cf. *2 Hen. IV*, 1. 3. 35); 1. 2. 137

LAZAR, leper; 1. 1. 15; 2. 1. 76

LEA, arable land (cf. *Temp.* 4. 1. 60; *Tim.* 4. 3. 193); 5. 2. 44

LEGERITY, nimbleness, activity; 4. 1. 23

LET, impediment; 5. 2. 65

LIBERTINE, 'one who follows his own inclinations' (O.E.D.); 1. 1. 48

LIBERTY, licence; 3. 3. 12

LICENCE, leave, permission; 4. 7. 70

LIE IN, depend upon; 5. 2. 77

LIEU (IN), in return; 1. 2. 256

LIFE, living semblance, exact representation; 4. 2. 54

LIG, lie, North. dial.; 3. 2. 112

LIKE (adv.), alike; 2. 2. 183

LIKELIHOOD, parallel, 'similitude' (Warburton); 5 Prol. 29

LINE (sb.), genealogy; 2. 4. 88

LINE (vb), reinforce, strengthen; 2. 4. 7

LINEAL, lineally descended; 1. 2. 82

LINGER, protract, prolong; 2 Prol. 31

LINSTOCK, staff to hold the gunner's lighted match (O.E.D.); 3 Prol. 33

LOB, hang down; 4. 2. 47

LODGING, lying down; 3. 7. 31; couch; 4. 1. 16

LOFTY, stately, high-born; 3. 5. 35

LOW-RATED, despised; 4 Prol. 19

LUXURIOUS, salacious (cf. *Macb.* 4. 3. 58); 4. 4. 20

LUXURY, lust (cf. *Ric. III*, 3. 5. 80; *Lear*, 4. 6. 119); 3. 5. 6

MAGNANIMOUS, brave; 3. 6. 6; 4. 7. 16–17

MAKE AGAINST, militate against; 1. 2. 36

MAKE ROAD, make inroad (cf. *Cor.* 3. 1. 5); 1. 2. 138

MANHOOD, courage; 4. 3. 66

MANNERS, morals; 1. 2. 49

MARCHES, the Scottish border; 1. 2. 140

MASTER, possess (cf. *Son.* 106. 8); 2. 4. 137

MEASURE, (*a*) metre, (*b*) stately dance (for a court), (*c*) amount; 5. 2. 137–9

MEMORABLE, commemorated, commemorative; 2. 4. 53, 88; 4. 7. 103; 5. 1. 71

METTLE, stuff, spunk; 3. 1. 27; 3. 5. 15, 29

MIND, call to mind; 4 Prol. 53

MIRROR, model, pattern; 2 Prol. 6

MISCREATE, illegitimate, spurious (cf. *create*); 1. 2. 16

MISTFUL, dim with tears; 4. 6. 34

MISTRESS, (i) 'authoress, creatress, or patroness of an

art' etc. (O.E.D. 7, citing Northbrooke, *Dicing*, 1577, 'Idlenesse...is the mystres and beginning of all vice'); 1. 1. 52; (ii) chief; 2. 4. 133; (iii) used equivocally at 3. 7. 44, 47 *et seq.*

MOCK, cheat (cf. *2 Hen. IV*, 5. 2. 126); 1. 2. 286, 287

MODEL, representation in miniature (cf. *Ric. II*, 3. 2. 153); 2 Prol. 16

MODEST, moderate; 2. 4. 34

MOIETY, half; 5. 2. 216

MONMOUTH CAP, 'a round, brimless cap with high, tapering crown, worn by sailors and soldiers' (Linthicum, *Cost. in Eliz. Drama*, p. 226); orig. made at Monmouth; 4. 7. 99

MOPE, wander aimlessly as if in sleep (cf. *Temp.* 5. 1. 241); 3. 7. 132

MORAL (sb.), (i) symbolical figure (O.E.D.); 3. 6. 37; (ii) 'application of a fable' (J.); 5. 2. 311

MORRIS-DANCE, a rustic dance in which the performers blackened their faces, were dressed in grotesque costume with bells, etc. Sometimes associated with the May or Whitsun Games in which Robin Hood and Maid Marian figured (v. Chambers, *Med. Stage*, i. 195–201); 2. 4. 25

MORTIFIED, killed (theol.); 1. 1. 26

MOTIVE, the means of 'getting a move on'; 2. 2. 156

MOUNTED (TO BE), soar (like a hawk); 4. 1. 106

MUSTER, the enlistment of troops; 2. 4. 18

NASTY. 'The orig. force of the word...has been greatly toned down in English use...but retained in the United States, where it is not commonly used by polite speakers' (O.E.D.); 2. 1. 50

NATIVE, (i) proper, rightful (cf. *Ric. II*, 3. 2. 25); 2. 4. 95; (ii) in one's own country; 4. 1. 165; 4. 3. 96

NATURAL, filial; 2 Prol. 19

NATURE, the natural feelings of humanity (cf. *Ham.* G.); 3. 1. 8

NEGLECT, despise; 2. 4. 13

NEIGHBOURHOOD, neighbourly feeling; 1. 2. 154; 5. 2. 350

NEW-TUNED, newly devised (as 'accompaniment' to their stale stories); 3. 6. 74

NICE, scrupulous, punctilious; 5. 2. 269, 274

NICELY, (i) sophistically; 1. 2. 15; (ii) 'too nicely' = too much in detail; 5. 2. 95

NOBLE, coin worth 6s. 8d.; 2. 1. 107, 114

NOOK-SHOTTEN, highly indented (v. note); 3. 5. 14

NOTE, sign; 4 Prol. 35

O, tiny circle, round spot. Used in the 17th c. for the small circular spangles on a dress (O.E.D. 2 *b*); 1 Prol. 13

ODDS, strife; 2. 4. 129

O'ERBLOW, blow away or over; 3. 3. 31

OFFER, offer violence; 2. 1. 38

ONLY (THE), the unique, peerless; 2. 1. 79

OPEN, reveal; 1. 1. 78; declare, advance (a claim); 1. 2. 16

ORDINANCE, (i) practice, usage; 2. 4. 83; (ii) cannon, ordnance (a syncopated variant of (i), the orig. meaning being 'arrangement in order'); 2. 4. 126; 3 Prol. 26

OSTENT, display; 5. Prol. 21

OUTRUN, escape; 4. 1. 165

OUTWEAR, waste; 4. 2. 63

OVERBEAR, conquer, suppress; 4 Prol. 39

OVER-LUSTY, too lively; 4 Prol. 18

PACTION, compact; 5. 2. 362

PALE (vb), enclose, encircle; 5 Prol. 10

PALFREY, 'a saddle-horse for ordinary riding as distinguished from a war-horse; esp. a small saddle-horse for ladies' (O.E.D.); 3. 7. 26

PARIS-BALL, tennis-ball (v. O.E.D. 'Paris'); 2. 4. 131

PART (sb.), (i) (*a*) 'the melody assigned to a particular voice or instrument in concerted music' (O.E.D. 10); (*b*) function, share (in a co-operative enterprise); 1. 2. 181; (ii) side, party; 1. 1. 73, 4. 7. 116

PART (vb), depart, die; 2. 3. 12

PARTICULAR (MISTRESS), belonging to one lover; 3. 7. 46

PASS, indulge in. Lit. 'pass the career' = run the course at full gallop; 2. 1. 126

PASSAGE, (i) channel, line of descent; 1. 1. 86; (ii) action, fighting; 3. 6. 90

PAUCA, i.e. pauca verba = in short; 2. 1. 79

PAVILION, encamp (cf. 4. 1. 27); 1. 2. 129

PAX. For the kiss of peace given at mass in the early church there was substituted in the 13th c. the practice of passing a tablet depicting the Crucifixion, called a 'pax', to the communicants to kiss in turn; 3. 6. 39, 44

PEER, come in sight; appear; 4. 7. 84

PEEVISH, silly; 3. 7. 131

PERDITION, losses; 3. 6. 95

PERDURABLE, lasting; 4. 5. 7

PERDY, by God, indeed; 2. 1. 49

PEREMPTORY, final, conclusive; 5. 2. 83

PERPEND, weigh; 4. 4. 8

PERSPECTIVELY, as through a perspective, i.e. either a glass so cut as to produce an optical illusion when looked through, or a picture which shows different objects when turned this way and that; 5. 2. 319

PETTINESS, insignificance; 3. 6. 127

PHARAMOND, a semi-mythical Frankish ruler of the early 5th c.; 1. 2. 37

PHRASE, phraseology; 3. 6. 73

PICK, select carefully; 2. 4. 86; 3. 2. 101

PIONER, sapper; 3. 2. 85

PITCH AND PAY, pay cash. Prov. (Apperson, p. 498), orig. meaning obscure; 2. 3. 47

PITH, strength, vigour; 3 Prol. 21

PLACE, (i) position in a row of figures (cf. Baldwin, *Petty School*, pp. 164–5); 1 Prol. 16; (ii) office in the state (cf. Bacon, *Essays*, 'Of great place'); 4. 1. 242

PLAIN-SONG, simple melody or theme without variations (fig.); 3. 2. 5, 6

PLEASANT, merry, facetious; 1. 2. 260

POCKET UP, put up (with). With a quibble; 3. 2. 50

POLICY, statecraft; 1. 1. 45; 1. 2. 221

POPULAR, of the common people; 4. 1. 38

POPULARITY, intercourse with common people; 1. 1. 59

PORING, tiring to the eyes; cf. Nashe, *Christs Teares* (McKerrow, ii. 89): 'I that haue poor'd out myne eyes vpon bookes' (O.E.D. 'pore' 3); 4 Prol. 2

PORTAGE, port-holes; 3. 1. 10

POSSESS, inspire; 4. 1. 110, 286

POWDERING-TUB. Lit. pickling-vat (cf. note *1 Hen. IV*, 5. 4. 112); 'humorously applied to the sweating-tub used for the cure of venereal disease' (O.E.D.); 2. 1. 75

POWER, army; 2. 2. 15; 2. 4. 1; 3. 3. 46

PRACTIC, practical; 1. 1. 51

PRACTICE, plot; 2. 2. 90, 144

PRACTISE ON, impose upon; 2. 2. 99

PRAISE, merit, desert; 1. 2. 163

PRECÉPT, writ of summons (cf. *2 Hen. IV*, 5. 1. 11); 3. 3. 26

PREPOSTEROUSLY, contrary to the natural order of things; 2. 2. 112

PRESCRIPT, prescribed; 3. 7. 45

PRESENT, immediate; 2. 1. 107; 2. 4. 67; 4. 2. 8

PRESENTLY, without delay; 2. 1. 88; 3. 2. 54; 5. 2. 80

PRETTY, lovely. Without mod. trivial sense; 4. 6. 28

PREY (IN), after, or engaged upon, prey (cf. *Lear*, 3. 4. 97, 'lion in prey'); 1. 2. 169

PRIVATE (adj. and sb.), one (*or* of one) not holding a public position; 4. 1. 195, 233, 234

PROJECTION, design; 2. 4. 46

PROPORTION (sb.), due relation of things to each other. Lit. symmetry, balance, harmony; 2. 2. 109; 4. 1. 144–5

PROPORTION (vb), be commensurate with; 3. 6. 124

PROPORTIONS, forces, estimated number of troops required; 1. 2. 137, 305; 2. 4. 45

PUDDING, stuffed stomach or guts, black pudding, sausage (cf. *Wives*, 2. 1. 27); 2. 1. 86

PUISSANCE, armed force, strength; 1 Prol. 25; 2. 2. 190; 3 Prol. 21

PURCHASE, booty (thieves' cant); 3. 2. 42

PUT UP, raise (O.E.D. 53*a*); 5. 2. 37

QUALITY, (i) profession; 3. 6. 135; (ii) efficacy, power; 5. 2. 19, 67

QUESTION, consideration, discussion; 1. 1. 5

QUICK, alive, living; 2. 2. 79

QUIT (vb.), (i) absolve; 2. 2. 166; (ii) rid; 3. 5. 47

QUITTANCE, return, recompense; 2. 2. 34

QUOTIDIAN, v. note, 2. 1. 119

RAUGHT, pret. of 'reach'; 4. 6. 21

RAWLY LEFT, unprovided for (cf. *Macb.* 4. 3. 26); 4. 1. 139–40

RE-ANSWER, compensate for, repay, atone for; 3. 6. 126

REBUKE, check; 3. 6. 119

REDUCE, restore; 5. 2. 63

REEK, rise like vapour. The word did not become offensive until the 19th c.; 4. 3. 101

RELIGIOUSLY, scrupulously; 1. 2. 10

RELISH, taste (cf. *Ham.* 3. 3. 92); 4. 1. 109

RENDEZVOUS. A mil. term, a retreat or refuge. Here (i) last resort; 2. 1. 16; (ii) home to return to (cf. 1 *Hen. IV*, 4. 1. 57); 5. 1. 82

RENOWN, bring renown to (cf. *Tw. Nt.* 3. 3. 24); 1. 2. 118

REPENT, regret; 2. 2. 152

RESOLVE(D), 'are resolved' = have our doubts or ignorance removed; 1. 2. 4, 223

REST, final resolve. The term for the reserved stakes in the card-game of primero; hence to 'set up one's rest' = decide to hazard all (cf. *Rom.* 5. 3. 110); 2. 1. 16

REVOLT, treason; 2. 2. 141

RIM, peritoneum or lining of the belly; 4. 4. 15

RIVAGE, shore; 3 Prol. 14

ROBUSTIOUS, violent; 3. 7. 146

ROPING, hanging like rope; 3. 5. 23; 4. 2. 48

ROUND, plain-spoken; 4. 1. 200

RUB, obstacle, hindrance. A term in bowls; 2. 2. 188; 5. 2. 33

RUN, discharge (cf. *Caes.* 2. 2. 78); 2. 1. 121

SACK, Spanish white wine (cf. note *1 Hen. IV*, 1. 2. 3–4); 2. 3. 26

SAD-EYED, 'with eyes severe' (*A.Y.L.* 2. 7. 155); 1. 2. 202

SAIL, 'show my sail of greatness' = to demean myself proudly (cf. O.E.D. 'sail' sb. 3); 1. 2. 275

SAND, sandbank; 4. 1. 97

SAVAGE, uncultivated, untamed; 3. 5. 7

SAVAGERY, wild growth; 5. 2. 47

SCAMBLE (vb.), scramble with others in a crowd for something; 5. 2. 205

SCAMBLING (adj.), scuffling, disorderly; 1. 1. 4

SCAULD, scurvy; 5. 1. 5, etc.

SCION, slip for grafting; 3. 5. 7

SCONCE, redoubt, earthwork; 3. 6. 70

SCOUR, (i) wash away (or poss.) purge; 1. 1. 34; (ii) (*a*) beat, punish severely (O.E.D. *v*.² 9); (*b*) clean a pistol with a 'scourer' = ramrod with a wad or sponge (O.E.D. 'scourer²' 5); 2. 1. 56

SECURE, over-confident (cf. *2 Hen. IV*, 1. 2. 44); 4 Prol. 17

SECURITY, confidence; 2. 2. 44

SELF, self-same; 1. 1. 1

SEQUESTRATION, seclusion; 1. 1. 58

SERVICE, military service, exploit; 3. 2. 46; 3. 6. 3, 69

SEVERALS, details, particulars; 1. 1. 86

SHALE, shell; 4. 2. 18

SHOG, move off (slang); 2. 1. 45; 2. 3. 43

SHREWDLY, grievously; 3. 7. 48, 150

SIGNAL, symbol, token; 5 Prol. 21

SIMPLY, absolutely; 3. 7. 96

SINISTER, left-handed, illegitimate; 2. 4. 85

SKIRR, scurry; 4. 7. 60

SLANDER, scandal, disgrace; 3. 6. 77

SLIPS (IN THE), on the leash; 3. 1. 31

SLOBBERY, sloppy, wet; 3. 5. 13

SLOVENRY, slovenliness; 4. 3. 114

SMOOTH, mild, bland; 2. 2. 3

SMOTHER UP, suffocate; 4. 5. 20

SODDEN, boiled (p. part. of 'seethe'); 3. 5. 18

SONANCE, sound; 4. 2. 35

SORT, (i) rank, degree; 4. 7. 134; 4. 8. 76; 'of sorts' = of various ranks; 1. 2. 190; (ii) style, array; 5 Prol. 25

SPARINGLY, with reserve; 1. 2. 240

SPEND ONE'S MOUTH, bark. A hunting term; 2. 4. 70

SPIN (of blood), gush out, spurt (O.E.D. 8); 4. 2. 10

SPITAL, lazar-house, a low-class hospital, esp. for the leprous and syphilitic (cf. O.E.D. 'spittle'); 2. 1. 74; 5. 1. 80

SPOIL (vb.), ruin; 4. 5. 18

SQUARE OF BATTLE, squadron (cf. *A. & C.* 3. 11. 40); 4. 2. 28

STAND OFF, stand out; 2. 2. 103

STAND UP, rebel (cf. O.E.D. 103, n.); 2. 2. 118

STATE, 'pomp and ceremony befitting' a king (O.E.D. 19); 1. 2. 274; 2. 4. 32

STERNAGE, 'to sternage of' = astern of; 3 Prol. 18

STILLNESS, silence, or poss. staidness; 3. 1. 4 (cf. *Oth.* 2. 3. 191)

STIRRER, 'early stirrer' = early riser; 4. 1. 6

STOMACH, taste, inclination; 2 Prol. 40; 3. 2. 52; 3. 7. 153; 4. 3. 35

STOOP, swoop (like a hawk) upon some object; 4. 1. 107

STRAY, beast found wandering; 1. 2. 160

STRIKE, fight (a battle), 2. 4. 54

STROSSERS, trousers; 3. 7. 53

STUBBORN, rude, rough; 5. 2. 227

SUBTLY, treacherously; 4.1.254

SUDDENLY, quickly; 5. 2. 82

SUFFERANCE, (i) suffering; 2. 2. 159; (ii) forbearance; 2. 2. 46; 3. 6. 123

SUIT (vb), clothe; 4. 2. 53

SUMLESS, inestimable, incalculable; 1. 2. 165

SUMMER (vb), lit. graze cattle in summer—hence, nurture (v. O.E.D. 2); 5. 2. 307

SUR-REINED, over-ridden; lit. over-reined; 3. 5. 19

SUTLER, one who sells provisions to the army. A camp follower, not an officer (from Dutch *soeteler*); 2. 1. 111

SWASHER, swaggererer, bully; 3. 2. 29

SWELLING, majestic (cf. *Macb.* 1. 3. 128); 1 Prol. 4

SWORN BROTHERS, 'companions in arms who took an oath according to the rules of chivalry to share each other's good and bad fortunes' (O.E.D.); 2. 1. 12; 3. 2. 44

SYMPATHIZE WITH, resemble; 3. 7. 145

TAKE, (*a*) strike, (*b*) take fire; 2. 1. 52

TAKE UP SHORT, give short shrift to; 2. 4. 72

TALL, brave. In Sh. 'generally with a touch of irony' (M.S.); 2. 1. 68

TARTAR, the classical Tartarus, the portion of the underworld where the wicked are punished; 2. 2. 123

TASK, occupy anxiously; 1. 2. 6, 310

TEMPER, mould (like wax); 2. 2. 118

TENDER, have tender regard for; 2. 2. 175

TENOUR, (in law) substance, purport; 5. 2. 72

TERMS, 'in fair' or 'good terms' = pretty thoroughly; 2. 1. 57, 69–70; position, situation; 3. 6. 72

TERTIAN, v. note; 2. 1. 119

THEORIC, theory; 1. 1. 52

THREADEN, made of thread; 3 Prol. 10

TIMES, eras, periods of history (O.E.D. 'time' 3); 2. 4. 83

TOWN OF WAR, stronghold, fortified place; 2. 4. 7

TROJAN, cant term for dissolute fellow; 5. 1. 31

TROPHY, token; 5 Prol. 21

TROTH-PLIGHT, formally betrothed (which in Eliz. days was almost as binding as being married); 2. 1. 19

TRUMPET, trumpeter; 4. 2. 61; 4. 7. 55

TRUTH, loyalty, fidelity; 4. 3. 14

TUCKET, (i) trumpet-call; 3. 6. 110 S.D.; (ii) trumpet-call as a 'signal for marching used by cavalry troops' (O.E.D.); 4. 2. 35

TUN, barrel; 1. 2. 256

TURN HEAD, stand at bay (of a stag). Technical exp. (cf. Turbervile, *Book of Hunting*, 1576, ch. 41, p. 126, foot); 2. 4. 69

UMBERED, lit. stained brown (cf. *A.Y.L.* 1. 3. 112); hence, shadowed, darkened; 4 Prol. 9

UNFURNISHED, without means of defence; 1. 2. 148

UNHIDDEN, manifest; 1. 1. 86

UNPROVIDED, unprepared; 4. 1. 171

UNRAISED, uninspired; 1 Prol. 9

UNTEMPERING, 'without power to soften a lady's heart' (M.S.); 5. 2. 225

URN. Vaguely used (esp. in poetry) for 'a tomb or sepulcre, the grave' (O.E.D.); 1. 2. 229

USE, treat; 3. 2. 124

VARY, express in varying terms; 3. 7. 31

VASTY, vast (often with a suggestion of 'waste'); 1 Prol. 12; 2. 2. 123; 2. 4. 105

VAULTAGE, cavern; 2. 4. 124

VAWARD, vanguard; 4. 3. 131

VENTURE TRADE, 'speculate in trade' (M.S.); 1. 2. 192

VILE, mean, of low rank; 4 Prol. 50; 4. 3. 62

VOICE, approval, 'to get the voice' = to be acclaimed; 2. 2. 113

VOID, quit; 4. 7. 58

VULGAR, common people; 4. 7. 76

WAIT UPON, attend; 1. 1. 98

WAR-PROOF, valour proved in war; 3. 1. 18

WASTEFUL, devastating; 1. 2. 284; 3. 1. 14

WELL-APPOINTED, well-equipped; 3 Prol. 4

WHELK, pimple; 3. 6. 100

WHIFFLER, officer who clears the way for a procession by flourishing a javelin or sword; 5 Prol. 12

WHITE-LIVERED, cowardly by nature. The liver was supposed the seat of courage (cf. *Macb.* 5. 3. 15, 'lily-livered'); 3. 2. 32

WIDE, (*a*) loose (O.E.D. 11*a*); (*b*) gaping; 3. 3. 13

WIND UP, lit. wrap something up in something else, hence fig. (of time) absorb, pass (cf. O.E.D. 'wind' 16, 22); 4. 1. 275

WINK, shut the eyes; 2. 1. 7; 3. 7. 141; 5. 2. 299, 304, 305

WORD, motto (cf. note *Ham.* 1. 5. 110); 2. 3. 47

WORKING-HOUSE, workshop (fig.); 5 Prol. 23

WORSHIP (vb.), honour; 1. 2. 234

WRACK, wreckage; 1. 2. 165

WRANGLER, adversary, disputant; 1. 2. 265

WRINGING, belly-ache, 'a griping or wringing pain, esp. in the intestines' (O.E.D. 3); 4. 1. 232

WRONG, (i) wrong-doing; 1. 2. 27; (ii) stolen goods (with quibble on (i)); 3. 2. 50

YEOMAN, freeholder under the rank of a gentleman; 3. 1. 25

YERK, (of a horse) lash out with the heels, kick; 4. 7. 79

YOKE-FELLOW, fellow-worker (cf. Phil. iv. 3, Tyndale's trans. of σύζυγος, the earliest use of the word); 2. 3. 52; 4. 6. 9